TAKE
THIS EXIT

TAKE THIS EXIT

Rediscovering the *IOWA* Landscape

Edited by

ROBERT F. SAYRE

Iowa State University Press / Ames

Manufactured in the United States of America
♾ Printed on acid-free paper

First edition 1989
Second printing, 1990

Library of Congress Cataloging-in-Publication Data

Take this exit : rediscovering the Iowa landscape / edited by Robert F. Sayre.
— 1st ed.
     p. cm.
   Includes index.
    ISBN 0-8138-0096-X. — ISBN 0-8138-0199-0 (pbk.)
    1. Iowa—Description and travel—1981- —Guide-books. 2. Landscape—
Iowa. 3. Prairies—Iowa. 4. Cities and towns—Iowa—Guide-books.
I. Sayre, Robert F.
F619.3.T35   1989
917.77'0433—dc19   89–1932

Book design by Joanne E. Kinney

To the people of Iowa,
makers and,
we hope,
preservers of its landscape

Contents

Preface

▽

"Something Iowa desperately needs," I wrote in June 1986 in the *Des Moines Register,* "is a good new state guidebook."

That winter had brought the worst of the farm crisis, and all over the state there was talk of foreclosures, layoffs in farm-service industries, and the need to develop new businesses — one of which was going to be tourism.

But these boosters had to be con-men or fools. Tourism? In *Iowa?*

People did not come to Iowa for their vacations or weekends; they left it — or quickly drove through it. Annually the state government spent less money on tourist development than any other state. Tourist information centers near the borders closed up in the fall, after the rush of summer drivers, and did not open again till late May. And most of the travel advertising in Sunday papers was for "Get Away" weekends in Chicago, St. Louis, Kansas City, and Minneapolis.

My argument, however, was not that Iowa wasn't interesting. It was that before Iowans tried to develop tourism and ran the risk of turning the state into a sideshow, they needed to do some very serious reviewing of their own landscape and that an intelligent travel guide would be a means. Here, I wrote, was "one of the most intensely domesticated, man-made landscapes in the United States," and yet nobody seemed to know it or how to look at it. "Nature" was in Wisconsin or the Ozarks or northern Minnesota. "Civilization" and "culture" were in New York or San Francisco. "Vacations" were to be spent in the mountains, at a lake, or at the seashore. "Beauty," to Iowans, was always supposed to be elsewhere. The Iowa landscape, they thought, was dull, monotonous, and flat — except for a few choice spots in northeast Iowa, which developers condescendingly referred to as "little Switzerland."

1

In these silly prejudices Iowans are not alone, of course. Many Americans hold them about Iowa and the Midwest. But people should not be ashamed of their home turf. Iowans, once as brassy as the *Music Man,* had become too sensitive to outside opinion. They had to stop believing what other people said about their hometowns.

The notion that only some choice morsels of the planet Earth are beautiful and the rest dull or ugly is one of the most noxious and insidious prejudices of today. It has condemned and is condemning the rest of the earth to urban and rural slums, industrial zones, and a kind of nameless oblivion while at the same time, paradoxically, drawing such hordes of people to the so-called beauty spots that the crowds destroy them. The problem exists from Walden Pond to Yosemite National Park. And it helps little to mount great campaigns to "save" such shrines. By then they are already lost, and the publicity ends up attracting more gawkers. Worse, such a concentration of attention on those shrines furthers the delusion that the rest of the world is less "historic" or "beautiful" or "natural," and it becomes more neglected. Precivilized humanity, from times before such easy travel and superficial sophistication, was prejudiced too—but only in favor of its homeland. Other places were alien, so people left them alone, except on pilgrimages or, if necessary, in war.

This prejudice about landscape is just as "galling," one writer has said, "as dismissing a certain kind of people because of the color of their skin or the beliefs they profess. It violates the biological urge toward multiplicity and diversity that energizes our planet" (Conger Beasley, Jr., "The Return of Beaver to the Missouri River," *Antaeus,* No. 57 [Autumn 1986], p. 196). The traveler who dismisses north central Iowa because it is flat has only a *Playboy* taste. The Iowan (or any other American) who stops at Walden to find inspiration beside Thoreau's glacial kettle hole ought to get back in the car and go study the kettle holes in Dickinson County. The true traveler begins at home. The true traveler does not go running off on African safaris or (as Thoreau put it) "to count the cats in Zanzibar."

This book, therefore, is a loosely organized traveler's guide to Iowa. Not a Michelin: we don't cover the state and we certainly don't assign three stars to this and one to that. Not a Fielding's: we list no hotels and no restaurants and are not after your money. Nor an *Iowa on $25 a Day,* because you do not need much advice on saving money in Iowa! Just eat at cafés and stay in small-town motels or at campgrounds. Or go on RAGBRAI.

But we do try to advise you on what to see and how to see it — the two most important functions of any good travel book. And yet neither of these is simple.

For too long Americans have been told (and complacently told themselves) that the only things to look for in Iowa were corn, hogs, and the small town where grandma and grandpa used to live. Nothing wrong with looking for corn and hogs, of course, except that they don't require much searching and looking only for them leads to boredom. And nothing wrong with seeking one's family roots. But not all our ancestors came from Iowa. So promoters lure the rest of us to some dead celebrity's hometown, instead. It is all kind of diverting and funky, but in the end it is as unreal as postcards of forty-foot ears of corn.

What people should look for in Iowa, as in any strange place (and the real Iowa is a very strange place to outsiders) are the things that are still characteristic or meaningful but which they do not know about. Thus from the titles of the essays in this book you can quickly see that we have introduced a dozen or more common features of the Iowa landscape that are not so commonly noticed or studied. For example:

- the remaining stands of the tallgrass prairies that once covered most of the state
- the mining and milling and railroad towns that were the beginnings of Iowa industry
- the Victorian shops and homes that have been preserved and restored in small towns
- the opera houses and art deco movie theaters
- bicycle and hiking trails
- antique shops and flea markets
- ethnic communities
- Mississippi River towns
- the architecture of farmhouses, barns, and other buildings

But really seeing these places also requires knowing *how* to look. To the uneducated eye a prairie looks no different from an overgrown pasture or weed patch. You have to know some basic botany and ecology and the names of flowers and grasses. In seeking ghost towns, you may not even find them unless you know where to look, and even then, you want to know what they did, when they flourished, and why they died. In looking at farms, you have to know enough about farm history and architecture to identify the different kinds of barns, when they were built, and what they have been used for. And as for small towns, they all look alike — until you know how to compare and study them, observing the kinds of buildings, their condition, location, and adaptation.

When one looks in these ways—ecologically, historically, socially, and economically—landscape becomes perhaps the most comprehensive human record there is. *Landscape* is land as it has been perceived and shaped by human use. It is not just something pretty or ugly, to go see and photograph, or drive by and ignore. You might just as well rudely dismiss the people living on it—or enthusiastically try to line them up and "shoot" them.

In fact, in our opinion, the whole emphasis among travelers, painters, and photographers on merely the pretty or ugly (and "exotic," "sublime," "picturesque," "harmonious," "colorful," and other evaluative terms) in looking at landscape is misguided. At the least, it is premature. Before the viewer can judge, the viewer must understand. And if the viewer does not understand, the judgment is going to be condescending, trivial, and ignorant. A landscape is like a book: you certainly cannot judge it by its cover; and before you can judge it at all you must read it very carefully, considering its context, its parts, and their relationships.

Not everyone would agree with us, of course. To other people a landscape is simply a dress. It changes with the seasons. You may like it in spring but not in the fall. It can be altered. It can be formal or informal, impressive or shabby. But our response to this is, Who made the dress? Maybe Mother Nature made the snow and the bright fall colors, but she did not make the towns and barns in Iowa, or plant the trees, or plow and plant and harvest the fields. All that took human work.

Thus the critic of the American landscape whose ideas have been most stimulating to some of the writers of this book is John Brinkerhoff Jackson, founder of the magazine *Landscape* and the concept of the "vernacular landscape." Vernacular, Jackson reminds us, means local and ordinary. As vernacular language is the language spoken by the natives, so is the vernacular landscape the landscape that has been shaped by the inhabitants' economic needs and daily rituals and behavior. In practice, Jackson goes on, most landscapes are a composite of the vernacular and the formal, political, or official, but in Iowa we feel it is the vernacular that is the most interesting and, up to now, least studied.

This preference for the vernacular also explains our neglect of subjects like courthouses, state parks, the locks and dams on the Mississippi River that were built by the Army Corps of Engineers, and most of the museums, colleges, and notable buildings in Iowa's larger towns and cities. These places are also better celebrated and advertised, whereas the "common" barns and farmhouses, main streets and side streets of small towns, industrial buildings, cafés, roadhouses, newer suburbs and shopping strips, state and county roads and roadsides, old railroad lines and grain elevators—these places that are Iowa's real heritage—have been neglected. And by and large, it is individual and community enterprise, as opposed to official authority, that built them in the first place and has recently led the campaigns to preserve and restore them. A person driving through or living in Iowa who does not appreciate all this simply does not know the territory.

An inconsistency in our selections, it may seem, is our inclusion of essays on prairies and "Indian Iowa"—what was once the "natural" or "native" landscape. But our reasons are good. First, the Indian landscape of Iowa was really the first vernacular landscape. It was not a wilderness. Second, there is no full understanding of what later Americans did without knowing what was there before. And third, the modern preservation and restoration of prairies is also human work. It is not necessarily vernacular. It has come about by the leadership of a few far-sighted farmers, botanists, conservationists, and public-spirited citizens. But it too has largely been unofficial and, until now, unrecognized by state and county governments, most of which were far happier to ditch and drain "swamps" than to save them, and to spray those "weeds" that survived along roadsides. Given the ease with which men and women today can dominate the environment—or try to—saving and recovering it usually takes the more dedicated and imaginative human work.

So these essays try to present the traveler with a new route to a true "Get Away" in Iowa (and maybe more of the Midwest as well): of getting away from clichés and frozen vision, of getting away from landscapist prejudices, and getting deeper into the Iowa landscape. *Take This Exit.*

But before exiting from this Preface, I want to thank people who made this book possible. First, Jay Semel, director of University House at the Oakdale Campus of the University of Iowa, serving as the catalyst of "Scholar City," brought some of us contributors together. Meanwhile, he and his secretary Lorna Olson provided us with a stimulating place to work. Jennifer Curry at the University of Iowa Foundation introduced me to Francis Miller at the Maytag Family Foundation, Newton, Iowa, and it generously made a grant in 1986 to pay for some of the costs of travel and illustrations. Mary Bennett, the curator of the photographic collection at the State Historical Society in Iowa

City, volunteered her comprehensive knowledge of Iowa's photographic history and has been of enormous help. Nina Metzner, my research assistant, paid by the University of Iowa Graduate College, has done hours of typing, editing, and seeking of maps and additional illustrations. Finally, thanks to many other people, not all of whom can be mentioned: Becky Peterson at the State Historical Society in Des Moines; Ron Johnson at the Department of Natural Resources; the staff of the Photo Service at the University of Iowa; Ron Clester of Albia; George Schrimper, director of the University of Iowa Museum of Natural History; Randy Brinkhuis and Richard Green at the Map Collection, University of Iowa Library; Jean Pryor; Bob Campagna; Drake Hokanson; Steve Ohrn; Fredrick Woodard; Kay Chambers; Don Drake; and Bill Silag and Lynne Bishop of the Iowa State University Press.

Finally, I want to thank the contributors who wrote it. Most I had not even met when I began to think about it, taking a promising detour from the traditional pursuits of an English professor. From their insights and knowledge I learned so much that I now wonder if I really have strayed.

What, after all, is the main road?

PART
I

Introduction

1

THE IOWA LANDSCAPE,
PAST & FUTURE

Robert F. Sayre

One hundred years ago, to immigrants from Europe or pioneers coming from the East, Iowa appeared to be one of the most beautiful sights in the world: millions of acres of fertile land, few steep hills, no rocks to break or damage plows, and bright, busy country towns. There were, as Willa Cather wrote in *My Antonia,* "burning summers when the world lies green and billowy beneath a brilliant sky, when one is fairly stifled in vegetation, in the colour and smell of strong weeds and heavy harvests; blustery winters with little snow, when the whole country is stripped bare and grey as sheet-iron." The landscape of Iowa and Nebraska was endless and repetitive, but that did not make it boring, any more than Americans today find mountains or seashore boring. They, too, are magnificent because they are endless and repetitive.

In fact, Americans found Iowa so attractive that in the half century after statehood in 1846, the population rose from 192,000 in 1850 to 2,232,000 in 1900, which is only half a million less than it is now. The area of the state is 56,290 square miles (an area one-fifth larger than the state of New York), and almost all of it was fenced off and converted from woods and prairie into towns and farms. The first state parks were not acquired until 1919, and even today Iowa is close to last among the fifty states in its area of public land. But the overriding reason for this is simple: the land was too good for parks; people wanted farms. Those 56,290 square miles equal 36,025,600 acres, and at an average of 160 acres that could mean 225,160 farms. The 1930 census actually counted 215,361 farms in Iowa.

Fig. 1.1. Iowa's man-made landscape: Malcolm, just north of I-80 in Poweshiek County, in the early morning. Although appearing to represent the essence of the American rural ideal—and therefore a landscape more "natural" than the city—everything in this scene has been affected by human activity. Note how the trees on this former prairie land are mainly in town or around farm houses; the only "wild" ones are along fencerows and creeks. (Photo by Drake Hokanson)

What these figures also tell us is that for all its rural appearance, Iowa is not a "natural" landscape. It is almost entirely a human-made one: measured and cultivated, planted and built upon by the men and women who live and have lived on it. The water towers and grain elevators; houses, barns, and farmsteads; towns and highways; fences and fields all represent human work; and so do the cattle, hogs, and other farm animals who mow the pastures and consume the crops.

Thus the way to look at Iowa is, from this perspective, closer to the way one looks at a city — in terms of its architecture and design and the social and technological forces behind them.

The land and weather must not be forgotten; they are Iowa's constants. But Iowa's *landscape* is human-made, a creation, as Robert Bunge explains in "Indian Iowa," that began with the builders of mounds, gardens, and wickiups and the control of the prairies and woodlands by fire. So, for thousands of years, even if but an instant in geologic time, Iowa's landscape has been largely what modern students of landscape call a vernacular one. It came to be this way by the conscious and unconscious choices, habits, and rituals of the inhabitants. Of course, wider political and economic forces have affected it too, from the Jeffersonian grid that was laid down by surveyors to the massive early railroad system. But within and sometimes even behind these forces are still the choices of the landowners. "It's my land," the classic Iowa farmer insists (however short-sightedly); "I'll do what I want." And the equivalent in a proud Iowa town is, "It's our town; if we all get together, we can make it great."

The dominant features of the Iowa landscape are its farms and small towns, and so learning to read this Iowa vernacular has to begin with them. Even today there are approximately 109,000 farms and no one really knows how many towns. In January 1988 the State Department of Transportation, which prepares the official highway map, reported 954 incorporated towns. A recent Post Office ZIP Code directory listed (by my count) 1,008, more than only four other states (Pennsylvania, Texas, Illinois, and California). In the summer of 1987 an Iowan named Ray Beyer, who had started a project of visiting every town in the state while a college student twenty years ago, reached his goal by visiting the town of Hawkeye, in northeast Iowa—his 1,168th.

Whatever constitutes a farm or a small town (see Jon Spayde, "The Edge of Town"), the fact is that the two are interdependent, and both are largely creations of those years between 1850 and 1900 when the present landscape of Iowa was begun. So as you look at Iowa today (or go to that re-created open-air museum outside Des Moines, Living History Farms), imagine what a farm and small town of 1890 looked like.

The typical farm, as Don Scheese shows in "Changes in an Iowa Landscape," practiced a combination of subsistence and market agriculture. It had a large garden where the farmer's wife and children raised all the vegetables the family would need for the year: beans, potatoes, corn, squash and pumpkins, beets, carrots, cabbage, turnips, and so on. Ideally, their ripening was staggered so as to provide fresh food all through the growing season, from onions and rhubarb in the spring to squash and pumpkins in the late fall. For fruits there were strawberries, raspberries, currants, apples, pears, and melons. The surplus was canned or stored in root cellars (which doubled as shelters in tornado weather). And if the farm was near a city and a railroad line, like the Dennis farm that Scheese writes about, it might also sell potatoes, apples, milk, and poultry. A farm wife also raised chickens and, if she was unusually enterprising, geese or turkeys, selling the eggs and extra birds in town—"egg money" or "turkey money." This gave the wife a slight measure of economic independence and might, to the husband's relief or embarrassment, save the family in hard times.

The husband, with help from his older children and one or more hired hands, depending on the size of the farm, raised the field crops—at first wheat, later corn—that were for sale. A large part of every summer was also spent in cutting, drying, baling, and storing the hay needed for his cows, cattle, sheep, and also horses. For farms were run by horsepower, and on large farms there might be whole teams of draft horses, plus others for riding or, if a farmer was rich, sport and show. Large cattle and dairy operations, as Lowell Soike explains in "Viewing Iowa's Farmsteads," required even larger acreages of hay and forage crops. The labor required skilled coordination of people, machines, and horses; and before there were balers, the loose hay had to be handled smartly. The skilled hand at haying time, in Iowa as in New England, was like Silas in Robert Frost's "The Death of the Hired Man":

> He bundles every forkful in its place,
> And tags and numbers it for future reference,
> So he can find and easily dislodge it
> In the unloading.

Thus the hot, back-breaking June, July, and early August labor of haying, and thus the huge wooden barns that became the signature of farms throughout Iowa and the Midwest.

The early settlers did not instantly convert the land to fields and crops, however. Scheese learned that "Indian Run" was once the place where Mormons made handcarts for their trek to Utah, and if similar land-use histories were to be done for other places, Iowans might find many surprises. Paul Christiansen, in "Prairie Past and Prairie Present," reminds us that many early farmers kept portions of the primordial woods and prairie. Some woodland, where it existed, was saved for slower consumption as firewood, and new trees were planted for windbreaks and shade. Some prairie was at first used for pasture or saved simply because it was too wet to be plowed. An estimated ten percent of Iowa was wetland prairie (much more in what geologists call the Des

Moines Lobe of north central Iowa), and the draining of this land by digging ditches and laying drainage tiles required decades of later work, generally not feasible until there were steam shovels and other earth-moving equipment.

Fig. 1.2.   Threshing oats on a farm northeast of Kalona in July, 1986. Since the Amish still practice "horse-farming," their farms give an idea of what farms were like one hundred years ago. This threshing machine is much newer, of course, but the shocks in the field and the horse-drawn wagons are barely changed. (Photo by Bob Campagna)

The first machines on Iowa farms that were not horse-powered were generally the steam-powered threshing machines that threshed wheat and oats in the 1880s. Descriptions of them and of the complex and tiring but also sociable and joyful work of operating them can be found in Hamlin Garland's evocative autobiographies, *Boy Life on the Prairie* and *Son of the Middle Border.* Later there were steam-powered tractors as well — ponderous smoking giants that can be seen throughout Iowa every Labor

Day weekend at such gatherings as the Old Threshers' Reunion in Mt. Pleasant. These machines, now maintained as hobbies, were, one might say, the first agents of the twentieth-century specialization of farming. They, along with other changes like hybrid seeds (that increased and standardized yields) and artificial fertilizers, enabled and encouraged farmers to devote more land to cash crops, thus ending the diversified farming of Iowa's early, formative years. Owning such machines required much more capital, and the way to get it was to raise more of the crops that threshers, combines, and tractors could service.

But we are getting ahead of our story. Some of these changes came much later.

The interrelationship of farm and town arose from the dependency of even the subsistence farmer on manufactured tools and equipment, banks, markets, and railroads. For the Iowa farm was not like the pre–Civil War southern plantation, with slave carpenters and brick-makers and the primitive tools that an on-site blacksmith could make and repair. It was not technologically self-sufficient. Most early Iowa farmers also regarded themselves as cultured, social people, wanting schools that were better than just one-room rural schoolhouses (though at one time there were an estimated fourteen thousand of these) and wanting books, newspapers, fancy clothes, and an occasional trip to a theater or circus. And so, step by step and county by county, with the plowing up and fencing off of the prairies into farms, came the building of the towns that supplied them with everything from barbed wire to mason jars, lumber to mortgages.

This fundamental commercial purpose may be the reason why towns in Iowa are called towns or small towns, not villages. A village is European—a quiet little place with just a church, a few shops, and no desire to grow. But a town, especially in the early days, was on the make. It may have begun with just a church and a grain mill, but with a name like Washington, Bonaparte, Paris, Madrid, Moscow, or Rome (or even Wheatland, Mechanicsville, or Lost Nation), it wanted a hotel, a theater, a railroad station, brick houses and mansions, and maybe a college or an academy, mines, quarries, and factories.

Indeed, as James Hippen tells in "Farm Towns and Factory Towns" and Harriet Heuskinveld tells in her tour of "Ghost Towns in the Central Des Moines River Valley," many Iowa towns started primarily because of industries like lead or coal mining. Others started as settlements of various ethnic groups or as service towns for railroads (see Dorothy Schwieder, "Patterns of Prairie Settlement" and Philip Webber, "German and Dutch Ethnic Communities"). In the prosperity of the 1880s, it was not long before hundreds of these towns had the amenities of nine-teenth-century civilization: a railroad station, a hotel, an Elks or Masons hall, an opera house, several grocery stores and butcher shops, a cigar-maker or two, a furniture store, livery stables, a harness shop, a millinery shop, an ice house, a post office, and possibly two or three competing newspapers and banks. Different churches appealed to the different ethnic groups, and they com-peted in building the most impressive sanctuaries. In the summer the churches might also compete (or combine) in supporting a chautauqua meeting, revival, or temperance lecturer.

Fig. 1.3.   Skean's Block on the courthouse square in Albia, a symbol that in 1889 Skean was a prosperous citizen. This building, like many in Albia, has been restored to its nineteenth-century elegance. (Photo by Robert F. Sayre)

On Main Street in the 1880s and 1890s the merchants tore down their hastily built wooden stores (or the stores burned), and in their place went up two-story brick buildings with two or more first-floor shops, one for the owner to occupy and the others to rent. The second floor would also be rented out—to lawyers, doctors, insurance agents, or maybe a music or dancing teacher. And just under the heavily ornamented, overhanging cornices would be the owner's name: Skean's Block or Armstrong Block. This did not mean that the building occupied a whole city block; it merely meant that it had been built as a unit and that the owner and his family were now substantial citizens.

On Elm Street, meanwhile, these same merchants, bankers, and owners of the local quarry or mill might build their Victorian mansions—at first Italianate but then variations of Gothic, Queen Anne, and Renaissance, until the purer styles of prairie architecture became popular in the early twentieth century. Meanwhile, local nurseries sold the trees and shrubs to landscape these lots, while also doing a winter greenhouse business in flowers and table lettuce.

If a town prospered to the degree that its population increased to three thousand people or more, it was no longer considered just a farm town. To reach these numbers it had to win out against neighboring towns, competing to attract railroads or to become the county seat. The legendary and outrageous boosterism that was later satirized by Sinclair Lewis had begun. Losers did not do so well. Their main streets remained shorter and buildings smaller; the railroads serving them were branch lines, not main lines; there were fewer shops; and the surrounding homes might be occupied by retired farmers rather than owners and employees of the shops and factories.

What kind of life did these towns provide their residents? Jon Spayde says that we today attempt to assess early small-town culture largely through literature, and the reports conflict. Writers like Hamlin Garland praised the comfort and refinement of the towns and pictured the farms as dreary and isolated; Sinclair Lewis romanticized the country and exposed the hypocrisy and sham of the Gopher Prairies. From early on, the towns must have been dominated by their bankers; the more prominent ministers, lawyers, and doctors; and the richer store and factory owners and their wives. Thus the character and outlook of the towns varied with the leadership, and some were no doubt narrow and priggish. They might distrust the farmers whom they served and resent all outside authority—beginning with the federal government and the railroads, unless they had a piece of the action. Once such a hierarchy was established, social mobility was slow, both up and down. Often the best way up, as Joseph Wall wrote in *Iowa, a Bicentennial History,* was out. Almost from the beginning the ambitious and restless young left — for college, for California, for the East, or for larger cities. But, generally, those who stayed behind and those who returned still had a good life. The later culture and prosperity of Iowa towns, the work of what we might call the second- and third-generation residents, is not in the literary accounts. (The authors, by and large, had left!) But the record is in the landscape, or townscape — a physical record in the later houses, churches, stores, and public buildings of many towns and small cities.

This record must be seen; you can rarely read about it. But anyone who can identify the prairie architecture (from about 1910 to 1955) in towns all over Iowa, from Dubuque to Sioux City, Mason City to Oskaloosa, and in the schools and colleges and art museums built in these and other towns can attest to it. People in such towns were not isolated and narrow-minded. They traveled (Iowans generally love to get out of town — they have all those relatives to see); they traded books and ideas as well as grain and cement; and they tried to improve their towns, while still keeping the small-town friendliness and quiet that they liked (and liked returning to).

This physical record of middleclass culture may not be so striking in smaller towns, which did not have so many successful citizens, yet the signs of small-town pride and friendliness are visible there too. You see it in the clean streets and well-kept homes, the annual town festivals ("Solon Beef Days," "Dixon Sweet Corn Festival"), the billboards on the edge of town advertising the recent victories of the high school athletic teams, and the hill streets that are closed to cars every winter so the kids can sled down them. While the kids are around, they are the best diversion in town. They also represent the town's hopes. For even if they leave, if they are to want to come back, they have to be given lots of good memories.

There are so many towns because in the pre-automotive age they had to be within four or five miles, a one- or two-hour wagon ride, of the farms they served. Farms were smaller, more numerous, and had more people living on them (all the children and hired hands, and possibly tenant families too), so they supported nearby tiny towns with only a church, a school, and a general store. Cosgrove, twelve miles west of Iowa City, was such a town, though today it has only a school and a lovely Catholic church. It is not on most maps. Its general store, once a center for the farmers' Saturday afternoon poker games, is vanished. On Saturday nights people gathered at different houses for supper and dancing. "You'd go upstairs," an old former resident once told me, "and all the beds were covered with coats and babies." A trip from Cosgrove to Oxford, the nearest railroad stop, was eight miles—a two- or three-hour wagon ride. A trip to the Johnson County courthouse in Iowa City would have required starting out very early in the morning and returning very late at night, with a prayer for good weather.

Thus, more and smaller and more densely populated farms supported even more small towns than today; the towns catered to them, and both depended on railroads. At one time, it is said, no point in Iowa was more than ten miles from a railroad, so that even travel within a county, say, from Oxford to Iowa City, could be by train, or interurban line.

Iowa had one of the most extensive railroad networks in the United States. It is hard to realize this today, but the alert hiker, bicyclist, and motorist can still find the abandoned rights-of-way of the branch lines, with their solid stone bridges and their level grades closely following a creek. These old routes are also likely to contain remnants of original prairie or to have become lined by encroaching trees. Some have been converted to hiking and cross-country ski trails, as John Karras writes in "Iowa: Bicycling Heaven," but even where they haven't, they make pleasant walking.

As one hikes along these abandoned roadbeds, with coal and cinders beneath one's feet, it is interesting to speculate, as Drake Hokanson does in "Travel in Iowa," on how differently the landscape appeared from a train than from a car. Willa Cather's evocative description of crossing Iowa in summer was written as if from the observation car of a train. She was not staring down a white line nor did she have to watch the speedometer. She could look where she wanted, read when she was tired, and talk to other passengers. "While the train flashed through never-ending miles of ripe wheat, by country towns and bright-flowered pastures and oak groves wilting in the sun," she could also reminisce, recalling pioneer days in her small town in Nebraska. Train travelers not only saw a historically different Midwest, they saw it from different perspectives: from river valleys, looking sideways rather than straight ahead, and from much higher up—above the fields of corn. They passed the backs and sides of farmsteads, not the fronts, and passed through the centers of towns rather than skirting their edges.

The dawn of the automotive age did not immediately change this landscape. Early in 1920, Iowa had only 25 miles of paved country roads. By 1925 this number had grown to 568 and by 1930, 3,350; but this was still a tiny fraction of the total miles of roads in the state. Consider that today any one of Iowa's ninety-nine counties has 900 miles of roads, most of them still gravel. And until an Iowa road is paved or well graveled, forget about driving on it, unless it is very dry or solidly frozen. So even though Iowa farmers were eager to buy Model Ts and trucks and tractors, the early motor vehicles were merely replacements for their horses and buggies. When the roads were bad, the car stayed in the barn; thus it did not immediately change the farmers' dependence on a nearby town. But in the 1930s and 1940s, as state legislators responded to calls to "Get Iowa out of the mud" and for farm-to-market highways, the rural landscape finally began to enter its automotive phase. Farmers could drive to the Oxfords, if the roads were frozen or fairly dry, and the creeks not flooded, and ignore the Cosgroves. Or they could drive to the county seats and not have to take trains.

About the time the roads began to improve, the farmers also got rural electrification, more and bigger tractors, more hybrid corn, more fertilizers, and the new wonder-crop of that time, soybeans, although soybeans really were not planted extensively until the 1950s. As telephone and electric poles went up along the

Fig. 1.4.   Mud on the Lincoln Highway near Ames, about 1919, an illustration of why the automobile made slow progress in rural Iowa. (Photo courtesy of Iowa Department of Transportation)

county roads, farmers took down or just abandoned the wind-mills that pumped water from shallow wells to their barnyards and pastures. They could electrify their homes and have radios and refrigerators; they could install force pumps in deep wells so as to have more reliable water supplies; and then they could install pressure tanks in their cellars to provide running water inside. They could dismiss the hired hands (if they had not already gone to town or joined the army) and rent or buy more land and still cultivate it all themselves. The fertilizers eliminated the need for manure, and soybeans provided a legume crop to rotate with corn (restoring the nitrogen the corn took out)—farmers could further specialize their operations. The new farm wife could give up the chickens and turkeys and gradually reduce her vegetable garden and orchard. All these things could now be brought out from town and stored in a refrigerator or freezer. For supplemental income she and even her husband could take a job in town for part of the year. And "town" could be ten, twenty, or even thirty miles away.

Henry Wallace, a major developer of hybrid corn and Franklin Roosevelt's Secretary of Agriculture, estimated in 1956 that a farmer with a horse-drawn plow required two or three hours of work a year to produce one bushel of corn. By 1926 with early tractors, the average was down to thirty minutes per bushel, and six minutes by 1956. So between 1926 and 1956, with the other transformations in electrification, road building, Depression austerity, and wartime and postwar prosperity came the closing out of tens of thousands of farms and the slow and painful decay of hundreds of small towns.

During the 1960s and 1970s these trends continued. Farm machinery got bigger and bigger; use of fertilizers, herbicides, and pesticides increased (as any one who was watching television advertising knew); and as farms were combined, the rural population declined and small-town businesses folded. Along country roads one could see old farmhouses abandoned and then bull-dozed and burned so that the new owner (usually a neighboring farmer) would not have to pay taxes on them. The barn might be kept if the storage space was needed. But by the 1970s farmers were buying the new hay balers that rolled the hay into the huge six-foot-round pillows that could be left in the fields—hay barns were becoming obsolete. Boards blew off the sides, roofs fell in, and they were abandoned or burned too, along with chicken coops and farrowing pens and other out-buildings. As Lowell Soike explains in "Viewing Iowa's Farmsteads," farm buildings that remained went through another major change: metal-sided, one-story pole buildings (so-called because of their internal support structure of a few upright steel or wood poles with horizontal braces) became the new look. At the same time, the prosperous farmers of those years were likely to move out of the two-story farmhouses into low ranch-style houses. Except for their characteristically bigger garages, these houses look quite suburban — the vernacular modification of Frank Lloyd Wright's "Usonian House" of the 1930s.

Another addition to the farm landscape in these decades was the farm pond, which was one way of controlling erosion and re-using eroded gullies. Modern bulldozers could easily build the dams. A pond in a pasture could supply water for cattle, and another could be stocked with fish and used for swimming — grass-enclosed successors to the ole swimmin' hole. Most such ponds do not yet look very picturesque, but they are still a lovely resource for farms that have them. Iowa-style lakes! Private versions of the Army Corps of Engineers and state park lakes. And reminders that prairies, too, were not all dry but included large sections of marshland.

Yet while the farmers of the 1960s and 1970s prospered, often at their neighbors' expense, the small towns did not because the rural population was declining and what was left of it was going to the larger towns and their new shopping centers. The U.S. highways and busier state highways were rerouted off Main Street onto bypasses, and then the bypasses became built up with new and larger businesses. In county seats the buildings around the courthouse square lost their second-floor tenants and even some of the ground-floor stores closed.

This generalized review of Iowa landscape-history should help the traveler to place the farm crisis of the 1980s in perspective. It is a town crisis as well, a rural crisis, and some of the underlying causes of it are the very technologies that for decades have been labeled "farm progress": bigger and more specialized machines, requiring bigger fields and bigger debts; better roads; more "efficiency"; more "labor-saving" devices; more "production" and "over-production" — all leading to lower prices, fewer farmers, and less business for small-town merchants. During the 1980s, the *Des Moines Register* estimates that one-tenth of the Iowa farms have gone under, and another tenth are currently facing bankruptcy. But these are only the latest blows in a battle that rural Iowa has been fighting for a long time.

The difficult battle for survival has also had some positive consequences. As John Harper reports in "Theaters of Iowa," the economic hard times have drawn people together and often have increased community activity. Community theater is an example, and the restoration of old movie theaters and opera houses is a tangible result that can be seen in scores of large and small towns. Concurrently, merchants along the main streets and courthouse squares of these and many other towns (Albia, Decorah, and Independence are good examples) have restored the fronts of their supposedly "dying" buildings. When they have torn off the facings of the 1950s or 1960s, they have found the original stone and brick of the 1890s. And the insides and outsides of the old Victorian houses on the Elm streets and Maple streets have undergone similar restorations.

David Gebhard and Tom Martinson, authors of a planned architectural history of Iowa, have found that Iowa has one of the nation's richest records of late nineteenth-century architecture. First, the wealth of that time was spread widely all over the state, and the competition between towns that we have been describing made them outdo each other in planning their banks, courthouses, libraries, and homes. But then the slower growth (and decline) of Iowa towns in the years since has been kind to these handsome old buildings. They have not been so disastrously "modernized" as in larger cities—or totally demolished by urban renewal projects. So as Iowa towns restore and preserve these buildings, they give their residents and visitors something to be very proud of.

Today, therefore, Iowa towns are not "all the same." For someone who can appreciate the styles of vernacular commercial and domestic architecture from the 1880s to the present, a century in which the midwestern prairie school led the nation, Iowa is an unexpected treasure trove. Such a person can set out in a car

Fig. 1.5.   Albia Courthouse Square in January, 1988. The "new" courthouse was built in 1902, when Monroe County was a very active coal-mining area. The two-story businesses around the square retain the old-town flavor. (Photo by Ron Clester)

from anywhere in the state, and because towns are so close together, in one day of meandering around with what Patricia Hampl calls "the aimlessness of perfect travel," one can come upon dozens of elegant old houses and well-preserved main streets.

I call this meandering "gunkholing," a term I learned in college when a roommate and I spent our spring vacations sailing his uncle's boat on Chesapeake Bay. There a "gunkhole" is a small creek or harbor so isolated that you have the sense that no one else has ever seen it. The gunkholer has, on a small and intimate level, that grand pleasure of travel, a sense of discovery.

Of course, gunkholers by car will, like those in boats, sometimes get muddy boots and find some places that are unfriendly or ugly. Iowans have known for a long time that their state is not always and everywhere beautiful. In fact, several years ago when some state legislators tried to put a boastful slogan on the license plates, "Beautiful Land" or "State of Minds," Donald Kaul of the *Des Moines Register* shot them down by running a contest among readers of his column to suggest better ones. "Land of Ten Lakes," "Gateway to Nebraska," and "Baja Minnesota" were some of the suggestions. Perhaps in reaction to the boosterism of their grandparents, Iowans today often prefer to be humorous, ironic, or just silent. Land of tall corn and a low profile.

The ugliest sights in Iowa are the signs of bad farming, such as fall plowing, which leaves the land exposed all winter to wind erosion, leading to "black snow." Farming "fencerow to fencerow," to squeeze extra bushels from every field, means cutting down trees and shrubs along the fence lines, eliminating what could be wind-breaks as well as cover for birds and small animals. Some modern farmers, in order to use bigger (and more expensive) plows and combines, are also eliminating the terraces their predecessors built on hillsides to stop water erosion. In the spring the fences on the downhill sides of these fields, as well as others that have not been wisely tended, are half buried in washed-down mud and silt. But just as ugly can be a field with no fences at all, because it is a sign, in most of Iowa, that the farmer is no longer using cattle and hogs to glean the field in the fall or planning to rotate it later into a pasture. Such fields are also likely to stink in the spring from the application of chemical fertilizers. The smell is like a thousand confined animals — but there are none in sight.

It is also depressing to drive into a once-thriving town and find everything closed up. The filling stations are shut (with the gas prices left at thirty-eight cents per gallon); stores are boarded up and some store buildings have been razed to lower the tax assessments; the bank building has become a rundown bar; and the last hardware store is now a ransacked antique and junk shop. As Amy Godine points out in "Iowa for Collectors," such towns (and a large part of the countryside around them) are selling off their final assets. The only active business may be a bright little plastic-roofed Casey's convenience store, and its cheer is somehow false. It is like a night-light in an empty house.

So what lies ahead, on down the road in the Iowa landscape?

This is, in a very real, ultimate sense, for the resident and the traveler to discover, but our best prophecy is that it is in preserving and restoring the variety that has traditionally been its greatest beauty and greatest economic strength. This applies to everything from the diverse and colorful prairies to the farms and towns.

In "Prairie Past and Prairie Present" and "The Loess Hills," Paul Christiansen and I and Connie Mutel, respectively, show that prairies were the complete antithesis of the monocultures of corn and soybeans that cover most of Iowa today. Scores of different grasses and hundreds of different flowers, or forbs, grew on the prairies. There were cool-season and hot-season grasses, some that flourished in wet summers when the prairie marshlands fanned out, and others that took over in droughts, invading the drying lowlands. All the while, the prairies also supported an equal variety of insects, birds, and other large and small animals. In this wildness, to adapt the words of Thoreau, was the preservation of the prairie world. And make no mistake: with its extremes of fire and blizzard, wind and rain and scorching sun, lyrical calm and thunderous conflict, it was some of the wildest land in all North America. Too many Iowans think that to experience wilderness they must go to Alaska. If they only knew how, they could find or grow wilderness on their own farms.

But these adventure-seekers are right, in a way. The Iowa landscape has become too domesticated. A great project that the state and private citizens might undertake in times of depressed land prices would be the restoration of tens of thousands of acres into representative prairie and forest preserves. If it is worth going to Africa to photograph lions, why not have buffalo to photograph in wild Iowa? As Connie Mutel says, in excess of seventeen thousand acres are being set aside to establish the Loess Hills Pioneer State Forest in Harrison and Monona counties. Similar or larger preserves with more wild animals could be established elsewhere.

Things to look for on farms are signs of greater diversification. Already, some people have planted apple and pear orchards, generally on north- and east-facing hillsides. (Hilly land is poor for crops, and south- and west-facing slopes warm so fast in the spring that trees may bud and then be nipped by late frosts.) Other innovators have planted berry farms where customers do the picking, and still others have gone into truck farming for the "Farmers Markets" that have been started in larger towns and cities. Where these fruits and vegetables are grown organically they are even more in demand.

Clearly these small operations are not for every farmer, nor will they alone fulfill political slogans like "Save the Family Farm." But a gunkholer who finds a new orchard or berry farm or place to buy sweet corn picked that morning has satisfactions the interstate driver never knows. Extensive diversification is difficult for many farmers because their present equipment is specialized and hard or impossible to adapt. The $75,000 combine that crawls along a highway or eats its way through an autumn field is a dinosaur in more ways than one. Thus what may happen over much of the Iowa landscape is that large farms that already have the huge investments that make superfarms profitable may get even larger, while diversification and innovation happen on smaller ones that can use or adapt smaller or second-hand equipment.

Another large variable in these changes is the structure of U.S. farm-support programs and farm exports. As any farmer or Iowa banker will tell you, policies made in Washington one year will have a direct effect on the Iowa landscape the next spring. A guaranteed price for a crop and/or a limit on its production will dictate what is planted, how it is fertilized and cultivated, and the value of the land it is grown on. This may seem like interference in farmers' independence, but in one way or another the national government has been involved in agricultural policy throughout Iowa's history, beginning with land sales and land grants to railroads, and all Americans have an interest in it. The never-ending challenge is to set policies that strengthen and improve the landscape.

Diversification for small towns means not just preserving their farm services, symbolized in grain elevators and feed stores, equipment dealerships and fertilizer distributors, but finding and keeping industry. On the edges of most thriving towns you will see a metal-sided modern factory building or warehouse—better yet, two or three. They are not necessarily attractive. With their windowless walls they seem cold and anonymous. You don't know what goes on in them until you read the name on the small office in front or on the low, brick-bordered sign along the road—and sometimes not even then, since it is only initials or the logo of a big conglomerate. But these buildings mean jobs, magnets that hold people in town and draw them from the surrounding countryside.

The prototypes of these combined farm towns and factory towns were the "Mississippi River Towns" that Loren Horton and I write about. From 1850 to 1890 sawmills in these cities cut up the pines from Wisconsin and Minnesota that were rafted down the river. From 1890 to 1930 they had hundreds of factories that made buttons from freshwater mussels. Towns in the interior and along the Missouri became centers for milling grain and for meat packing: Waterloo, Cedar Rapids, Ottumwa, Council Bluffs, and Sioux City. But some of the most spectacular small-town success stories came from local inventors and entrepreneurs. The Sheaffer Pen Company in Fort Madison started in the back of a jewelry store in 1908. Businessmen in Newton started making primitive washing machines in 1898, marketing them through the countryside. In 1911 F. L. Maytag and the inventor Howard Snyder, who had started making their washing machines as a sideline, added electric motors, and by the 1920s Newton was a washing machine boom town. In Cedar Rapids in 1931 Arthur A. Collins began making ham radio equipment, the origin of Collins Radio Company. It became part of the Rockwell International in 1973, and today with 7,700 employees, the Collins divisions are the largest employer in Cedar Rapids and the third largest in Iowa.

Dyersville, near Dubuque, suddenly prospered in the 1970s with the growth of Ertl toy wagons and tractors. At the same time the little town of Conrad (population 1,113) in Grundy County prospered from Ritchie Industries, maker of livestock watering tanks. Mt. Pleasant, the county seat of Henry County, has since the 1960s followed a policy of attracting many small industries so that it will never be dependent on just one big employer. By 1986 it had twenty-five factories, none with more than six hundred employees.

But when looking at the shining sides of a new factory, look, too, at the areas marked "Zoned for Industry" and "Future Industrial Park" that have nothing but weather-beaten realtors' signs. They symbolize the frustrated hopes of the local Chamber of Commerce — and the often ill-advised tax concessions and low-interest loans some towns will make in order to attract any business. Some towns would be better served (and saved) by a new café or bed-and-breakfast (B & B) house. Such places do not have to have rare antiques, although that is an attraction of many new B & Bs; and the restaurants should not have to be gourmet. The best hamburgers, soups, and pork tenderloin sandwiches (*the* Iowa specialty) are already in small-town cafés, and a gunkholer's delight. We also want to save the roadhouses and supper clubs where we can get good steaks. But it would be a decided improvement if such places had windows that overlooked the river or some natural landscape behind them or were in town, facing the park or courthouse square.

Towns could also help themselves and the state by developing regional recreation trails and advertising good biking or hiking trips in their area. Iowa has excellent pheasant and deer hunting, and were there more cover on farms, the farmers and nearby towns would attract more hunters. When rivers are cleaner and more accessible, the fishing will improve too. More boat landings (and getting rid of the fences that sometimes cross Iowa rivers!) would be an aid to both fishermen and canoers. And we are not proposing this just for "the tourist" but for residents of the Hawkeye state itself.

Tourists, let's admit it, have never been particularly drawn to Iowa. People have come here not to travel and play but to live and work, and that, in most respects, is an admirable heritage. The Iowa landscape has not been cluttered with the junk that lines the highways of a lot of the United States. Instead, one still sees farms and towns, the working vernacular landscape we have been describing. But in a world that no longer wants *all* the produce this land can grow, or even *all* the factory products its towns might make, Iowans often find themselves frustrated and puzzled. As an Iowa minister said recently after a particularly painful rural tragedy, "We who live in rural America are in trouble, Lord—not because we have been lazy or irresponsible or because we have not worked long and hard. As a matter of fact, Lord, the harder we work, the more desperate the situation becomes."

This, in a few solemn words, is the present paradox of Iowa: a vernacular landscape made by work in which there is less work of the old kind to be done. Too much corn and soybeans, too many farmhouses and small towns, too many county roads; thus the old landscape is decaying and changing, and it will inevitably change more. Travelers can see this and may, indeed, see it more clearly than the natives. The natives, in turn, are beginning to want the travelers, as natives do everywhere when their old industries give out. But this should not become the occasion simply for "tourist development." What is needed is rural redevelopment, a rural renaissance, both for natives and visitors. If we only work and exploit the land, it will no longer sustain us; in fact it may kill us. We need to learn to enjoy it. Today in Iowa travelers and natives have a common interest in appreciating the past landscape and shaping a new one in which to work less destructively and play more constructively, more re-creatively.

PART
II

The Land

2

CHANGES IN
AN IOWA LANDSCAPE

Don Scheese

The United States lies like a huge page in the history of society
. . . a palimpsest.
> Frederick Jackson Turner, *The Significance of the Frontier in American History*

Wilderness and wildlife, history, life itself, for that matter, is something that takes place somewhere else, it seems. You must travel to
witness it, you must get in your car in summer and go off to look at
things which some "expert," such as the National Park Service,
tells you is important, or beautiful, or historic. In spite of their
admitted grandeur, I find such well-documented places somewhat
boring. What I prefer . . . is that undiscovered country of the
nearby, the secret world that lurks beyond the night windows and
at the fringes of cultivated backyards.
> John Hanson Mitchell, *Ceremonial Time: Fifteen Thousand Years on One Square Mile*

Once in his life a man ought to concentrate his mind upon the
remembered earth, I believe. He ought to give himself up to a
particular landscape in his experience, to look at it from as many
angles as he can, to wander about it, to dwell upon it. He ought to
imagine that he touches it with his hands at every season and
listens to the sounds that are made upon it. He ought to imagine
the creatures there and all the faintest motions of the wind. He
ought to recollect the glare of noon and all the colors of the dawn
and dusk.
> N. Scott Momaday, *The Way to Rainy Mountain*

"Where the hell you gonna hike in Iowa?"

That was the way a friend in Idaho responded when I told him that my wife and I would be moving from the Pacific Northwest to the Midwest. I had to admit it—the question was on my mind, too. We were abandoning the Oregon coast, the volcanoes of the Cascades, the lake and deep forest country of the Idaho Panhandle, and the high desert of eastern Oregon and Washington. And for what? A return to the b.s. of grad school and student poverty, and the monotonous cornfields of Iowa.

Were we in our right minds?

Perhaps not. But my wife and I had grown up in eastern Pennsylvania and felt we needed a change from the eight months of interminable drizzle in western Oregon. Having grown up with cold, snowy winters and sensual, humid summers, we were sort of nostalgically looking forward to experiencing them again.

Still, when we arrived at a campground near Iowa City around midnight one evening in late August of 1984, unable to sleep in our tent because of the double whammy of sweltering humidity and a thunderstorm directly overhead, we had some initial doubts about our new home. They were quickly confirmed as we confronted a fundamental fact about Iowa: ninety-seven percent of the state is under cultivation. Now there is a truth about the landscape that is hard to ignore. One could hike in Iowa, certainly, but not very far, at least not without walking in circles. The trails I discovered and later walked were not really hiking trails, they were courses along which one meandered. They snaked through woods, all right—but the woods were only shelterbelts between farms or along creeks and rivers. The "topo" maps I looked at indicated sparse tree cover, mainly along the thin blue lines that signified the drainages. There were no national forests, large or small, in Iowa, only a couple of small (by western standards) state forests, around eight thousand acres.

One such parcel of forest lies about one hundred yards from our apartment, at the western edge of Iowa City off Mormon Trek Boulevard. Actually it's a park—Mormon Handcart Park: some prairie, a hardwood forest bordering Clear Creek, a quarter-mile paved foot trail, a few interpretive signs, and a concrete monument. Very unpretentious. And there are some other trails, too, paths worn through the gallery forest of locust, oak, hickory, and cottonwood, no doubt tramped into distinction by local kids who needed a play area commensurate with their expanding imaginations.

I began to explore this four-acre tract. I would come home from school with terrific headaches from all the palaver of academia—talk, talk, talk. So it soon became a ritual for me to head for the park, read the signs, walk the paved trail, then angle off into the brush and under the tree canopy, look around and do nothing except get into my senses, as Thoreau did on his daily saunters. Some days I was more receptive to my surroundings than others, taking an hour to tune in to the environment. One day it took spooking (and getting spooked by) three White-tailed deer, their cottony rumps barely visible as they disappeared into a bottomland thicket, to snap me out of my sensory doldrums. Another day I was tramping mindlessly along when, happening to glance up into a tree, I snatched a glimpse of the silhouette of a Great horned owl, its horns plainly evident, before it disappeared. Such incidents stunned me; they made me realize how far away from the woods I could be while walking through them. All the same, it was therapy.

Fig. 2.1. The entrance to Mormon Handcart Park today. Note the restored tallgrass prairie in the middle distance, above the sign. (Photo by Don Scheese)

Eventually, I began to find a way to relate what I was doing after school to what I was becoming increasingly interested in *in* school—the history of the landscape, a term J. B. Jackson in *Discovering the Vernacular Landscape* defines as "a synthetic space, a man-made system of spaces superimposed on the face of the land." In other words, land is transformed into landscapes by human activities. In a course on the making of the American landscape I read a work entitled *Changes in the Land,* an ecological history of New England from 1500 to 1800. I was taken by the idea of studying the process of how various cultures had shaped a particular landscape. I soon learned that others had done the same kind of study of other regions. However, what is needed, said a professor of mine, is a study of one square mile of land over a long period of time. As it turned out there was in fact such a work: John Hanson Mitchell's *Ceremonial Time: Fifteen Thousand Years on One Square Mile.* On his turf in Massachusetts ran a procession of glaciers, prehistoric and historic Native Americans, colonial and modern farmers, and engineers and computer wizards who manufactured synthesizers for radio satellites.

From such works I learned that social history and environmental history are closely intertwined. That is, where people live in part determines how they live, and how they perceive their environment plays a major role in the eventual shape of the landscape. All this seems quite obvious after only a little thought; but nowadays as people and their work become farther and farther removed from the land, few people examine how they have shaped and been shaped by the place where they live.

I looked hard for landscape histories of areas in the Midwest, but found none. This was not too surprising. "Why no environmental studies of Iowa?" another professor of mine asked rhetorically. "Simple—they aren't sexy enough." What he meant was that the physical geography of the Midwest is generally perceived as dull (untrue—but conventional wisdom dies hard); it was also assumed that its environmental history, that is the reshaping of the landscape, was also dull. Intending to debunk these notions, I became intrigued with the idea of doing a landscape history of . . . what was my turf's name? I needed something catchy, like the "Scratch Flat" of Mitchell's *Ceremonial Time.* Then, in reading a local history of Coralville I ran across an anecdote told by Elizabeth Fellows Dennis, the daughter of the first white settler to officially lay claim to land that is now part of Mormon Handcart Park. She referred to the area about Clear Creek as "Indian Run—meaning a straight, quick path from Indian land to where they wished to go." Indian Run—it had a ring to it.

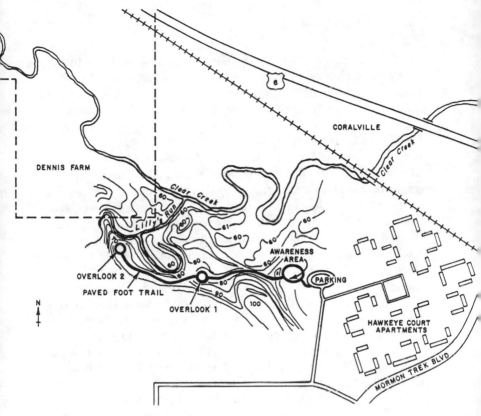

Fig. 2.2. Map of Indian Run, showing the park and its relation to the Dennis Farm, Clear Creek, Coralville, and university property on the west side of Iowa City. (Map by Kay Chambers)

As I have said, Indian Run is not a spectacular landscape, but it does have some interesting human history. Most noteworthy is the fact that for several months in 1856 and 1857, twenty-five hundred Mormons camped on it before continuing west for Utah, carrying their belongings in handcarts. This temporary occupation while being organized into handcart "companies" eventually led to the establishment and naming of the park in 1980. Prior to the Mormon encampment members of the Sac and Fox tribes lived nearby and traveled through the area, and before, during, and after the Mormon occupation the land was cultivated by farmers. Today Indian Run is used by recreationists — people out for a half-hour stroll through a historical park.

The point is, Iowans have nothing to be ashamed of and muⅽh to be proud of concerning the history of their landscape. Admittedly, we do not have mountains or a coastline — just a land subtly beautiful, a land rich in human history. It deserves our attention.

In the spring of 1985 a new wing of the University of Iowa's Museum of Natural History opened. Short of walking the landscape itself, Iowa Hall provides the next best thing to being in the field. Its exhibits trace the geologic and cultural history of Iowa, allowing the visitor entry into the state's complex past. When I became interested in studying the making of Indian Run, I made it a habit to tour Iowa Hall, so that I could get some graphic, lifelike images of what it may have looked like during various stages of history. One of the most striking exhibits portrayed a scene from the Devonian Period, some 420 million years ago, when the entire continent was under water. Behind the glass walls swam a nine-foot-long armored fish, which was about to dine on a school of much smaller fish. A cross-sectional view of the area floor showed how the remains of trilobites, snails, corals, sponges, and other sea organisms of the period accumulated in the mud. Over time these accumulations became fossiliferous limestone — which is how Coralville got its name. Let me explain.

According to a pamphlet written to commemorate Coralville's centennial celebration in 1973 (*Coralville, Iowa: Centennial Year 1873-1973*, State Historical Society, Iowa City), when the federal government surveyed the Mississippi River Valley in the 1850s, coral formations along the Iowa River attracted the attention of geologists. Word of them reached Louis Agassiz, then America's most prominent natural scientist and a professor at Harvard. Agassiz came to Iowa and delivered a series of lectures on the formation of the coral deposits, and one week later local residents coined a new town name: Coralville. On December 19, 1866, an Iowa City newspaper declared that "so far as our knowledge extends there is no other town in the wide world of the same name."

Little of these deposits is visible at Indian Run, though a mile north (just north of I-80) a limestone quarry is evidence of the continued economic importance of the formations. I took great pleasure in these discoveries, knowing that events of over 400 million years ago were still in plain evidence, still relevant to what people did on the land today. The sense of continuity was reassuring.

By further touring Iowa Hall and reading Wayne Anderson's *Geology of Iowa,* I became aware of even more conspicuous evidence of geologic history on and near Indian Run, in fact just about everywhere in Iowa. Being a newcomer to the Midwest, I was struck by the dominant feature of the landscape — its endless farmland. Its productivity is traceable to developments during the Pleistocene Epoch, otherwise known as the Ice Age, which began two to three million years ago. Glaciers drifted over Indian Run, depositing glacial till, and when they retreated (around twenty thousand years ago) the action of the ice grinding on exposed rock produced a fine powder, called loess, which is rich in nutrients. This powder was blown by the wind over Iowa until in places such as Johnson County it reached a depth of as much as sixteen feet. The loess concentrations plus favorable climatic conditions determined Iowa's future as a farm state.

Of course, agriculture—rather, monoculture, as it exists today in Iowa—is a very recent development, geologically speaking. According to the fossil pollen count, between nine thousand and thirty-two hundred years ago two warming trends occurred during which the "Prairie Peninsula" was established. Long prior to pioneer farming, then, a wedge of grassland environment appeared and eventually dominated an area as far north as Minnesota and as far east as Ohio. The prehistoric prairie may have been perpetuated by humans through the deliberate use of fire, since game such as bison thrived in such habitat, and the burning of the grass promoted its growth and kept out trees. At any rate, based on information secured in the federal land surveys in the mid-nineteenth century, much of Iowa remained grassland at the time of Anglo-American settlement in the 1830s. Only along the drainages did oak and hickory forests predominate.

After touring Iowa Hall and reading works of geology I would return to Indian Run, happy to get back to "fieldwork." It occurred to me that to the unknowing eye Mormon Handcart Park, with its heavy tree cover along Clear Creek and tallgrass prairie, might represent a remnant of "virgin" Iowa. Such a perception would be incorrect, however. As I researched the more recent history of Indian Run, I learned that the forest has returned only after extensive cutting by the pioneer farmers and Mormon emigrants and that the tallgrass prairie has actually been re-created, the result of efforts by environmentally conscious Iowans wishing to save and restore a small fraction of the state's original ecology.

So much for the geologic history of Indian Run. More interesting to me was the prospect of tracing its human history, that is, the way in which various cultures had shaped the landscape to make it more productive and comfortable to live in. This process began some twelve thousand years ago when humans first appeared in Iowa, but for Indian Run itself the first reports of human occupation come much later, in 1673 with the coming of Joliet and Marquette. The Ioway Indians, after whom the state was named, were a Plains tribe whose material cultural remains have for the most part been discovered in the western part of the state and who dominated Iowa until the early eighteenth century.

But it was the Sac and Fox tribes, who entered the area in 1733 to escape punitive raids by the French in Wisconsin, that provide the best evidence of American Indian inhabitation of land near Indian Run. They lived along the Iowa River near its confluence with Clear Creek, very close to the area that later became Mormon Handcart Park.

By the beginning of the nineteenth century the Anglo-American frontier was advancing westward. Unknown to the Sac and Fox (to whom the idea of formally exchanging land between different peoples was inconceivable), the fledgling nation of the United States had become the "owners" of their territory in 1803, the year Louisiana was purchased from France. Thus we know about the Sac and Fox presence near Indian Run through anecdotal evidence provided by the invaders, pioneers who first settled Johnson County beginning in 1838.

Before I could do meaningful research on this aspect of the human history of Indian Run, I had to shed some of the stereotypical notions many white people have about Indians, past and present. Although I had spent eight years living in the West, I had had little contact with any of the tribes there, and like a typical environmentalist, I mythologized Indian relationships with nature, assuming they had always lived "in balance with the land" — whatever that meant. From noble savages to noble ecologists — I began to realize we really had not advanced much in our understanding of Native American culture. So I had to be quite wary of accounts of pioneers and my own preconceptions.

In addition to consulting local histories and visiting the exhibits of Indian life in Iowa Hall, I read relevant portions of volume 15 of the *Handbook of North American Indians*. As far as I could determine, there was little archeological evidence of Sac and Fox inhabitation on or near Indian Run, nor did they leave much in the way of written accounts — and the few that do survive were recorded by white pioneers, and thus read like excerpts from the *Leatherstocking Tales*. In truth, it was difficult to obtain a nineteenth-century Indian's point of view on how the landscape might have appeared.

When pioneers first came to Iowa they perceived it as a wilderness because the landscape did not conform to what a settled area should look like. But what they failed to realize was that the Indians had manipulated the landscape, had transformed it, albeit on a small scale. The Sac and Fox were hunter-gatherers, planting corn, beans, squash, pumpkins, and melons along the river bottomlands in spring and summer, and hunting bison (until around 1820) and deer in the fall and winter. With the advent of Euro-American encroachment they participated in the fur trade,

exchanging deerskins and beaver and muskrat pelts for metal artifacts such as kettles, knives, and guns. They lived in summer
dwellings, which consisted of pole scaffoldings forty to sixty feet
long by twenty feet wide and covered with elm bark. During the
winter they moved to dome-shaped structures with cattail mats
serving as roofing and walls.

According to one local history (C. R. Aurner's *Leading
Events in Johnson County),* four Sac and Fox villages were located along the Iowa River in the 1830s, all within fifteen miles of
Indian Run. As the fur trapping frontier was replaced by the
farming frontier in eastern Iowa, conflicts between the tribes and
settlers proved inevitable, and beginning in 1824, the Sac and Fox
were forced to relinquish portions of land in formal treaties with
the U.S. government. The dispute was essentially over land use:
the tribes wanted to continue to hunt game and do subsistence
farming, while the settlers wanted to practice intensive agriculture, with the hope of eventually producing a surplus for market.
By 1851 the Indians of Iowa had ceded their last foothold in the
state, by which time disease, alcoholism, and general cultural
erosion had reduced the population of the Sac and Fox from six
thousand (in 1833) to fourteen hundred. Since then the descendants of the two tribes have made a remarkable recovery, but that's
another story (see "Indian Iowa").

Nathaniel Fellows emigrated from Indiana with his family
and was one of the first settlers near Indian Run. He befriended
the local chief, Poweshiek, who subsequently gave him some land
near the confluence of the Iowa River and Clear Creek. His
daughter Elizabeth was quite the raconteur and in the early part
of the twentieth century recounted pioneer life to local historians.
She recalled that occasionally angry tribesmen appeared at the
backdoor of the family's homestead and demanded food in retri-
bution for their land. She also reported that they continued to
hunt in the forest along Clear Creek after 1837, when the tribes
ceded another large portion of eastern Iowa.

By that time it was clear to the Sac and Fox that they had to
retreat westward once again. Poweshiek is said to have delivered
the following plaintive speech in 1839 when invited to a celebration at a nearby trading post to mark the recognition by the
federal government of Iowa's territorial status:

> Soon I shall go to a new home and you will plant corn where my
> dead sleep. Our towns, the paths we have made, and the flowers
> we love will soon be yours. I have moved many times and have
> seen the white man put the earth into fields and gardens. I know
> that I must go away and you will be so glad when I am gone that
> you will soon forget that the meat and the lodge-fire of the Indian

have been forever free to the stranger and at all times he has asked
for what he has fought for, the right to be free.

I found this speech in the local history written to commemorate the Coralville centennial. Its florid, Cooperesque style masks
an important development in the history of Indian Run — the
transformation of the land about to be wrought by American
pioneers. It could be said that the Indians were conservationists
by default in the sense that they had neither the numbers, the
technology, nor the economic system to significantly affect their
environment. Their dispossession marked the beginning of an entirely new era of land use.

This new era produced a dramatic change in the nature and
amount of historic materials. In studying Indian land use I was
faced with the problem of too little evidence, but just the opposite
was the case for the subsequent history of the area. Indeed, the
problem became what to cull from the wealth of information.
This disparity in the amount of evidence of course reflected a
fundamental difference in culture between the Indians, who depended on oral tradition and memory, and the whites, who depended on the written word and extensive record keeping.

In *The Land Office Business* and *The Trans-Appalachian
Frontier,* Malcolm Rohrbough chronicles the expansion of the
United States in the nineteenth century. Pioneer farmers were
lured to the Midwest by promotional literature celebrating the
richness of the prairie soil — once it was discovered that the tree-
less terrain was indeed very fertile. But before a territory could be
opened up for settlement two steps had to be carried out, according to the Northwest Ordinance of 1787. First, the resident Indian
tribes had to cede their land to the federal government; and second, an official land survey had to be carried out. But so rapid
was the influx of immigrants into this region that would become
the Iowa Territory that squatting proved inevitable. By 1839 there
were an estimated ten thousand illegal settlers in eastern Iowa.
The federal government retroactively sanctioned this activity by
passing a permanent Preemption Act, allowing a squatter the
right to purchase up to 160 acres of land at a minimum price of
$1.25 an acre. The official survey of the territory was then done
between 1836 and 1859, with the six-mile-square township as the
basic land unit. Indian Run thus acquired a new reference: it lay
in the northeast quarter of section 7, and the northwest quarter of
section 8, in Township 79 North, Range 6 West.

By imposing straight lines on the undulating, drainage-dom-
inated terrain of eastern Iowa, the township system stamped the
Anglo-American sense of order upon the land. Over time the

landscape itself came to reflect this state of mind, as anyone who has flown over the Midwest can testify. The checkerboard pattern etched by roads and property boundaries in conformity with section lines is a distinct trademark of the midwestern landscape. In fact, as Walter Sullivan remarks in *Landprints,* the term "section" is itself an Americanism that is rarely translated into other languages.

Enough of the big, aerial perspective — I wanted to know about the individual settlers of Indian Run. As I have mentioned, Nathaniel Fellows was among the first emigrants to arrive in the area, and was given land by Chief Poweshiek. The statement of Fellows's claim (found in the Coralville centennial history) reveals how a pioneer farmer in the 1840s read the landscape:

> Claim made by me June 1838. Beginning on the west bank of the Iowa River about five miles above Cleer Creek beginning at a Tree thence meandering the [Iowa] River up to the mouth of a Small Creek then running to a Southerly direction across the Hill to the first mentioned bound. said Claim is timber with Sugar tree [maple?] oak lin [the genus linden?] and various kinds of Timber February 26th 1840 said Claim is supposed to contain three lots handed in March 14th 1840.

In 1843 Fellows's daughter Elizabeth married Isaac Dennis, an emigrant from Ohio, and together they assumed ownership of the farm. (The land remained in the Dennis name until 1943, according to plat books, and continued to exist after that in the minds of locals through the 1980s, as indicated in their references to "the old Dennis farm" when I inquired about the history of Indian Run.) By 1859, the date of the earliest extant landowner's map (available in the State Historical Society library), the Dennis property included the land on both sides of Clear Creek, in sections 6 and 7 of Township 79 North, Range 6 West.

When Elizabeth Dennis was interviewed by local historians in the early part of the twentieth century (she was then in her 90s), she recalled an idyllic existence as a member of a pioneer farm family. She described her new home as "a land of milk and honey," with the milk provided by the family cow and the honey gathered from hollow trees along Clear Creek. Data from the Agricultural Census for the period 1850 to 1880 (available in the State Historical Society microfiche collection) confirmed that the farm was experiencing flush times. It took little time for the Dennis farm to make the transition from subsistence to market agriculture.

The 1850 Census reveals that three milk cows produced enough milk to provide 100 pounds of butter and 900 pounds of cheese. The total value of the livestock, which included 15 swine, was $186. Crops included Irish potatoes (130 bushels), oats (190 bushels), and Indian corn (1,200 bushels). Even at this early stage Johnson County farmers were surpassing the production figures of subsistence farming, undoubtedly due to the fertility of the soil and the proximity of major transportation routes: the railroad (which extended only as far west as Iowa City at the time) and the Mississippi River. In 1850 the Dennis farm was actually below average in terms of its cash value, $1,330, as compared to the average worth of a farm in Johnson County of $2,343, but would not remain so for long.

With the advent of new and improved farm technology, Iowa farmers began to increase their farm production and acreage. Sodbusting became a specialized occupation as mechanics developed special plows to dig furrows through the thick, tough prairie sod. According to Allan Bogue in *From Prairie to Corn Belt,* corn gradually replaced wheat as the bumper crop when pests damaged winter wheat crops in the 1840s. But the Dennis farm (and others in Johnson County) remained diversified through 1880, with wheat, oats, Irish potatoes, hay, and Indian corn continuing to be grown in significant quantities. Dennis also raised more swine (40 in 1860) and slaughtered more (for a total of $500) than in previous years, and in 1870 his orchard produced $50 worth of fruit and 20 gallons of wine, and his beehive produced 200 pounds of honey. Perhaps most significantly, in 1870 and 1880 he sold timber products harvested from the woods along Clear Creek: in 1870 $900 worth of forest products, and in 1880 30 cords of wood sold for $120.

The figures from the 1880 Census are the most detailed. The Dennis farm then totaled 250 acres: 160 tilled; 10 in orchard, pasture, vineyard, and meadow; 50 in woodland; and 30 in old fields. The total value of the farm had climbed from $1,330 in 1850 to $10,000. Farm implements accumulated to a total value of $840 (up from $120 in 1850). Isaac Dennis began to hire outside labor as the farm grew in size, activities, and worth. Someone had to help tend his 15 horses, 7 milk cows, 14 head of cattle, and 200 chickens. His star also began to rise in the community. He became trustee and county supervisor of West Lucas Township, and his farmhouse was a local landmark, constructed of walnut shipped all the way from Muscatine.

Certainly in its long history, Indian Run had never before been the site of such intensive human productivity. The landscape had been transformed from a prairie and forest "wilderness" to an orderly pattern of fields and fences. Yet though farming was the dominant land-use activity on the land from 1838 until the

1960s, it was not the most memorable. In fact, had farmers been the only users of the land following the removal of the Sac and Fox, undoubtedly Indian Run would have remained like ninety-seven percent of Iowa: farmland. But the encampment of twenty-five hundred Mormons on the land in 1856 and 1857 changed its destiny.

In 1856 the railroad extended no farther than Iowa City. This was the crucial fact in determining the Mormon occupation of Indian Run. Many of the Mormon emigrants heading west to the newly discovered kingdom of Deseret (later Utah) could not afford the price of passage from Scandinavia and England or the train fare from New York City; so they agreed to work for the church as a form of payment. But because the Mormon Emigration Fund was exhausted by an overwhelming number of converts, many were then forced to travel on foot from Iowa to Utah, pushing their belongings in wooden handcarts thirteen hundred miles across the midsection of the continent.

The State Historical Society of Iowa library holds a number of documents related to the Mormon occupation of Indian Run. As I read through them, I realized that once again (as in my study of land-use practices of the Sac and Fox) I had some mental obstacles to overcome — this time some liberal prejudices concerning twentieth-century Mormon politics. But what my ZPG- and feminist-minded friends failed to realize was that as a pioneering people in the nineteenth century, the Mormons were quite successful in their communitarian approach to settlement in the arid West. Their politics aside, I came to a much better understanding and appreciation for this quintessentially American religious movement as I studied Mormonism in general and their occupation of Indian Run in particular.

I learned the general history of Mormonism from the standard history of the movement, Leonard Arrington's *Great Basin Kingdom.* Joseph Smith founded the Church of Jesus Christ of Latter-day Saints in 1830 when he published *The Book of Mormon,* after having gathered a following by proselytizing in up-state New York. Persecution soon followed, however, as some of the more unorthodox practices accepted by the church, such as polygamy, antagonized local residents. Smith and his followers attempted to establish the church in Ohio, Missouri, and Illinois, but were met everywhere with open hostility. Finally with the assassination of Smith in Nauvoo, Illinois, in 1844, Brigham Young assumed power and moved the faithful to the Great Basin country in 1847. From there he later issued this proclamation:

Let all the Saints who can, gather up for Zion, and come while the

way is open for them; let the poor come, whether they receive aid
or not from the Emigration Fund; let them come on foot with
hand carts, or wheel barrows; let them gird up their loins and walk
through and nothing shall hinder or stay them.

And come on foot with handcarts they did. From the
journals kept by several of the emigrants, a detailed picture
emerges of the tent city the Mormons established on Indian Run.
Five separate companies arrived in 1856 and two in 1857, each
numbering between 150 and 576. John D. McCallister, the com-
missary for the 1856 encampment, wrote this entry upon arriving
in Iowa City:

> Wednesday 14th A.M. Commenced hauling our luggage to camp
> by wagons and handcarts. All was safely lodged in camp by 11
> o'clock. Many wet to the skin for it rained very fast. Brother
> Ferguson and I overtook a family and carried two of their little
> fellows into camp, it was located on a beautiful hill about three
> miles from the center of the city. Plenty of wood and water.

Being a theocratic communitarian society, the Mormons imposed a degree of discipline and order upon the landscape surely
unknown in the history of Indian Run. They built a granary and
mechanical shop, hired locals to perform some of the necessary
work, sent the women out to work for local farmers, and put the
remainder of their force to work on the handcarts. Archer Walters, a forty-seven-year-old carpenter from Sheffield, England,
brought along his wife and five children. His special skills kept
him busy in camp; "still working at the handcarts" is a frequent
refrain in his journal. The handcarts, constructed of hickory and
oak, were built to hold no more than seventeen pounds of posses-
sions, the maximum amount of luggage allowed each family.

Conditions in the camp were less than ideal. Daniel D.
McArthur, captain of the second handcart company in 1856,
mentioned in his journal that meetings were held to emphasize the
importance of maintaining sanitary conditions. This may not
have been easy, since as many as twenty people slept in a tent.
Frequent thunderstorms also contributed to the emigrants' discomfort. All three journal-keepers noted in the entry for May 26,
1856, the occurrence of a severe lightning storm that pounded the
area for three hours. Fever and malnourishment afflicted the emigrants as well.

At least six people died during the 1856 encampment, most
of them infants. Walters had the unenviable task of constructing
crude coffins for the deceased. (As late as 1975 the gravesites were
still noticeable.) According to plat books, no one owned the land

on which the Mormons camped, though the Dennis property bordered it. Elizabeth Dennis commented about its general conditions:

> [The Mormons] were destituted of provisions, presenting a sight truly pitiable. Deaths were frequent and births were infinitely pathetic. From a log, the bark would be stripped in half cylinders, the bodies would be placed between them and then laid in a shallow trench or cast out upon the waters of the Iowa. After the burial there would be a prayer, a hymn, then a futile attempt to mark the spot where the loved one had been left. At the bank of the creek women washed the soiled garments of their families. A smoke rose into the air from the thousand campfires.

Obviously, Dennis was not an objective observer. She also recalled helping a young Mormon girl of questionable faith escape from the camp, and she expressed her delight over the fact that the girl later married a local Christian. But in general there is little evidence to suggest that relations between the Mormons and the local residents were openly hostile, probably due to the fact that it was understood that the Mormons were itinerants, not prospective inhabitants. Indian Run was but a way station for them.

I have often wondered: Had the handcart pioneers been able to complete their thirteen-hundred-mile odyssey without incident, would the site of their encampment have later been set aside as a park? For much greater tragedy befell the Mormons during their continental trek, and mass death has a way of sanctifying historical events and places. The fourth and fifth companies of 1856 did not depart Indian Run until July 15 and July 29—much too late to avoid a winter crossing of the Rocky Mountains. Disaster struck. More than 200 of the 500 emigrants of the fourth company perished in winter storms, and between 135 and 150 of the 576 of the fifth company died also. Little wonder then that their numbers dropped sharply in 1857, with only two companies, of 149 and 330, making the trip—this time without difficulty.

In 1858 the railroad was extended to Florence, Nebraska, and so Indian Run as a campsite for the Mormons ended. The land immediately along Clear Creek eventually returned to woodland, replacing the trees that the Dennises and the Mormons had cut; the remainder continued to be cultivated by farmers. In fact the farmscape dominated well into the twentieth century, though monoculture of corn and later soybeans destroyed the earlier diversity, even as Indian Run itself emerged as an island of woodland surrounded by farmland, a railroad corridor, a commercial strip, and high-density housing. The Mormon campsite remained buried until its figurative and literal excavation in the 1970s.

That excavation began with the planning of the Coralville Centennial celebration. In 1973 a local Boy Scout troop proposed to Richard Gibson, director of the Office for Facilities Planning and Utilization at the University of Iowa, that they be allowed to build a short, crude historical trail on Indian Run to commemorate the experience of the Mormon handcart pioneers. The university agreed, and many of the descendants of the emigrants gathered later that year to pay their respects.

It was to the Office for Facilities Planning and Utilization that I turned for information on the actual creation of Mormon Handcart Park. A sign at the trailhead read "Erected in 1979 as a cooperative effort of The Church of Jesus Christ of Latter-Day Saints and The University of Iowa," and I became curious about this collaboration. Dick Gibson's office was happy to turn over to me the files on the creation of the park, and once again I was

Fig. 2.3. Banks of Clear Creek today. Here, or near here, the Mormons of 1856 and 1857 drew their water and did their washing, while the handcarts were being built for the trek to Utah. (Photo by Robert F. Sayre)

faced with the prospect of transforming lots of facts into a coherent land-use history.

The university began to acquire land near Indian Run in the 1960s. A golf course replaced farmland to the southeast, followed by apartment complexes for students, but the woodland along Clear Creek remained an unofficial natural area. The university discussed the possibility of developing hiking trails there, since, according to one official, "in this day of concern over the environment and the preservation of natural areas . . . consideration should be given to developing the rougher areas on the old Dennis farm . . . into small beauty spots or parks which would be available for students to go to on foot." The influence of the so-called "Environmental Decade" was afoot — an era during which the slogan "Parks Are for People" became popular. Not until 1973, however, did sufficient impetus materialize to transform Indian Run into an official park. Following the Coralville Centennial, the Mormon Church became actively involved in promoting Indian Run to park status. Donald Doty, a university professor and local church activist, met with Gibson to discuss this possiblity. The plans were finalized when the Mormon Church agreed to provide the funding to develop a park site. The State Archaeological Office then conducted a surface study of the 1856–1857 campsite but found no artifacts, though the report mentioned that a small cemetery was clearly visible. Given the written evidence, the report concluded, it was likely that the Mormons had indeed camped in the area. The lack of material evidence was explained by the frequent flooding of Clear Creek, which would have washed away the remains of the camp.

The decision to establish Mormon Handcart Park came just in time, for in 1976 the university built a trailer court for students immediately south of the woodland along Clear Creek; and according to a report in the files of the Facilities Planning Office, Indian Run had begun to serve the ignoble functions of carwash site and garbage dump. (Remains of the latter are still visible along the creek bottomland.) It was clear that in the mid-1970s development and its residue were encroaching upon this tiny parcel of forest.

The park was officially dedicated on August 1, 1980. Landscape architects constructed a quarter-mile paved trail with a historical monument and interpretive signs at two overlooks, and in consultation with Paul Christiansen, a professor of biology at Cornell College, re-created a tallgrass prairie near the parking lot and along the final portion of trail. On nice weekends strollers walk the official trail, pausing at the signs to read about the area's ecology and history.

Fig. 2.4.   Paved trail through the woods along the
south edge of the handcart site. Part of the trail also
forms a boundary between the woods and the restored
grassland. (Photo by Drake Hokanson)

On August 10, 1982, University of Iowa president James
Freedman received a letter from Clara Oleson, a lawyer representing the Iowa Civil Liberties Union, requesting information
about the cooperative effort between the Mormon Church and the
university. She and the group were concerned about the First
Amendment implications of this collaboration.

The matter was referred to Richard Gibson, who in turn
referred it to a lawyer for the university. He quickly dispatched a
letter to Oleson in which he expressed his opinion that there had
been no illegal or unconstitutional acts involved in the cooperation between church and state, either in the negotiations leading
up to the cooperative agreement or in the creation of the park
itself, and cited a 1971 Supreme Court decision to uphold his
opinion.

Donald Doty received copies of the letters in this exchange,
and his two subsequent responses to Dick Gibson suggest a new
perception of Indian Run—one reflecting the kind of protec-

tionist posture people automatically assume today when a nearby park is threatened in any way. "Why," he wanted to know, "do people have to be so critical of something that is as nice and as beneficial to the people of this community as is that little historical site?" He now hoped that the university lawyer's response "will put a quiet end to the truly unnecessary and unwarranted criticism of this nice development that we have made available to the people of our community."

In the early fall of 1986, I decided to take a walk in the nearby woods. By that time I had completed my research on the history of Indian Run but, having been gone all summer, had not had an opportunity to do fieldwork for a while. As I left the paved trail and plunged into the forest heading for Clear Creek,

Fig. 2.5.   An unmarked trail in the lower level of the park, kept open mainly by hikers' feet. The small size of the trees indicates that this land was only recently a field or pasture. (Photo by Robert F. Sayre)

the distant roar from a university football game was replaced by woodland noises. Golden-shafted flickers cried out as they flew from snag to snag; on an oak I noticed a White-breasted nuthatch climbing downward, whistling its low, nasal notes; and in the treetops there were the unmistakable, insistent calls of Cardinals, perhaps guarding their territories. I was in my element again—a wild landscape.

Approaching a slough of the creek, I tried to be quiet while wading through the understory. Although it was fall, Indian summer prevailed and, yes, on some protruding logs lay several Box turtles, indolently sunning themselves. I glassed them and then moved on past an ancient cottonwood of tremendous girth to an oxbow in the creek, where I spooked a Great blue heron feeding along the bank. The water was so low that I could lie on an exposed sandy beach, and like the turtles I indulged myself, soaking up the lovely autumn weather.

After a spell—who knows how long?—I moved upstream, noting the extensive beaver work, the young hardwoods gnawed and dropped into the water, some of the woodchips quite recent. Near the confluence of Clear Creek and the small tributary of Lily's Run, the site of the Mormon encampment, Fox squirrels and groundhogs scampered through the brush. I noted more birds: a Brown creeper, Black-capped chickadees, and a Hairy woodpecker. Then I leaped across Lily's Run and continued farther up-creek where the forest grew thicker, wilder. I startled two White-tailed deer and followed their trail until the creek bent sharply again; a Red-tailed hawk flew off from the top of a tall cottonwood at my approach. Coming back, I saw through the tangle of treetops a Barred owl nestled in the bare branches of the forest canopy. Once again the woods had proven to be good therapy for taking my mind off school.

I stopped as I usually do to climb a tree in which some deerslayer had constructed a hunting stand. I wanted to reflect on the history of "my" turf, now that my research was mostly over and I was seeing it fresh again after several months' absence.

I was no longer merely another visitor, occasionally strolling down its paved path and glancing at the interpretive signs. I had become another of its long history of inhabitants; this landscape was my home, part of my daily routine. True, I did not depend on it for my physical subsistence as had the Sac and Fox and the Dennises. Nevertheless, Indian Run was important to me as a place where I could stretch both my legs and my mind. Looking down on part of it from my perch, I realized the cycles the landscape had gone through, the continuities in the character of the land and the general land-use activities that had endured. Even today, it dawned on me, certain aspects of it persist. Every two or three years in the spring park personnel burn off the prairie, as Native Americans did, to promote its regrowth. The fire blackens the surface but does not affect the long roots of the grasses. In a couple of weeks the ground will be lush green, and by late summer the prairie again will be "horse high," recalling the seas of grass the pioneers described when they crossed the midwestern frontier. And with a little imagination, the woods along the creek still have the feel of wildness in them, representing part of the tiny portion of Iowa that is still wild. I thought of some of the last exhibits in Iowa Hall, depicting woodland-prairie scenes, places where a little of Iowa's natural heritage survived. How nice that the scenes in the exhibit could actually be re-created in nature, and were not irretrievable, forever lost, like the passenger pigeon! And how ironic that a wilderness could be reborn!

At least in the mind of one observer, then, Indian Run has come full circle: from a wilderness of prairie and forest to farmland back to a wild place. History does repeat itself, sometimes in strange and mysterious ways.

3

PRAIRIE PAST
&
PRAIRIE PRESENT

Paul Christiansen and Robert F. Sayre

Driving across Iowa today, staring at miles and miles of even rows of corn and soybeans, you have no idea of the beauty and terror of early Iowa—unless you happen to be caught in a tornado or a blizzard or to find yourself in one of the rare patches of surviving prairie.

"The whole of the surface of these beautiful plains," wrote one visitor in 1840, "is clad throughout the season of verdure with every imaginable variety of color. . . . It is impossible to conceive a more infinite diversity, or a richer profusion of hues."

And so it was, as Lewis and Clark, James Audubon, Margaret Fuller, Judge James Hall, and any number of early visitors to the prairies of Illinois and Iowa all wrote—an "ocean" of grass and flowers. The land rolled like subsiding waves of a great storm. The grass rippled in the wind. And the flowers burst, from May to October, in whites, blues, reds, and yellows. (That *wasn't* like an ocean.)

Yet if the fogs of early spring rolled in and you could no longer see the Lone Tree or Pilot Grove you were headed for (the buoys in this ocean—now remembered in the names of a few Iowa towns), you were as lost as a sailor without a compass. Or if you were a child and fell out of the family prairie schooner, you were "drowned"—as children still are every summer when they wander into tall corn. To spot a child or a man or an ox who had sunk into that rippling ocean, you had to stand up on the saddle of your horse—and even then you couldn't scan more than a few hundred feet. Not after late July, anyway. For by then the tall grasses like big bluestem and the flowers like rosinweed and compass plant were six to eight feet high, tall enough to reach over the head of a horse, or be tied in a knot across the horse's back.

It really was oceanic—hundreds of thousands of square miles of this, from what is now western Ohio to eastern Nebraska, from Saskatchewan to Texas. Nothing divided it but rivers, bordered with oaks and hickories and other hardwoods, and occasional stretches of lakes and marshes—what we now call "wetlands," though most of them are gone too. It was terrifying. And all the more so because, unlike an ocean, it burned. In a dry spell at almost any time of year, though especially spring and fall, when struck by lightning or ignited by Indians or some foolish traveler or settler, it could suddenly become an ocean of fire.

"Till I saw this," wrote a pious Methodist preacher in Illinois in 1835, making the best comparison he could, "I could never understand . . . the scripture. The cloud which overspread the camp of Israel and kept off the rays of sun by day, was a *pillar of fire by night*. It was literally so with the smoke which rose from these fires."

Think of that as you sit in front of your motel and watch the lightning of an approaching storm. Or go to one of the tiny remnants of prairie on a windy September afternoon and stand on the highest hump of sod you can find—you will feel like an abandoned sailor, with your eyes just high enough to see the horizon. But crouch down and you are closed in by the thicket of stems, and you cannot see more than a few feet. After sunset you will have no guide but the stars. Around you are turtles, foxes, snakes, hundreds of mice, and thousands of mosquitoes. Not a very welcome place to sleep. If fire came, you would burn to death, for you cannot run like a deer or go to your burrow like a mole. Yet in the morning you will hear hundreds of birds, Bobolinks and crows and geese, and think you are in a garden, a garden of the gods, a new Eden—as you are, or were.

For this was the Iowa of only 150 years ago: an ocean as hot as the tropics in summer and as numbing as the poles in winter, a garden of strawberries in spring, and an almost impenetrable mat of dried flowers and grasses in the fall. And at any time between the Moon of the Falling Leaves and the Moon of the Snowblind (late November to early April), a blizzard could rush in, dropping temperatures twenty degrees in an hour and bringing snow so thick that a man could get lost between his house and barn. There was nothing to stop the winds, and they howled, as Hamlin Garland said, "like ten thousand tigers."

Fig. 3.1.   The towering flames and smoke from a controlled burning of a replanted prairie give some idea of the awesomeness of prairie fires. (Photo by Bob Campagna)

No wonder the early travelers and settlers told such conflicting stories of these tallgrass prairies. Their observations varied according to what season they came, their own purposes, and just their own psyches. For as with oceans of water, people see them in many different moods, from many different perspectives — and not everyone likes them.

About tallgrass prairies, however, people from the East knew even less than they knew about the Atlantic and the Pacific. They knew few names for the grasses and flowers, and they knew nothing of the complex geological and ecological history that had made this desert/garden. Many thought that the only land that was good for farming was forestland, which is why many pressed on to Oregon or California. The rest settled at first only where there were trees. They chose the river banks, often taking the land the Indians had just been forced to vacate, or they went to what they called "oak openings," groves of bur oaks. The bur oak could survive prairie fires because of its thick, corky bark, and so grew up leaving densely shaded groves where the grasses could not grow. So to many travelers and settlers these openings were welcome "islands," with a low cover of bright flowers in the spring and dried leaves in the fall. Here they were likely to build their first cabins, cutting the wood for buildings, fences, and fuel, while also beginning the tedious, exhausting labor of "breaking" the sod.

John Muir, later the explorer of the California Sierras, grew up on a frontier farm in southern Wisconsin, and in *The Story of My Boyhood and Youth* he wrote a detailed description of this sod busting.

> Most of these ploughs were very large, turning furrows from eighteen inches to two feet wide, and drawn by four or five yoke of oxen. [Often they were owned and driven by men who did this for hire, but Muir did some of it himself.] They were used only for the first ploughing, in breaking up the wild sod woven into a tough mass, chiefly by the cordlike roots of perennial grasses, reinforced by the taproots of oak and hickory bushes, called "grubs," some . . . more than a century old and four or five inches in diameter. In the hardest ploughing on the most difficult ground, the grubs were said to be as thick as the hairs on a dog's back. If in good trim, the plough cut through the wood and turned over these grubs as if the century-old wood were soft like the flesh of carrots and turnips; but if not in good trim the grubs promptly tossed the plough out of the ground.

Fig. 3.2. An oak grove being used as spring pasture for hogs. The intermediate size of these trees suggests that about one hundred years ago this was prairie. (Photo by Robert F. Sayre)

Muir explains that before the farmers came, fires had kept most of these grubs from ever growing above ground. But once fires were contained by ploughed fields and roads, the grubs in the still unploughed land (some of which was kept for pastures) soon "grew up into trees and formed tall thickets so dense that it was difficult to walk through them . . ." Thus did some prairie surprisingly turn into thicket and forest—the origin of some of the magnificent oak and hickory groves in Wisconsin, Iowa, and Illinois today. Romantically, some people are likely to ask if this is "virgin timber," but unless it is one of the remaining oak openings or "savannahs" (now extremely rare), these stands were probably once prairie. It is the trimming by livestock and the occasional thinning and pruning by men that have cultivated them as woods.

Overall, however, Iowa probably had less of these tree roots in its soil than neighboring Wisconsin, which is why the Iowa prairies were more rapidly converted to cropland. They were somewhat easier to plough, and once ploughed, the roots of the grasses and flowers (called forbs) decayed sooner than the grubs. Thus the once mislabeled "barren prairie" became ideal, after the year or two it took the roots to decay, for the settlers' first crops of wheat and oats. These, after all, were but domesticated "grasses," well suited to the same soil. The same was true of the corn they planted later, while soybeans were another legume with which to replace the many species of wild legumes that had grown on the early prairies. In fact, Iowa was so well suited to crops and pastures, as well as to orchards and vegetables, that by 1900 almost all the original prairie and woods were gone. It was one of the fastest environmental changes that men and women had up to that time caused, the epic "taming of the prairies," as they called it. But from an ecological standpoint it was also like a plague, a plague of ploughs. Could John Muir return today and visit Iowa, he would find far fewer acres of original prairie here than acres of redwoods in California. They are less than one-tenth of one percent, a fraction that becomes more precious every year.

What we have learned, in the interim, is that prairie ecology is just as complex and delicate as forest ecology. And a new or replanted prairie takes just as long to become well established as does a new forest. But to understand this we must study some of the precious remnants, and so the balance of this essay will be a kind of tour of some of them, with lists of places to go and the flora and fauna to look for. All seekers of prairies should equip themselves with one or more of the field guides listed at the end of this essay, because the forbs and grasses are not easy to identify. To the novice (as to the early settlers), many look alike. In addition, prairie seekers should wear long pants and long-sleeved shirts (many of the grasses are like tiny hacksaws) and carry field glasses for looking at the birds. Finally, visitors should be respectful of these plots. A horde of photographers, all crouching down in the same place to photograph the same rare plant, can damage the surrounding plants, destroying the immediate environment that the plant depends upon. But if more people begin to appreciate the prairies, sentiment will grow for their further preservation and replanting—the subject of the remainder of this essay.

Prairies remaining in Iowa are few and far between. However, through the efforts of the Department of Natural Resources (DNR), County Conservation Boards, The Nature Conservancy, Iowa Natural Heritage Foundation, and other organizations and private individuals, most parts of the state have preserved repre-

TABLE 3.1. SOME PRAIRIE PRESERVES IN IOWA

Name	Location	Size (acres)
Ames High School Prairie	Story County in Ames	7
Anderson Prairie	Emmet County near Estherville	200
Cavler Prairie	Dickinson County near Spirit Lake	160
Cedar Hills Sand Prairie	Black Hawk County near Cedar Falls	35
Dineson Prairie	Shelby County near Harlan	20
Fairmont Park	Pottawattamie County in Council Bluffs	10
Fish Farm Mounds	Allamakee County near Lansing	3
Five Ridges Prairie	Plymouth County near Sioux City	500
Hayden Prairie	Howard County near Lime Springs	240
Hoffman Prairie	Cerro Gordo County near Ventura	30
Kalsow Prairie	Pocahontas County near Manson	160
Kish-Ke-Kosh Prairie	Jasper County near Newton	17
Loess Hills Wildlife Management Unit	Monona County near Onawa	200
Manikowski Prairie	Clinton County near Goose Lake	40
Ocheyedan Mound	Osceola County near Ocheyedan	24
Rolling Thunder Prairie	Warren County near New Virginia	123
Sheeder Prairie	Guthrie County near Guthrie Center	25
Shield Prairie	Muscatine County near Muscatine	80
Sioux City Prairie	Woodbury County in Sioux City	80
Steele Prairie	Cherokee County near Larrabee	200
Turin Loess Hills Preserve	Monona County near Turin	100
Waubonsie State Park	Fremont County near Sidney	50
Williams Prairie	Johnson County near Oxford	30

sentative prairies. To help you locate prairies near you or your route a list is given (Table 3.1). Four prairies (Hayden, Kalsow, Steele, Cayler), all state preserves located across the northern one-half of Iowa, are excellent examples of Iowa prairies. All are mesic prairies; that is, they are neither extremely wet nor dry and have adequate but not excessive moisture throughout most of the growing season.

Hayden Prairie, in northeast Iowa in Howard County, was purchased by the state of Iowa in 1946 and named after Dr. Ada Hayden, a botanist at Iowa State University. Dr. Hayden was instrumental in alerting Iowans to the rapid disappearance of prairie remnants in the 1930s and 1940s. She and a committee from the Iowa Academy of Science identified more than one hundred remaining prairies at that time. Hayden Prairie was the first of several to be purchased by the state. Of Hayden Prairie's 240 acres, 160 acres, or one-quarter of a square mile, are upland prairie. More than two hundred different kinds of plants have been located. Firebreaks are mowed through the prairie that also serve as paths into the middle of the prairie. (Two forty-acre parcels to the south and southwest of the large tract are lower and wetter and are recovering from grazing and invasion by quaking aspen.)

Kalsow Prairie, in Pocahontas County and west of Fort Dodge, is a quarter section of mesic prairie with a swale, a wetter area, running north-south across the middle of it. In the northwest corner of the prairie is an area that was once heavily grazed. Since 1949 when Kalsow Prairie was purchased, prairie species have been reinvading this grassy area. As you walk toward the undisturbed prairie you will see more and more prairie species, which will gradually become the dominant vegetation.

Steele Prairie, northwest of Larrabee in Cherokee County, is the newest addition to Iowa's prairie preserves. Purchased jointly by The Nature Conservancy and the DNR in 1987, its two hundred acres hold a number of rare prairie species. The preservation of this prairie, resulting from its being used as wild hayland instead of plowing it up to grow corn and soybeans, illustrates the dedication of the Steele family to our natural heritage. Steele Prairie, with a drainage-way running from north to southeast, provides habitats for mesic as well as wet-prairie species.

Cayler Prairie, 160 acres, is located a few miles west of West Lake Okoboji in Dickinson County. It is in the "knob-and-kettle" country that borders the Des Moines Lobe, the last area glaciated in Iowa. Knobs with gravelly soil are habitats for some of Iowa's most drought-tolerant prairie species. On the other hand, pot holes, undrained depressions, are often very wet and have marsh-edge plants in them; between are expanses of mesic prairie. In certain places in Cayler Prairie you can walk down into a pot hole and not be able to see any evidence of humans, such as buildings, power lines, or cultivated fields. Only a contrail from an airplane passing over might break the spell of what it was like to be on the prairie before European settlement.

Prairie remnants across Iowa vary greatly in the kinds and numbers of plants growing on them. The nature of the soil, the lay of the land, and the amount of rainfall all help to determine which species will be successful. Where the soil is sandy or gravelly little moisture is held and grasses such as little bluestem and junegrass do well. In low-lying areas where the soil contains large amounts of clay, water drains through very slowly and switchgrass and sloughgrass are likely to be dominant. On the "goat prairies" (so called because they are so steep) of northeastern Iowa and the western Loess Hills, the summer sun blazing down on the southwest-facing slopes creates a very dry environment. The variations in soil type, slope, and rainfall help to produce an ever-changing mosaic of prairie plants across the state.

Prairie Through the Seasons

To fully appreciate the diversity of the prairie one must visit it several times throughout the year, from spring, through summer, into fall, and even in winter. Plants and animals live by the seasons—active during some, dormant in others, with none occupying center stage at all times. A visitor to a mesic prairie in early spring would be greeted by hoary puccoon, with yellow-orange flowers, and violet wood-sorrel. Star grass, a tiny yellow flower with hairy grasslike leaves, and blue-eyed grass, with tiny blue flowers on a slender stalk several inches tall, are also out early in the spring. In the northeastern third of Iowa, shooting star, a pointed flower with petals folded back, ranges in color from purple to white. The leaves are all at ground level, and the flowers droop at the tip of a stalk that is more than a foot tall. Other spring flowers are golden alexanders and prairie violet. Within the daisy family prairie ragwort and dwarf dandelion both bloom in the spring. Prairie ragwort has yellow heads, much like a tiny daisy and is often seen growing in patches in roadside ditches. Dwarf dandelion has flowers similar to dandelion but the heads are on taller stalks and the petals are more orange in color. On drier prairies pasque flower is the first bloom of the season in mid-April, with pale blue petals forming a miniature solar collector that gives a place for tiny insects to warm up during cool spring days. Pasque flower reduces the windchill by slowing the movement of air with a forest of tiny hairs on its stem and leaves. Close upon the heels of pasque flower is early buttercup. The tiny butter yellow flowers stay close to the ground, just above the dead grasses of the previous year. Other dry prairie spring flowers are narrow-leaved puccoon, lousewort, and bastard toadflax. Birdfoot violet has leaves that are divided into narrow segments, which resemble a bird's foot and whose flowers are more flat-faced than other violets (it is sometimes called the pansy-faced violet). Several milk vetches, members of the pea family, bloom on dry prairies in the spring; milk vetch with light yellow flowers is found on the Loess Hills. Ground-plum has light purple flowers that develop seed pods resembling plums by midsummer. Usually pods from previous years are still under the plant unless a prairie fire has burned them up.

In northeastern Iowa long-plumed purple ayens blooms on moist prairies in early spring. The small white petals are surrounded by dark red sepals that are far more showy. When the cluster of seeds in each flower matures, each seed develops a gray feathery hair, producing a tuft of "whiskers," suggesting the names "old man's beard" and "prairie smoke." Another wet prairie spring flower is swamp saxifrage with a cluster of tiny green flowers on a sturdy stalk and with large, hairy leaves next to the ground.

The spring season is also an interesting time to watch birds on the prairie. Both Eastern and Western meadowlarks nest in the prairie grasses. They perch on dead stalks of the tall plants of the previous year and sing to advertise their territories. Bobolinks are found on larger prairies, especially those that are in the wet range of mesic. Stop and listen to the din they create as they begin nesting. It alone is worth a trip. Sparrows of various sorts, such as the Lark bunting, LeConte's sparrow, Grasshopper sparrow, Savannah sparrow, Sharp-tailed sparrow, and Swamp sparrow are all active in the spring and all nest on the prairie. Henslow's sparrow is spotted sporadically across the state and is the most rare of the prairie sparrows.

As the season progresses and the vegetation gradually grows taller, the spring flowers are hidden by the summer-blooming plants, which in turn will be over-topped by the fall plants. During each season the flowers ready for pollination are found above the other plants. Once pollination has occurred they cease growing and form seeds while the later-blooming plants pass them by. This way all season long the prairie has some plants blooming, some that have finished and are forming seeds, and others that will bloom later.

Summer on the prairie is a time for an even wider variety of plants to bloom. In June on mesic prairies purple coneflower (daisy family) is very prominent because its large heads stand well above other plants. The drooping purple petals stay on the head for more than a month. Small, dark-colored butterflies called Skippers feed on the nectar of the coneflower. Later they lay eggs on the lower leaves of little bluestem grass.

Ox-eye, or false sunflower, is another member of the daisy family. Its large heads with yellow petals and yellow centers begin appearing in mid-June. The flowers are long-lived and remain on the plant. (When grown in a garden, ox-eye makes a very good cut flower because the blooms last for weeks in a vase.) Ox-eye is very aggressive, even weedy, and often is a pioneer into disturbed areas such as gopher mounds. For this reason it is often used when planting a prairie.

Prairie phlox is also a very conspicuous flower in early summer. Clusters of five-petaled flowers bloom at the top of short, leafy stems. Their color varies from purple to almost pure white with only spots of purple at the base of each petal. These spots are called "nectar guides" because they help insects find their way to nectar in the flower. Many flowers have nectar guides, the color usually contrasting with the background color of the petals. In some cases, such as on black-eyed-susan, the petal is not spotted but rather the outer portion of each petal reflects ultraviolet light, which insects can detect, while the inner portion of the petal absorbs ultraviolet light. Thus, the center of the flower appears as a bull's-eye marking the area where nectar is available.

Wild strawberries, members of the rose family, are native prairie plants. They nestle close to the ground and therefore must bloom early to attract pollinators. Later they produce delicious but small fruits with tiny seeds embedded in the surface. Another rose family member blooming in the summer is the wild rose, Iowa's state flower. Actually, three species of wild rose are found on prairies: *Rosa arkansana* and *R. carolina* on mesic prairies, *Rosa blanda* on wet prairies. Arkansana and carolina are very similar, with pink flowers and spiny stems, and both develop red hips (fruit containing the seeds) in the fall. Blanda has similar flowers and hips, but its stem is almost spineless and deep red in color.

Cream false indigo is a stunning plant with large, cream-colored sweet-pea-type flowers on a bushlike plant. The plant grows very rapidly in the spring and reaches about two feet before producing flowers in early June. Sprays of flowers grow sideways from the plant, later developing dusky gray inflated pods about two inches long. Most of the time the pods are infested with weevils and insect larvae that consume the seeds before they have a chance to drop from the pod.

The tall grasses that the prairie is famous for do not bloom and produce seeds until fall. However, several early summer, or "cool-season," grasses are an important part of the prairie. Porcupine grass has very long, narrow leaves and seed stalks about three feet tall. Few seeds are produced but they are quite large, about one-half inch long, and very sharp at one end; the other end has a bristle attached, which is more than three inches long. An odd habit of the bristle is to twist as it dries out and untwist as it is rewetted. When the seed drops off the plant and falls into the tangle of leaves, stems, and dead plant material near the ground, it manages to work its way through to the soil by twisting and untwisting with every change in humidity. Seeds have been known to twist their way into the flesh of sheep when the seeds were caught in their wool and sometimes even push their way through a paper bag after they were collected.

A much less conspicuous grass is rosette panicgrass. Named for the habit of producing large leaves close to the ground, a rosette, these grasses stand about one foot tall. Each plant produces a few roundish seeds in early summer. Although never a dominant grass, rosette panicgrass is important in filling spaces and invading disturbed areas.

On dry prairies an important cool-season grass is junegrass, which grows in tufts or bunches (a bunch grass), mostly in sandy soils. Often growing with it in the eastern half of Iowa is goat's-rue, a plant of the pea family. Flowers are sweet-pealike with a large, pink lower petal and yellow side petals; leaves are divided into many leaflets. As the pods mature they split and twist, throwing the seeds out. In the western quarter of Iowa, especially in the Loess Hills, another dry prairie plant is locoweed. Stalks of blue flowers appear in early June on plants having large basal leaves with very narrow leaflets. Horses and cattle grazing locoweed become disoriented and stagger or even fall down, sometimes eventually dying from the poisons in the plant.

Another interesting plant of the Loess Hills is the yucca. It has long, narrow leaves that droop and a central flower stalk that grows to three or four feet with large white flowers attached along its length. A very large seed pod develops (two to three inches long by one and one-half inches in diameter) with six rows of flat seeds stacked in each pod. The flower is pollinated by the Yucca moth, which flies at night. The moth gathers pollen, packs it on the stigma of the flower, and then lays eggs in the ovary of the flower, the same chamber within which the seeds develop. When the larvae hatch they have a ready-made food supply. They eat their way through the seeds, usually only consuming the richest part, the embryo, until they have reached full growth. At this point there are usually a few seeds left to attempt to produce new plants. However, it is not crucial that the yucca or any other perennial prairie plant produce seeds every year. Most perennial plants will come up year after year, and if seed production is not successful one year there will be other years. Over the years each plant has to produce only one successful seedling to replace itself to maintain the same population, so yearly seed production is not critical.

Thimbleweed is a type of coneflower with drooping yellow petals from an elongated or thimblelike head. The plant is not more than one foot tall and is found on dry prairies in the western half of the state. Rush-pink, or skeleton weed, is also a plant of the western Iowa dry prairies. Although the plant has no leaves, the branching stem is green and produces the plant's food. The plant is in the dandelion group within the daisy family. Flowers are in heads, usually with only five flowers with pale pink petals, making the head resemble a pink such as Depford pink. Rush-pink often is infected with insect galls, one-quarter inch or more in diameter. (The insect lays eggs within the stem, and the plant responds by developing a growth around the egg, which later serves as food for the developing larvae. The insect tricks the plant into producing the growth by secreting a material that resembles plant growth hormones, stimulating the plant to make the gall.)

The prairies have a number of milkweeds, which will vary depending on the moisture and the type of soil. Common milkweed, found in mesic prairies, unused places, and sometimes in crops, has pale pink flowers (with a delightful aroma) and develops "hairy" seed pods. Butterfly weed has bright orange flower clusters in flat-topped sprays at the top of the stem; these are the most colorful of the milkweeds, and the sprays can be seen for hundreds of feet. The green-flowered milkweed has green to white flowers, is usually one to two feet tall, and has small, sometimes narrow, leaves. The wet prairies have the swamp milkweed, which has rosy red flowers, tall stems, and long, narrow leaves. Another denizen of the wetter prairies is Sullivant's milkweed. This has clusters of flowers similar in shape and color to, but not nearly so dense in each cluster as, the common milkweed. The leaves are narrower than those of the common milkweed but are without hairs on the surfaces; the seed pods also develop without hairs. Blunt-leaved milkweed, often found on sandy prairies, is a

large-leaved milkweed in which the leaf edges undulate somewhat. The purple flowers are in round, diffuse clusters at the tip
of the plant. Often growing in the same habitat is the large-flowered beard-tongue, a plant about two to three feet tall with leaves
attached opposite each other on the stem. Near the top are large,
light pink flowers also arranged in opposite fashion. The beard-
tongue refers to a hairy stalk, a sterile stamen (pollen-producing
structure), within the flower. (The drug digitalis is derived from a
relative of large-flowered beard-tongue.)

There are fewer than a dozen shrubs on the prairie, and wild
roses, some shrubby willows, and New Jersey tea account for
most of them. New Jersey tea grows on dry prairies across the
state. In the southwest half of Iowa *Ceanothus ovatus* is found,
while *C. americanus* is in the northeastern half. Both species have
hairy leaves and produce bunches of tiny white flowers at the tips
of the branches. Ovatus blooms in early June while americanus
blooms a month later. When the seeds mature they are shot from
the seed pods thus foiling insects that would begin burrowing into
the seeds.

Wet prairies have their own set of summer-blooming plants.
Bluejoint grass, a sod-forming grass, forms extensive stands in
many wet prairies. In spite of its name the joints, or nodes, on the
stem never appear blue in color. Tiny seeds develop on a fine,
branched plume at the top of three-foot stems.

*Fig. 3.3.   In July the orange flowers of Turk's-cap
lily are easy to spot on moist prairies. (Photo by Paul
Christiansen)*

In early June the white flowers of Canada anemone often cover the ground. The seeds later develop into spiny heads at the tip of each flower stalk. Canada anemone spreads by underground stems and often forms large patches. A very familiar flower, blue flag, a wild iris, grows close to the border of prairie marshes and often forms a ring around the marsh just about where the soil becomes quite wet. It is often found near swamp milkweed.

As summer passes into July the prairie lilies come into bloom on wet prairies. Both wood lily and Turk's-cap lily are bright orange in color with several flowers at the tip of a leafy stem about two feet tall. Wood lily blooms slightly earlier and points its flowers upward, while the flowers of Turk's-cap lily bend over and face downward. The prairie lilies can be distinguished from the tiger lily, introduced from Asia, by their lack of tiny bulbs growing at the base of some of the leaves.

Fig. 3.4.   Yellow coneflowers and purple prairie clover sharing a prairie near Boone in midsummer. (Photo by Paul Christiansen)

The July mesic prairie has several well-known and important plants blooming. Most people recognize black-eyed susan, a member of the daisy family with stiff yellow petals and a pointed dark head in the center. While almost all prairie plants are perennial, coming up each spring from the roots, black-eyed susan is biennial, growing from seed the first year and producing flowers the second year only to die at the end of that year about the same time yellow coneflower blooms. Yellow coneflower is also in the daisy family but is taller, perennial, and has drooping yellow petals and a brown rounded head. These two plants often are found in roadsides and unused grassy places as well as prairies. Both are slightly weedy in nature and make good candidates for prairie establishment. Compass plant, named for the habit of orienting its large leaves (one to two feet long and having fingerlike margins) facing east-west, apparently to keep them cool in the summer heat, also blooms in mid-July. The few heads are large and attached to stalks up to six feet tall. Only the outer two or three rows of flowers in the head produce seeds. Compass plant seeds are remarkable in their ability to germinate after being kept cool and moist for several weeks. Sometimes nearly one-hundred percent of the seeds germinate.

We generally think of thistles as bad weeds and state law designates thistles as noxious weeds. However, Hill's thistle is restricted to prairies in the southeastern two-thirds of Iowa. It has very spiny leaves and one or a few large heads with red flowers at the top of the stem. Flodman's thistle, which occurs on drier prairies and has its leaves covered with a dense mat of white hairs, is found in the northwestern third of Iowa. Field thistle and tall thistle also occur on prairies, but they are more weedy in nature and do get into pastures and disturbed places. All of these thistles are biennial. Among the thistles, only Canada thistle, a weedy introduced species, is perennial.

In late June and July three important pea family plants come into bloom on mesic prairies. Lead plant, a small shrub with its leaflets covered with hairs, giving them the color of lead, has elongated heads of small purple flowers at the ends of its branches. Because the stamens produce bright yellow pollen it is easy to spot the pollen sacs on bees as they work these flowers. Tick-trefoil, named for its spiny seeds and three-leaflet leaves, has sprays of pink flowers in early July. The individual flowers resemble sweet-peas and the pods are flat with wavy edges. Tiny hooked hairs on the surface of the pod make them ideally suited to hitch a ride on a passing animal, or on clothing. White prairie clover resembles the domestic red clover only superficially. The heads, in addition to having white flowers, are narrow and elongated, one to two inches long, and the leaves usually have seven narrow leaflets. Purple prairie clover, a close relative and most abundant on drier prairies, has flowers similar to white prairie clover, except for the color, but the leaves are finer with threadlike leaflets.

One of the more bizarre prairie plants is rattlesnake master. Its leaves are long and narrow with widely spaced spines on the edges, very similar to yucca. The flower stalks have several spiny heads with inconspicuous flowers at the tops. Perhaps someone fancied that a person could beat off a rattlesnake with the spiny flower heads.

Wild bergamot is a mint with heads of pink to purple flowers at the top of the stem. The leaves are set on the square stem opposite each other in pairs. The strong minty odor can be released by crushing the leaves.

As July draws to a close prairie blazing-star, also called Kansas gayfeather, comes into bloom. The tight, elongated clusters of purple heads on two- to three-foot stalks make them easy to see. The grasslike leaves become progressively shorter toward the top of the stem. A week or two later rough blazing-star comes into bloom. The color of its flowers is similar but the heads are somewhat larger and not as tightly clustered.

As summer fades into fall, it is the time for the plants of the daisy family. Goldenrod, sunflower, aster—all flower in profusion. The goldenrods have small heads with a few yellow flowers. Experts have identified many kinds of goldenrods. Canada goldenrod, which grows on roadsides and waste places as well as in prairies, is the most common. The flowers of rigid goldenrod are somewhat larger and the heads are gathered into flat-topped clusters. Sunflowers also abound. Showy sunflower, with purple flowers in the center of the head and yellow-petaled flowers around the edge, is perennial, not annual as are the weedy sunflowers. The stems are often rough and dark-colored. Jerusalem artichoke, another sunflower, has wider leaves and thickened underground stems, which form tubers. Tasting somewhat like potato, their starch is not digestible.

Like the goldenrods, there are numerous kinds of asters on the prairie. Several examples will give some idea of their range of characteristics. New England aster has red-purple heads, which attract honey bees in the fall. Azure aster has light purple heads, smooth blue aster has blue heads and smooth stems, and panicled aster has small white heads on a much-branched plant.

The last of the flowers to bloom on mesic prairies is downy gentian. Its deep-blue flowers are almost hidden among the taller grasses and flowers of fall.

Late summer and fall is the major time for grasses to bloom and set seeds on the mesic prairie. In late July Canada wildrye has hairy spikes of seeds, which droop down. In August the major warm-season prairie grasses begin their flowering. Big bluestem is the best known and most abundant grass on the tallgrass prairies of Iowa. It produces long leaves that arise from ground level during the summer. When getting ready to flower the stem elongates rapidly, to six or eight feet, and seeds develop on short spikes, usually three, at the ends of the branches. Sometimes the plant is called turkey foot because the three spikes radiating from a common point resemble a bird's foot. Indiangrass is another warm-season grass that is common on Iowa prairies. It has a contracted plume of rich, golden brown seeds at the top of its seed stalks. It often is the first grass to invade roadsides from its native habitat. Prairie dropseed is a bunchgrass, meaning that it does not spread by underground tillers; it makes a tight cluster of stems that enlarges very little from year to year. The leaves of prairie dropseed are very long, very fine, and very numerous, forming a fountainlike mound from which arise a few very fine stems that branch near the top and produce small round seeds.

On the wetter prairies warm-season grasses include slough-grass and switchgrass. Sloughgrass grows in patches, largely to the exclusion of other plants. It grows an extensive system of underground stems, which occasionally produce leafy shoots. The young shoots are very tough and sharp as they penetrate the soil, and for this reason sloughgrass is not killed by siltation. Switchgrass also spreads by underground stems, but its colonies are more hospitable to other species. Switchgrass has become important as a roadside and summer pasture grass. Clumps, evident because of their height and brownish color, are prominent in the fall along most state and interstate highways.

In addition to the grasses just discussed, the wet prairies have many flowers. Flat-topped aster, sneezeweed, and big-toothed sunflower are daisy family flowers found on wet prairies. Flat-topped aster is one of the first asters to bloom, usually in late July. The flower heads are white, and as the name implies they are arranged in a flat spray at the top of the plant. The heads of sneezeweed are yellow with each petal having a shallow notch at its tip. Big-toothed sunflower is well named, both commonly and scientifically. The leaf edges have several teeth per inch while the yellow head is typical of the sunflower, with long petals on the outer flowers and small yellow flowers in the center. The stems and leaves are very smooth, in contrast to showy sunflower. Sunflowers are well known for their ability to hybridize—it is not uncommon to come upon a plant that does not fit all the criteria of a particular species but seems to be intermediate between the two parents.

Also growing in wet prairies is licorice root, named for the flavor and odor of its roots. The plant is typical of the pea family in leaf and flower. However, the mature pods are covered with short, but stout, hooked hairs, which assist in their dispersal by attaching on passing animals.

Meadow sweet is a small shrub that grows in the wet prairies. It has bunches of tiny flowers at the ends of the stems. A close relative that is found around many homes is bridal wreath. When dried the leaves give off a "sweet" odor. Also found in wet prairies is spotted water-hemlock, a member of the parsley family, which has light purple spots on the stems. It is a very poisonous plant, as Socrates found out.

Several mints grow in wet prairies, all of which have square stems and leaves that are attached opposite each other on the stem. Germander has pink flowers in a spike at the top of the stem — when examined closely it becomes evident that the flowers have no upper petals, only the three lower ones. Virginia mountain mint grows in patches, often excluding grasses and other plants. The small white flowers with pink nectar guides are in small clusters. The leaves are short and narrow with a wonderful minty aroma when crushed.

Blooming in late fall, the gentians are the last flowers of the season. On wet prairies closed gentian has several pale purple flowers in a cluster. The tips of the petals are pleated together, but bumblebees are able to force their way into the flower and pollinate it.

The most common grass on dry prairies in the fall is little bluestem. It is about two feet tall, the seeds are very feathery on short single stalks, and the stem and leaves turn rusty-red. Little bluestem, like prairie dropseed, is a bunchgrass. It is the major species on the Loess Hills as well as on gravelly and sandy prairies across the state. Often side-oats grama is found along with little bluestem. Its seeds are clustered in tiny, tight spikes, with many spikes attached in a row down the two-foot stalk, all hanging to one side of the stalk. Other grama grasses are found on the driest prairies in Iowa. Blue grama and hoary grama are shorter with their seed spikes tightly grouped looking something like an eyelash.

Gray goldenrod is restricted to dry prairies, its long lower leaves becoming progressively shorter toward the top. In August it blooms with yellow heads clustered in a cylindrical fashion at the top of the stem. At about the same time the dotted blazing-star blooms. Like other blazing-stars, its heads are purple; how-

ever, they are small and tightly clustered. The plants usually produce many shoots that sprawl outward. The dots of dotted
blazing-star are tiny thin spots in the leaves, which can be seen
when holding the leaves to the light. Maximillian's sunflower has
typical large yellow heads. The key to identifying it is the leaves,
which are similar to other sunflowers except that they are folded
along the midrib.

Fall brings false boneset into bloom on the dry prairie. This
plant usually will be missed until it is dispersing its seeds, which
are in small, white, fluffy balls at the top of the plant. When seen
with the sun in the background they seem to glow like tiny light
bulbs. Another fall flower is tall wormwood. This is one of the
sages found mostly in the West. Wormwood has whitish leaves
and very tiny flower heads; it usually grows in patches with scattered plants. The last daisy family flowers of the fall are the
asters. On dry prairies heath aster, or many-flowered aster, is
common. It has many, many quite small, white flower heads.
Silky aster is well named, with its leaves covered with tiny, silky
hairs making them very smooth to the touch. The flower heads
are fairly large with purple petals and yellow centers.

Partridge pea has yellow petals with brown stamens. The
leaves are made up of many tiny leaflets and the stem reaches two
and one-half feet tall. The long brown pods twist as they dry and
scatter squarish black seeds. This plant is an annual and must
grow from seeds every year, usually where the soil is sandy.
Round-headed bushclover also grows in dry prairies, producing
heads of small, inconspicuous, white flowers at the top of a three-
foot stem. The seeds develop in one-seeded pods, which are hidden in the brownish flower parts.

On sandy prairies hairy puccoon has showy clusters of yellow flowers in June. Typical of the puccoons, it develops small,
white, very hard seedpods within the base of each flower. An
evening primrose grows in the same type of soil and blooms at
about the same time. Its flowers are yellow with four petals and
are scattered along a stem up to three feet tall.

Tall cinquefoil grows on dry prairies. It has large, very hairy
leaves partially divided into leaflets and white flowers similar to
strawberry flowers. Seeds develop in the center of the flower but
are protected by sepals. Later, seeds can be easily collected by
tipping the dried flowers and pouring the tiny brown seeds into a
bag. Snow-on-the-mountain is in the spurge family along with
poinsettia. Instead of having red leaves below the flowers like
poinsettia, the margins of the upper leaves turn white. A close
look at the mature flowers reveals a three-chambered seedpod
hanging from the flower on a short stalk. Later, the pod pops

open and scatters the three seeds.

Through the seasons the prairie changes in the flowers that are in bloom and in the height of the grasses and other plants. From week to week it provides new discoveries for the casual or serious visitor.

Prairie Soil

Iowa owes the prairie a huge debt of gratitude for developing the excellent soil that has served as the basis of its agricultural supremacy. Almost from the beginning of settlement, farmers realized they were working with a soil far better than they had encountered in the eastern United States or in Europe. They understood the deep, black topsoil was a treasure of nutrients and an excellent environment for root growth. Perhaps they also realized that the prairie they were destroying was responsible for the soil's excellent characteristics of water retention, permeability of air, and nutrient storehouse.

Two attributes of prairie plants, being perennial and being herbaceous (having soft stems that die back to the ground each fall), along with adequate rainfall and generally mild summer temperatures all contributed to producing a topsoil up to three feet deep. Rainfall was adequate for luxurious plant growth, but not so much that it carried away nutrients as in the soils of the southeastern United States. Nor were summer temperatures so warm that they promoted excessive and rapid decomposition of dead plant material. On the other hand, deep soils did not develop in Iowa's forests.

Forest trees and shrubs have woody roots that die and decay only with the death of the tree. Leaves fall to the ground each autumn, but they are incorporated into only the upper few inches of the soil, resulting in a shallow topsoil of low quality. On the other hand the underground stems and roots of perennial prairie plants have a life span of just a few years. Each year older roots die and new ones grow to replace them. When these underground parts die they decay in place. Roots of the grasses are very fibrous, very abundant, and extend several feet into the soil. With the yearly dieoff and decay of roots the organic matter gradually builds up. Prairie soils are at least several thousand years old. Over that long span of time small increments of organic matter each year gradually developed into the soil the first pioneers found.

The high level of organic matter that makes the soil black contributes to soil quality in several ways. First of all, particles of silt and clay are glued together by the organic matter into "crumbs," which help to provide air spaces in the soil. Just as a pile of basketballs would have larger spaces between the balls than a pile of golf balls, so the soil with large particles also has larger air spaces. The spaces allow air and water to move easily through the soil. Organic matter also soaks up water within the soil. This water can be absorbed by plant roots as they need it. In this way plants continue to get water from the soil long after the last rain. Without organic matter much of the water would either drain away deeper into the soil or would be held so tightly by clay particles that plants could not use it.

Prairie Animals

Perhaps because of their wariness, prairie animals have always been fascinating to prairie visitors. While plants simply stand their ground and get stepped on, eaten, or pulled up, animals are generally difficult to find. Even if we do not see an animal we are pleased at spotting some sign—a mouse run in the grass, a fox den on the side of a hill, or a discarded snake skin. In spite of the fact that we seldom see them, there are a number of familiar animals that make themselves at home on the prairie. Red fox and badger have been able to adapt fairly well to occupation of the prairie by farmers. They still inhabit prairie remnants, but they are at home in pastures, on roadsides, or other less-disturbed places. The Thirteen-lined ground squirrel also has adapted well and is probably more plentiful now than in presettlement times because of the short grass provided by close grazing and mowing in pastures and lawns. Certainly the Pocket gopher has not required prairie vegetation to proliferate. However, Franklin's ground squirrel and Richardson's ground squirrel have not fared as well. Franklin's ground squirrel is restricted to prairies and its population is very low. Richardson's ground squirrel used to occupy a small portion of northwestern Iowa, but it has not been seen in Iowa in the past several years.

Mouse-sized animals are much more abundant on prairies than we imagine. They spend their time on the ground, below the dead grasses making up the litter layer. They are vegetarians and do very well, even on small remnants of prairie. The most common are the Meadow vole, a mouselike animal with a blunt nose and small ears, and the Deer mouse with white feet and tail. The Meadow jumping mouse is rusty brown with a long tail and seems to prefer moist parts of the prairie. Several other mice are less common, such as the Western harvest mouse, which prefers dense vegetation near water, and the Plains pocket mouse and the Northern grasshopper mouse, both of which are on the state endangered species list.

Two insect-eating mammals, shrews and bats, are sometimes found on prairies. Shrews are mouse-sized animals that eat large quantities of insects, worms, and other small animals. They have adapted well to replacement of prairies by fields and pastures and are found in every fencerow and roadside. Several species of shrew are commonly found, including the Short-tailed shrew, Common shrew, and Pygmy shrew. Bats are more spotty in their distribution, depending upon the availability of suitable roosting sites, such as caves or trees, as much as on the availability of suitable food sources. The abundance of caves in eastern Iowa contributes to the population density, while the development of farm groves in western Iowa may have contributed to increases in bat populations there.

Where temporary water sources are available toads can be found on prairies. The American toad is found across Iowa while the Great Plains toad and Rocky Mountain toad come into extreme western Iowa from the west. Skinks, small lizardlike reptiles, also live on prairies. They are very fast and seldom does one get a good look unless the skink assumes its stock-still stance in the open where it can be observed. In the northwestern two-thirds of Iowa the Northern prairie skink can be found, especially on dry prairies. The Great Plains skink is found in the extreme southwestern part of the state.

Several kinds of snakes live on prairies: Prairie kingsnake, Western fox snake, Bull snake. In former times rattlesnakes also lived on prairies. The Massasaugas was found across the southeastern half of Iowa while the Plains rattlesnake was in far western Iowa. At the present time the two snakes are extremely rare and sightings are unusual.

The study of insects has been associated primarily with those that affect our crops or ourselves, and prairie insects are not well studied. However, butterflies are so conspicuous they demand the attention of amateurs and professionals alike. Monarch, Viceroy, Swallowtail, and Fritillary are all familiar prairie butterflies. Smaller and less highly colored species are also prairie inhabitants: Skippers are usually brown with knobs on their antennae; Baltimores are quite rare but are closely tied to the prairie. They are always found close to turtlehead, which grows in wet prairies.

No image of the prairie is complete without including the American bison. Both in size and numbers bison dominated the prairie although their numbers in Iowa may not have been as great as in the Great Plains. Wandering about the landscape, the bison helped to give the prairie its character by browsing and rubbing trees out of existence, by creating wallows where weedy plants could get a start, and by creating migration trails followed by other animals. With plowing of the prairie the bison herds were soon driven from the prairie or were killed. Presently, several private herds are kept in Iowa but no public parks or refuges have herds.

American elk also roamed the prairies of Iowa, browsing on shrubs and trees, as well as grazing, in larger herds than bison. They also were quickly driven from the prairie. As with bison several private herds are raised in Iowa. White-tailed deer inhabited much the same type of cover they occupy today. Keeping near woodlands they often moved into the prairie to graze and rest. They have made the transition to the domestication of the prairie lands and coexist quite satisfactorily with heavy concentrations of humans.

Large predators such as the Prairie wolf and Grizzly bear were even less tolerated than bison and elk, being viewed by settlers as predators of domesticated livestock. Lewis and Clark, on their trip up the Missouri River, often wrote of encounters with or sightings of Grizzly bear, something we don't often include in our image of the prairie. The Coyote, like White-tailed deer, has made the transition to domestication of the landscape; its population and range continues to increase.

Prairie Reconstruction

Iowa's native prairies have nearly disappeared. Yet, many of us want to be closer than a drive of an hour or more to get to a prairie. Our only solution is to discover an unknown local prairie or to plant our own. Occasionally a small patch of prairie is discovered, but the chances of doing so diminish every year. On the other hand the information and materials to reconstruct a prairie accumulate year by year. All over the state planted prairies are appearing — some as small as the size of a garage, others several to many acres. And they are planted for a variety of reasons. Some people want an easy-to-care-for ground cover, some want a cover to prevent erosion, some want a place for wildlife to live, and some want to enjoy the beauty of the grasses and flowers. For whatever reason or combination of reasons, reconstructing prairies is gaining in popularity.

Many individuals and institutions across the state have established prairies. The John Deere Administration building in the south part of Cedar Falls has forty acres of prairie adjacent to the building and parking areas. In West Des Moines the Iowa Farm Bureau Federation has prairie planted around the perimeter of their grounds. The conventional lawn near the headquarters building meets the taller prairie in sweeping curves making a very attractive landscape. Specimen plantings of about a dozen different prairie species are also laid out nearby with labels so visitors can identify them. The Biology Department at the University of Northern Iowa has a large planting near the campus, and a small prairie is adjacent to Science II on the campus of Iowa State University. In West Branch along Interstate 80 seventy acres of prairie have been in place since the early 1970s as part of the Herbert Hoover National Historic Site. Scattergood School, two miles to the east, has about forty acres of prairie adjacent to the interstate.

Fig. 3.5. The tall, shaggy prairie flowers and grasses encircling the conventional lawn of the Iowa Farm Bureau Federation offices in West Des Moines: an attractive and economical newly established prairie. (Photo courtesy of Iowa Farm Bureau)

The Iowa Department of Transportation has used prairie grasses and flowers at several locations along primary and interstate highways in Iowa. On I-80 at the westbound rest stop just west of the Wilton interchange, an excellent specimen prairie has been planted and is unusually rich in prairie species. Near the

western border of Iowa on I-680 the grounds of a scenic overlook
are planted to prairie grasses, and on I-35 at the Osceola exit
south of Des Moines prairie grasses have been planted along the
roadsides. Also on I-35 about ten miles north of Ames, a prairie
remnant with lots of little bluestem can be reached from the
southbound lanes. Several counties have used prairie grasses on
roadside plantings. In Linn County north of Lisbon, two miles of
prairie grasses have been in place since 1971. Black Hawk and
Cerro Gordo counties, among others, are also using prairie
grasses on roadsides.

The Iowa Department of Natural Resources uses prairie
grasses extensively in wildlife refuges; this cover has been found
to produce more pheasants per acre than bromegrass. Summer
pastures planted to switchgrass, indiangrass, or big bluestem are
being encouraged by the Soil Conservation Service. While cool-
season grasses such as bromegrass and Kentucky bluegrass are
dormant during July and August, warm-season prairie grasses are
making most of their growth, providing excellent hot weather
pasture. Individuals are also planting prairies. Aaron Basten,
who lives near Solon, has more than one hundred prairie species
in a one-acre prairie. Many, many other Iowans have similar plots
where the blossoming of every species is noted throughout the
season.

Three cardinal rules apply to successful prairie reconstruc-
tion: one, all perennial plants on the area to be planted must be
killed to avoid excessive competition with the seedlings of prairie
plants; two, the soil must be firmed or packed after planting to
provide good contact between the seeds and the soil to insure
good germination; and three, the prairie planter must be patient
as the prairie plants become established because annual weeds
will be the most obvious plants as establishment begins.

Planting a prairie is much like planting a lawn: the soil is
prepared by tilling and raking; seeds are scattered by hand for
small areas or by using a hydroseeder or especially equipped drills
for larger sites; then the soil is firmed with a roller or packer.
Next, the explaining begins. Neighbors and visitors want to know
why you chose to establish a prairie, and then they want to know
why your effort is so unsuccessful. Prairie plants develop slowly,
putting most of their effort during the first year into growing a
good root system with only enough top growth to provide the
food for root growth. By contrast, annual weeds do just the
opposite, growing just enough roots to nourish the plant while
putting all their effort into producing leaves and eventually seeds.
The first year the prairie plants are small and spindly and largely
hidden by the weeds. Most people in our culture know only two

or three ways to stop weeds — pull them out, cut them off, or spray them with herbicide. The idea that prairie plants, so tiny the first year, could eventually choke out the weeds is beyond their imagination. Yet, that is what will happen, almost without fail, after two, three, or four years. That may be a long time to wait for someone with a highly visible area where there is pressure to be conventionally presentable. However, there are two ways around this dilemma — either be very persuasive that eventually the area will look better or do the job quickly by using transplants rather than seeds.

Although transplanting prairie plants is a rapid way to establish a prairie, it is very labor intensive and buying plants is expensive. Plants must be set out not more than twelve inches apart with a ratio of about seventy grass plants to thirty flower plants. After transplanting weeding will have to be done several times during the first year, but the reward will be "instant" prairie. Many species will flower the first year and during the second year the prairie plants will be in charge, with little weeding being necessary. Seeded prairies can be weeded too, but the problem is knowing which are the weeds and which are the prairie plants. It is not difficult to distinguish between weed and prairie seedlings if you know what to look for, but it takes good observation and practice.

The rewards of a reconstructed prairie are many. The parade of flowers and grasses through the spring, summer, and fall that occurs on the native prairies will be seen in miniature. Wildlife attracted to the cover and food provided by your prairie will be a source of joy. The long hours behind the lawnmower, the odor of engine exhaust, and the assurance that the same exercise will have to be repeated week by week all summer long will be avoided. The opportunity to learn about Iowa's native prairie and the possibility of teaching others is yet another source of satisfaction.

In a small way Iowa is returning to its prairie past. The appropriateness of prairie as a ground cover is beginning to make more sense. As we use more and more prairie in our pastures, roadsides, and front yards, and recognize its many advantages, we learn more of Mother Nature's wisdom in designing prairie as the plant community to inhabit Iowa. As you travel about Iowa be on the lookout for big bluestem and compass plant. They are the greeters who will help you rediscover Iowa's prairie past and point to Iowa's prairie future.

Selected References

Burt, W. H., and R. P. Grossenheider. *A Field Guide to the Mammals,* 2d ed. Boston: Houghton Mifflin Co., 1964.

Conat, R. *A Field Guide to Reptiles and Amphibians.* Boston: Houghton Mifflin Co., 1958.

Copper, Tom. *Iowa's Natural Heritage.* Des Moines: Iowa Natural Heritage Foundation; Cedar Falls: Iowa Academy of Science, 1982.

Dinsmore, J. J., T. H. Kent, D. Koenig, P. C. Petersen, and D. M. Roosa. *Iowa Birds.* Ames: Iowa State University Press, 1984.

Peterson, R. T., and M. McKenny. *A Field Guide to Wildflowers.* Boston: Houghton Mifflin Co., 1968.

Weaver, J. E. *North American Prairie.* Lincoln, Neb.: Johnsen Publishing Co., 1954.

Weaver, J. E. *Native Vegetation of Nebraska.* Lincoln: University of Nebraska Press, 1965.

Wilson, W. H. W. *Landscaping with Wildflowers and Native Plants.* San Francisco: Ortho Books. Chevron Chemical Co., 1984.

4

IOWA'S LOESS HILLS

Cornelia F. Mutel

To the motorist, much of Iowa appears as flat or gently rolling pastoral land, cloaked in summer by bright green fields of crops and by tailored farmsteads, towns, and roadsides. But approach Iowa from the west by crossing the Missouri River valley, and a distinctly different view meets the eye. From miles distant, a row of precipitous bluffs appears to pierce the horizon as a range of mountains in miniature. As you draw closer, details of this small mountain range become more obvious. Their ragged covering of grayish green herbs and shrubs, interspersed with patches of bare yellowish brown soil, contrasts with the flat-topped, evenly planted, rectangular fields of corn and beans that fill the valley bottom. And trees seen in the valley bottom, primarily in farmsteads, form forests that creep up ravines even to the crests of some of the taller hills. Here and there small farms nestle into bowl-shaped valleys. Cropland, if seen at all, is irregularly shaped, winding along the flatter bottoms of wider valleys. Cattle graze the sloping grasslands, their roan torsos seemingly bisected by trunks of interspersed trees.

Leaving Interstate 80 to climb into the hills by one of the smaller roads, you immediately sense entrance into another world, where time flows according to the needs and ways of wild species. A world of great beauty and natural variation in color and form. A drier world, reminiscent of the stubble-covered grasslands of western states. A hotter world, especially on the grass-covered open slopes facing toward the south and west. A wilder, more elemental world where humans are called to walk gently. Climb to the top of a bluff and look across the roughly corrugated, sharp-crested hills to the east; then turn back to the west and view the flat valley below. Sense the freedom of thinking that you are on top of the world, looking from a timeless wilderness down to the clock-regulated human world at your feet. Examine how the valley floor is ruled off into straight lines: roads, fields, channelized rivers. Then remembering that nature abhors straight lines, turn back to the hills and observe that curves flow everywhere—curves separating forest from prairie, curves of ridge crests, curving plants bent by the constant wind. Skylines where knobbed landforms are girded in undulating clumps of grasses, forbs, and trees. Linger here and sense why Indians buried their dead here, and used the bluff tops as sacred calling sites.

Fig. 4.1.   The Loess Hills rise abruptly from the Missouri River valley as an intricate network of angular, narrow-ridged hills and prairie grasslands. Today invasion of the prairies by trees has all but obliterated native grasslands in the far-southern Hills. (Photo courtesy of State Historical Society of Iowa)

This land apart is the Loess Hills (pronounced "luss" – of German origin meaning loose), a rugged landform shaped from amazingly deep wind-borne and water-carved soil. From west to east it is a narrow land – the massive bluffs and sharply dissected landforms giving way within a few miles to more gently rolling farmland. And because most roads follow the interspersed valleys or quickly cross the Hills, they may seem insignificantly small to the motorist. But if you walked the bluffs you would be impressed by their extent, for they stretch approximately 160 miles from the Missouri border (near Hamburg) up through six counties to Sioux City, with equally impressive hills (although less rugged bluff faces) reaching northward to Westfield in adjacent Plymouth County. In all places the division between the Missouri's flood-plain and the Loess Hills is razor sharp, the land changing in shape, human use, and vegetation within a matter of feet.

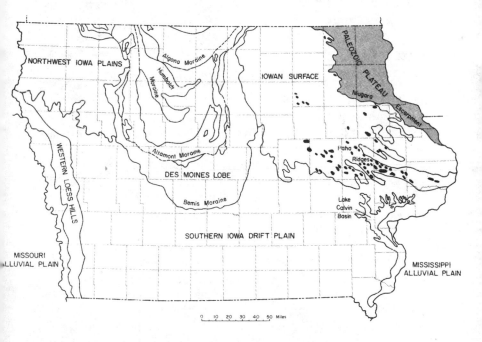

Fig. 4.2.   Landform regions of Iowa. (Map from Jean Cutler Prior, A Regional Guide to Iowa Land-forms, *1976)*

Natural historians throughout Iowa agree that the Loess Hills stand out in numerous ways. Geologists point out that this deep loess creates a landform unique in North America, and that it is duplicated in only one other place in the world: along the

Yellow River in Kansu Province, People's Republic of China. Exposure and drainage properties of the loess create a near desert for the Hills creatures. Archaeologists state that western Iowa was home to some of Iowa's first horticultural Indians, who formed permanent settlements here approximately one thousand years ago. These Indians and some now-extinct animals left a wealth of remains unsurpassed elsewhere in Iowa. Biologists explain that while Iowa, botanically speaking, formed the heart of the tallgrass prairie, only here can over a thousand contiguous acres of prairie still be found. What's more, the biologists look at the *type* of prairie that flourishes on the bluffs: a prairie containing many species more typical of western grasslands than of Iowa. The fact that western and eastern grasslands meet here on the last of Iowa's large prairies, and also intermix with patches of eastern woodland, lends an unusually large diversity of plants and animals to the region, and explains why a goodly number of Iowa's endangered species make the Loess Hills their last refuge. The Loess Hills truly are one of the state's natural sanctuaries — a refuge for some of our finest and rarest natural elements, an area worthy of preservation.

Although the Loess Hills are renowned for their natural features, they are by no means pristine. From the start of Euro-American settlement in the mid-1800s, people have left their mark on this unusual assemblage of species and landforms. Most settlers regarded the Hills as an obstacle, something to be reshaped into a useful and habitable form. Sioux City's hills were described as "one of nature's freaks," and seventy feet of loess were scraped from hilltops into adjacent valleys by horse-drawn graders. Virgin timber was cut until (ironically) some feared that the firewood supply would disappear. Bedrock underneath the loess was quarried, and loess was used for fill at construction sites and for building roads across the lowlands. Early in settlement, even the steeper hillsides were plowed for row crops. Only a few decades later, after the mighty Missouri and its tributaries were relegated to diked channels thus freeing the floodplain for intensive agricultural use, the Hills prairies often became overgrazed pasture. Within the loess, caves were dug to serve as small stables, wine cellars, lime kilns, and the like. Today, modern subdivisions, dirt bikes, and cattle eat into the faces of the bluffs.

Because the rugged Hills have posed a physical barrier to human activities, attempts to transform them into a "usable" form have been extreme; because of their fragility, such attempts have been devastating to the natural features. Yet their ruggedness, which has prevented total conversion to agricultural use, also has meant that here, unlike in most of Iowa, there is something left to preserve. Only three to five percent of the original Hills prairies are estimated to exist today, but this is far more than the less than one-tenth of one percent remaining elsewhere in Iowa. Many Loess Hills species have been pushed to the brink of extinction, yet they *still* survive here. Though the shape of the Hills is being altered by accelerated erosion, they remain, massive and free. And despite changes, the essential character of natural areas in many places remains intact. These Hills await efforts to preserve their natural character through additional acquisitions of high-quality natural areas, through continued growth in understanding and cooperation among private landowners, and through effective management of both private and public lands.

Examining the natural features of a region as complex as the Loess Hills would require a treatise much larger than this chapter. Even unlimited space would not allow all questions to be answered, since recent research projects have opened many new doors for future exploration. But within the constraints of present-day information, a number of stories can be told. This chapter focusses on three of these: the formation of the Hills, the natural features of the Hills, and the future of the ecosystems.

Fig. 4.3.   Sioux City's Loess Hills were viewed as obstacles by settlers and early residents, who reshaped the loess with horse-drawn equipment. (Photo courtesy of Sioux City Public Museum)

If you wish, the chapter may be used as a field guide — as a tool for examining the Hills in person, in more depth than would be achieved by an armchair reading of the text. Throughout the text and in Table 4.1, sites for viewing particular features and additional educational resources are listed. Virtually all land outside the parks and preserves is in agricultural use. Make the effort to locate public land where you can wander without fear of trespassing. Be sure to travel with good-quality state or county maps. The state highway map (in Part VI) also may be helpful when reading the text and touring the area.

Also consider driving the road that twists along the western face of the bluffs for much of its length. This road is especially beautiful in the autumn. One unusually nice section in the southern Hills extends from Thurman (in Fremont County) south on L-44, joining L-48 and continuing past Waubonsie State Park. A second, in the central Hills, starts in the region of the Loess Hills Wildlife Area and goes south on L-14 to the base of Murray Hill; here take F-20 east into the Hills, turning south onto Highway 183 at Pisgah and following the Soldier River, in one of the many large valleys that cut through the bluff line. You can follow the bluffs to Missouri Valley.

TABLE 4.1.   SELECTED PARKS AND PRESERVES
OF THE LOESS HILLS

FIVE-RIDGE PRAIRIE: Plymouth County, 790 acres
Location: follow H-12 N 6 miles from Stone State Park, take K-18 N 3.5 miles, follow sign to W, proceed 1 mile on dirt road.
Description: state preserve; hiking and cross-country skiing trails, hunting permitted; prairies and woodlands; one of the largest remaining roadless areas in the hills, must hike into preserve from parking area.

STONE STATE PARK: Woodbury County, 1,069 acres
Location: in NW Sioux City; bounded by H-12 (on W) and Talbot Road (on E).
Description: picnic areas, hiking trails, bridle trails, nature trail, campground, nature center (summer weekends); forests, bluff and ridgetop prairies.

SIOUX CITY PRAIRIE: Woodbury County, 150 acres
Location: in NW Sioux City; access from Briar Cliff College parking lot (into NE corner of prairie), or Talbot Road (runs along W side of prairie).
Description: hiking trails, monthly guided nature walks; hill prairie.

LOESS HILLS WILDLIFE AREA (northern section): Monona County, 2,504 acres

> *Location:* NE of Onawa; take L-12 N and follow signs to E, or from Castena (H-175), follow signs 3.5 miles to W.
>
> *Description:* largest publicly owned section of the Loess Hills; parking areas, hiking trails, hunting, primitive camping allowed; bluff and hill prairies, woodlands; Loess Hills Prairie Seminar held here each spring.

TURIN LOESS HILLS PRESERVE (southern section of Loess Hills Wildlife Area): Monona County, 220 acres

> *Location:* on L-14; 1.5 miles N of Turin.
>
> *Description:* state preserve; same activities as in Loess Hills Wildlife Area, but no established hiking trails; bluff and hill prairies, woodlands, managed as a nature preserve; take special care in where and how you walk here.

PREPARATION CANYON STATE PARK: Monona County, 344 acres

> *Location:* approximately 5 miles SW of Moorhead; follow signs from H-183 to W, or take E-60 E from Blencoe, follow signs to E.
>
> *Description:* picnic areas, hiking trails, no camping; mostly woodlands, some nonnative grasslands.

MURRAY HILL OVERLOOK: Harrison County, 3 acres

> *Location:* on F-20; 4 miles W of Pisgah and 2 miles NE of Little Sioux.
>
> *Description:* only bluff face crossed by a major highway; parking area, trail to top of bluff; bluff prairie, wonderful view.

WAUBONSIE STATE PARK: Fremont County, 1,209 acres

> *Location:* on H-2; 2 miles W of U.S. 275 and 5 miles E of I-29; enter via H-239.
>
> *Description:* picnic areas, campground, hiking trails, nature trails, bridle trails; primarily woodland, some ridgetop and hill prairies, magnificent bluff prairies along L-48.

LOESS HILLS PIONEER STATE FOREST: northern Harrison and southern Monona counties, eventually 17,190 acres

> *Development:* land is now being purchased by Iowa Department of Natural Resources.

Note: All distances in table are approximate; traveling with a good state map or county maps is advised.

Only larger or more ecologically significant areas, and those areas more easily found, are included.

Many additional public-use areas in the Loess Hills are owned by county conservation boards and by the cities of Sioux City and Council Bluffs; some of these contain significant natural features. Consult city or county maps, city governments, or county conservation boards.

Formation of the Hills

Had you lived a century ago, you may have been aware of a heated scientific debate that lasted for decades concerning the formation of the Loess Hills: How, exactly, had these gigantic mounds of loose soil been created? Some felt that they had been deposited directly by water, perhaps being washed into place in violent floods, or perhaps as sediments settling to the bottom of prairie ponds, lakes, or sluggish streams. Charles White (who, as state geologist, explained his views in 1870 in the first report of the Iowa Geological Survey) described the Hills as "miniature mountain ranges of dried mud" (p. 114). He felt that in distant times, muddy waters heavily laden with sediments produced by the grinding action of glaciers had flowed into a broad lake covering much of western Iowa. The sediments settled to the bottom, quickly filling the basin to the height of the tallest bluffs. In later years the extensive deposits were carved first by downcutting by the Missouri River and later by erosion into today's landforms.

By the turn of the century Bohumil Shimek, one of the state's first and most respected natural historians, hinted that Hill-forming particles had been lifted by the wind rather than carried by water. And by 1910 Shimek had established the modern theory of Hill formation. In the Annual Report of the Iowa Geological Survey (Vol. 20:401), he stated that "the source of the loess materials is . . . plainly discernible." He described gazing from bluff tops out across the Missouri River valley and seeing "columns and clouds of dust" lifted by the wind from river deposits. On windy days the atmosphere was dense with enormous quantities of such dust, which was then deposited on the uplands as loess.

What discoveries prodded Shimek's formulation? A major piece of evidence was his study of the abundant small snail fossils that are buried throughout the loess. Identifying these fossils Shimek realized that the vast majority were terrestrial rather than aquatic species, deposited on old upland surfaces that they had inhabited; if indeed these earliest inhabitants had lived on uplands, then loess could not have been deposited under water.

Today geologists agree that Iowa's loess (which as a deposit covers much of the state) consists of particles brought into the region as outwash of the last two major glaciations, but lifted and carried into place by the wind. Massive, moving glaciers ground rock into powder, which flowed downstream with melting water from the margins of glaciers. Although the massive continental glaciers lay far to the north of today's Loess Hills, these glaciers fed tremendous volumes of sediment-laden water into the Missouri River. During warm summers, this water covered miles-wide floodplains, but cold winter temperatures slowed the glacial outwash to a trickle. The exposed finely ground rock was free to be picked up by strong winter winds, and clouds of particles rose into the sky, later to be dropped on upland surfaces. (This same process can be seen today in certain Alaskan valleys draining large glaciers.)

A common deposit in the Midwest and in other parts of the world, loess covers much of Iowa to depths of several feet and today forms some of our most fertile agricultural soils. But the deepest North American loess was deposited immediately adjacent to the Missouri River between what is today Sioux City, Iowa, and Kansas City, Missouri, where the valley floor ran perpendicular to prevailing winds. Here deposits generally in excess of sixty feet (although deposits of 150 to 200 feet have been recorded) were laid down, major deposition occurring 30,000 to 12,500 years ago. Why are these Missouri River deposits so unusual? Because only here and in northern China has loess built up to sufficient depths to bury and obscure preexisting landforms, leaving instead a topography determined by characteristics of the loess.

The unusually great susceptibility of loess to erosion has been of prime importance in forming today's landform. Over the millennia the original wind-drifted, rounded dunes of fine-textured silt were reshaped by running water, which cut into and washed away large quantities of the loess, leaving the characteristically finely dissected, steep-sloped, unique Loess Hills.

Although we appreciate the intricate patterns of water-washed hills, the destructive power of erosion also must be recognized. The reshaping of the Hills by water erosion, a natural and ongoing process, has been dramatically accelerated by human activities. Since settlement in the mid-1800s, naturally high erosion rates have been exacerbated by substituting structures and cropland for prairie; numerous fenced cattle for smaller numbers of roving bison; and channelized, fast-running rivers for sluggish, meandering streams. Today the Hills claim a national reputation for high rates of erosion and sediment loads of streams—rates of thirty tons per acre (over three times the state average for cropland erosion) are not unusual. No easy solutions have been found.

Natural Features of the Hills

"Reading the landscape" is a skill often practiced by people trained in the natural sciences. But even if you lack such training, you can learn to look at the countryside, identify geological processes at work, point out major types of ecosystems, state their probable history of land use, and predict what organisms are likely to be present. Developing this skill as a hobby tremendously increases your pleasure in traveling by car. Rather than looking out of the window at a random and boring assemblage of plants, hills, and houses, the scenes you pass fall into place in a predictable manner, composing an open history book to be read in whatever depth you choose. Rather than waiting impatiently for the next village or city, you start to observe natural communities—associations of plants and animals native to the area that live in the same place because of their similar requirements for water, sunshine, soil nutrients, and other life-determining factors.

This section gives you basic information necessary for practicing landscape-reading skills in the Loess Hills; read it in the field and visit some of the recommended sites if possible. Remember, tread lightly and leave all natural features and organisms as you found them. If you are at home use your imagination and take a mental trip through the Hills. If you are motivated to look deeper into the natural history of the Hills, start with the following guides: *Iowa Conservationist: A Special Loess Hills Issue* (43:4, April 1984), available in libraries throughout the state, or request a copy from the *Iowa Conservationist,* Department of Natural Resources, Wallace State Office Building, Des Moines, 50319–0034; *Wildflowers, Grasses, and Other Plants of the Northern Plains and Black Hills (third edition)* (1983), by Theodore Van Bruggen, published by Badlands Natural History Association, Interior, South Dakota. (This guide, with its many colored pictures, is excellent for the beginner.)

Landforms

Start your journey by analyzing the largest features: look at the shape of the Hills. Seen from the air, the Loess Hills form an intricate network of narrow ridges with angular crests; extending from each central ridge are numerous spurs, which are equally sharp-featured. The result is a landscape that can be seen nowhere else on the continent—a finely dissected landscape, consisting of steeply pitched ridges intersected by troughs or broader valleys. Looking upward from the base of the bluffs, irregular ridge tops skirt the skyline and knobs of loess awkwardly protrude upward.

Characteristic shapes are most pronounced where the loess is deepest—immediately adjacent to the Missouri River valley. Look especially in the "heart of the loess," Harrison and Monona counties. Features fade into more gently rounded forms as you cut eastward through the Hills, this fading process occurring most rapidly south of Harrison County.

The finely dissected, angular landscape is in effect a dense drainage network, the result of very high erodability of loess and its ability to hold nearly vertical slopes of great height. These features are displayed most graphically by deep, perpendicular-sided gullies cut into valley floors throughout the deep loess region. Note also that where roads cut through the loess, the often sizeable roadside banks of loess stand for years without maintenance. Both people and nature routinely carve these vertical banks. When passing banks in wooded areas, stop to enjoy the delicate patterns formed by downward-reaching tree roots. Vertical loess cuts are one of the few places that tree root systems are exposed and can be readily examined.

Although vertical faces are extremely cohesive and well able to bear their own weight when dry, saturated loess dissolves like sugar, which can lead to disaster: slabs of bluffs slip downward to cover roads, and landscaped terraces collapse overnight.

The pointed side ridges typical of inland hills do not extend outward onto the floodplain. Instead, the floodplain is lined by broad, precipitous bluffs as high as three hundred feet. These were molded when the Missouri River, free in past ages to meander back and forth across the floodplain, washed away the outward-extending spurs, cutting backward into the more massive bluffs. Broad, steep bluff faces are prominent near Waubonsie State Park and in the areas of the Loess Hills Wildlife Area and Murray Hill.

By this time, you may have noticed that some hillsides seem to be horizontally ruled into multiple parallel lines. A close look at these will reveal that they are actually numerous small terraces called "catsteps" extending stepwise upslope. Some say that these catsteps have been cut by hooves of cattle in search of forage, but most geologists feel that catsteps are created naturally as gravity pulls the steeply sloped soil downward. Loess tends to sheer from hillsides in vertical faces forming these miniature cliffs. Look for catsteps on steep upper slopes throughout the Hills; one good site is near Murray Hill. (Do not confuse catsteps with the much larger bare-soil terraces seen in pastures on lower or upper slopes, formed when grazing cattle accentuate soil slumping and erosion.)

Fig. 4.4.   Characteristic shapes of the Loess Hills as seen from the air. (Photo courtesy of Geological Survey Bureau, Iowa Dep. of Natural Resources)

Geology

Looking beyond the shape of the Hills into the loess itself, a cursory glance reveals that this deep silt is uniform in particle size and color. If you have toured the Hills, you have undoubtedly experienced the fine dry dust permeating your car and clothing. Unfortunate tourists may have discovered that wet loess is like a sea of mashed bananas. You are not adequately introduced to the Hills until your car has uncontrollably slipped off the road. Fortunately the porous, well-drained loess dries rapidly.

In places, effects of weathering and remnants of previous epochs are visible within the loess. You may locate a collection of white, rocklike, knobby balls, which are called loess *kindchen* (a German term for small children). These are formed when water percolating through loess dissolves grains of carbonate. Lower in the loess, the carbonate solidifies into irregularly shaped nodules up to the size of a grapefruit. Look along Murray Hill roadcuts or anywhere else for these; however, if you leave these in place in the loess, others will be able to enjoy them in the future.

Solid rock underlying the loess can be seen in limestone quarries and roadcuts in the Council Bluffs area southward, in the shale quarries of the Sioux City area, and in the roadcut just south of the east entrance to Stone State Park (along Highway 12). This rock was formed from layers of sediments deposited when shallow marine seas cyclically covered the region. From Harrison County southward, rocks are 300-million-year-old Pennsylvanian deposits, remnants of massive coal-forming swamps. Near Sioux City, deposits are approximately 200 million years younger, formed during the Cretaceous period. Fossils of ancient marine organisms exist in both deposits, but only Cretaceous deposits contain remnants of modern flowering plants — leaf fossils of sassafras, willow, magnolia, and the like.

Also under the loess, you may notice angular stones, pebbles, and cobbles held together with clay. These are remnants of Iowa's earliest Ice Ages, glacial tills regarded as at least a half million years old. Being ancient they may be difficult to pick out, but look in Monona County along County Road L-14 in the roadcut just south of the entrance to the Turin Loess Hills Preserve.

Several miles farther south, on the Harrison-Monona county line (about one-half mile south of the entrance to the Little Sioux Fishing Access on L-14), look for a whitish streak about one foot thick that stands out in contrast to darker surrounding deposits. This is volcanic ash, blown across the Great Plains from major eruptions of now-extinct volcanoes in what is today Yellowstone National Park: volcanic ash deposits in roadcuts widely scattered in the Hills have been dated as 610,000 to 2 million years old.

Patterns of Plant Communities

Turning your attention to the living features of the Hills, focus on the *natural* assemblages of plants and animals that resemble presettlement Iowa — rather than on cropland and pasture planted and molded by human hands. Natural ecosystems remain where the most rugged topography has prevented conversion to cropland — primarily as a north-south band encompassing the bluff faces and the immediately adjacent hills. The width of this band varies. Where bluffs become small enough to allow intensive agriculture, the width of the band diminishes to next-to-nothing. Elsewhere, where tall steep hills and remote ridge crests extend farther to the east, the band of natural ecosystems widens. Plymouth County is an anomaly. The loess forms rolling hills lacking a steep bluff line, but some of the largest and most pristine prairies remain here.

Fig. 4.5. The mosaic of forest and grassland is
patterned by the availability of moisture. Trees, which
require more water than the grasses, are generally on
the cooler and wetter north- and east-facing slopes;
the prairie plants, masters of drought tolerance, prevail on the south- and west-facing slopes. (Photo by
Don Poggensee)

Stand back and observe any steep ridge in the central Hills.
The mosaic of forest and grassland becomes immediately apparent, a mosaic patterned by the availability of moisture. Trees,
which require greater amounts of water than grasses, cover the
cooler, wetter, north- and east-facing slopes, the ravines, and
some of the troughs running up dry hillsides. Prairie plants are
masters of drought tolerance. They have held the upper hand on
the very steepest slopes and on ridge tops, which are driest because they are best drained. Prairies prevail on the south- and
west-facing slopes, especially those immediately adjacent to the

Missouri River floodplain. These slopes are extremely dry because they are most exposed to intense, direct sunlight (which heats and dries the soil), and also to the prevailing drying winds. To observe the correlation of plant communities and slope exposure, climb Murray Hill; look to the north and the Loess Hills appear to be dominated by grasslands. Turn 180 degrees and look south; nearly solid forest meets the eye. This same difference of impression is created when you drive first north and then south along the base of the bluffs.

Take your eyes from the Hills of today and imagine yourself in the mid-1800s, when this region was first being settled. Roaming the Hills then, you would have wandered through much more extensive prairie, finding shelter only in scattered hillside groves and in streamside timber, which sometimes crept upward on moister slopes. The knobs of prairie-covered loess were first described in the 1804 journals of the Lewis and Clark expedition as "Bald Hills," an impression later affirmed by other early surveys, journals, and artists.

Even then, the border between forest and prairie was a tense battleground, each type of community claiming the other's territory when climatic conditions allowed. Fire—set regularly by Indians and by lightning—aided the naturally fire-hardy prairie plants in retaining the upper hand. Suppression of fire by settlers, possibly combined with a trend toward a wetter climate, shifted that balance. In the last century or so, woodlands have invaded the prairies en masse, obliterating many Loess Hills prairies with their unique collection of plants and animals. Woodland expansion continues today, pushing a number of prairie species to the brink of extinction in Iowa. At present rates of invasion and barring human intervention, the unique Loess Hills bluff prairies are predicted to disappear completely by the middle of the twenty-first century.

Prairies historically were more extensive in the far northern Hills, where lower annual precipitation and other climatic conditions favored growth of grasses. In the south, climate and the availability of forest and shrub seeds have hastened tree invasion. Today forests dominate nearly all slopes in far southern Fremont County, prairies being relegated to a few of the most westerly bluffs and to narrow bands along the ridge crests. In contrast, grasslands still roll without interruption down one slope and up another in parts of far northern Plymouth County, which is drier and more conducive to growth of prairie plants.

When looking at the forest-grassland mosaic, you may notice a line of shrubs interfacing the two communities. These shrubs are likely to be rough-leaved dogwood or smooth sumac.

Shrubs are the harbingers of change. Drought tolerant enough to grow out into prairies that line the woodlands, these shrubs shade out and eventually kill the sun-loving grasses. Shrubs also provide a sheltered site for shade-loving tree seedlings to thrive. The trees eventually extend above the shrubs, which are replaced by other forest species. The forest makes one more step forward.

Prairies

From a distance, one grassland may look like any other. But hike through grasslands and you will notice that in some places plants are tall, elsewhere they are close-cropped. Some prairies have many species, others have only a few. A flower seen in one place is absent elsewhere. Bare soil, obvious on one slope, is hidden by litter and vegetation on another. The grasslands are responding to differences in physical properties of each hillside, and to differing histories of human land use.

Three factors make Loess Hills prairies stand out from Iowa's more typical tallgrass prairies: the presence of certain western grassland species, the dominance of midheight (rather than very tall) grasses, and the absence of many moisture-loving broad-leaved plants typical of other Iowa prairies. Although within the region of tallgrass prairie, the drier Hills prairies are similar to the mixed-grass prairies of the westerly Great Plains. This unusual peninsular extension of drier prairie species occurs in the Loess Hills because of the area's dryness.

Loess soil, naturally deep and well drained, is desertlike on the steepest bluff slopes with western and southern exposures, those most exposed to sun and wind. Here native prairies are most sparse, and patches of bare soil abound. These driest prairies are most likely to contain the approximately forty drought-tolerant species for which the Loess Hills are known — plants typical of the dry grasslands eighty-plus miles to the west, which cannot be found east of the Hills. A number of these extend their range eastward only in a narrow finger along the Hills, not extending farther eastward. Even the names of these plants — yucca, cowboy's delight, tumblegrass, skeleton weed, locoweed — ring of the West. Several of these plants are rare or endangered in Iowa.

In general Hills prairies become lusher and taller as one travels eastward and sites become more protected. The two dominant Hills grasses, little bluestem and side-oats grama, may mix in places with tallgrasses (big bluestem, Indian grass). Tallgrass species become evident on inland hills with eastern or northern exposures, especially in Plymouth and Woodbury counties. Look along ridge tops just north of the central Loess Hills Wildlife

Area's central parking area, and note how tallgrasses appear immediately after crossing onto east-facing slopes. Taller grasslands probably abounded prehistorically in lowlands and on moister slopes, but these areas were first to be invaded by trees or plowed for row crops.

Most grasslands within the rugged, westernmost bluffs are neither pristine prairie nor planted fields, but instead the result of mixed natural and human elements. Moderately grazed prairies, overgrazed prairies, prairies cut for hay, pastures of planted brome, and pastures or abandoned cropland returning to prairie all are present. How can these be differentiated?

Native prairie throughout Iowa bears several distinctive features. Most prairie grasses are "warm season grasses" that retain their dormant dried appearance until early summer and do not set seed until August or September. Introduced species, in contrast, green up early in spring and set seed by midsummer. Most midheight prairie grasses are bunch grasses, maintaining a distinctive clumped appearance. Pastures of introduced sod formers, lacking the prairie's undulating surface and mixture of plants of many sizes, appear smoother and more uniform throughout. The rich cinnamon or russet color of fall and winter prairies is distinctive enough to identify from an airplane; other grasslands are a gaudier, brighter green in summer, fading in fall to the washed-out tan of a dry cornfield. Identify healthy native prairie by examining the steeper slopes for these traits and adding identification of the few key species mentioned earlier.

Light to moderate grazing may not adversely affect the prairie; roving bison grazed prairies for millennia. But graze a prairie too long or too intensely and the vigor and diversity of prairie plants decrease. Plants become close-cropped. Bare soil increases and soil slumping or erosion may become a problem. Tallgrasses and certain forbs decrease or disappear. One grass, side-oats grama, may increase for a while, but then it too decreases. Other species—hoary vervain, mullein, thistles among others—increase and may come to dominate a pasture. Even though not purposely planted, species introduced to the area by settlers may invade a pasture and proliferate; examine the grasslands speckled with red cedar, not a native to the area. Virtually all prairies other than those in parks or preserves are grazed and demonstrate these traits to a greater or lesser degree. If you climb Murray Hill by hiking the fenceline that outlines this preserve, compare features of ungrazed prairie with those of the grazed grassland on adjacent private land.

Prairies can be found throughout the Hills, with the best quality and largest found in northern preserves. The Sioux City

Prairie, Five-Ridge Prairie, Loess Hills Wildlife Area, and Turin Loess Hills Preserve offer the best opportunities for prairie observation.

Fig. 4.6. *Overgrazing can destroy the prairies, reducing the native plant cover to nearly nothing and exposing the loess soils to serious erosion. (Photo courtesy of Ron Johnson, Iowa Dep. of Natural Resources)*

Forests

Loess Hills forests are no more homogeneous than grasslands. They too have been affected by differing microenvironments and histories of human use. Although most postdate 1850, their ages differ greatly. Some have been logged or grazed, others are the result of prairie invasion, still others have taken over abandoned cropland, and a few have been purposely planted. The resulting forest mosaic awaits clarification through future research.

Forests are dominated by species of oak, with hickory, basswood, walnut, elm and ash species, and ironwood also abundant. Bur oak, the only oak that grows throughout the Hills, often is seen near the tops of ridges. Older bur oaks have a thick, corky bark that prevents damage by fire. Sections of presettlement prairie may have been speckled with these trees.

The Hills forests are one of the westernmost extensions of the Eastern Deciduous Forest, a major plant community to the south (in Missouri), in eastern Iowa, and throughout more easterly states. Many woody plant species reach their limits of distribution in the Loess Hills. They are able to grow in southern counties but find life in northern counties too harsh; thus tree diversity is greatest in southern Fremont County and decreases as one travels north.

A walk along the trails in Stone, Preparation Canyon, or Waubonsie state parks allows exploration of the Loess Hills woodlands.

Animals

What about the animals? The species that are most likely to be seen are common throughout Iowa: Fox squirrel, Eastern cottontail, Mourning dove, Blue jay, coyote, raccoon, skunk. Other species are not obvious because they are now rare or are well camouflaged or nocturnal, or because they burrow into the soil in an attempt to escape the sun's heat. Larger, more conspicuous species — Black bear, Grey wolf, cougar, wapiti, bison, and pronghorn — were eliminated from the area early during settlement.

But if you were able to assemble a Noah's ark of Loess Hills species, the diversity would be amazing. This diversity results from what ecologists call the "edge effect," the interfingering of prairie, shrubland, and woodland, which provides an abundance of habitat for animals that require any or all of these plant communities.

As Loess Hills forests become more extensive, the rich assemblage of woodland animals also expands. Woodland species such as the White-tailed deer are increasing, especially in the southern counties where forest animals are most common.

Loess Hills prairies, with their extreme temperatures and lack of standing water, present an especially harsh environment for any inhabitant. As with the plants, the animal assemblage has a decidedly western flavor unusual in Iowa, reflected in names such as the Great Plains toad, Plains leapfrog, Plains spadefoot, Plains pocket mouse, and Prairie rattlesnake, whose last Iowa refuge is in the northern Hills. A number of these are limited to only a few locations or are found in very low numbers. Elimination of their habitat (in particular the replacement of prairie by forest and cropland) has been devastating to Hills prairie animals. Only prairie preservation combined with careful prairie management will avoid local extinction.

Certain prairie butterflies are among the most host-specific of animals; they will lay their eggs on only one or two types of prairie plants. Because of the decimation of Iowa's prairies a number of butterflies are abundant only in the Loess Hills. Skippers, small and inconspicuous, are not likely to be noticed, but watch for the brilliant orange regal Fritillary, whose caterpillars depend on a few species of prairie violets.

Bird watchers are in for a treat in the Hills, where woodland birds (Red-bellied woodpeckers, Eastern wood peewees, Black-capped chickadees, and many others) mix with grassland birds (Grasshopper sparrows, Field sparrows, Dickcissels) and forest edge or shrubland species (Indigo bunting, Rufous-sided towhee). Western species (Western kingbird) and southern species (Chuck-will's widow, Summer tanager), rare elsewhere in Iowa, can be seen here along with several species on the National Audubon Society's "Blue List" of declining or special concern species (Bell's vireo, Upland sandpiper). Nesting Bank swallows flit in and out of holes carved into roadside cuts; migrating raptors are thought to be attracted by the thermal updrafts; waterfowl and eagles migrate along the Missouri River, stopping at Desoto Bend National Wildlife Refuge, about twenty miles north of Council Bluffs. Here, astounding numbers of birds attract tourists from throughout the state. As many as 200 thousand Snow geese grace the sky in mid-November, at the peak of fall migration, re-creating some sense of the incredible richness of bird life found along the Missouri before this great river was channelized.

The richest bird diversity occurs in Loess Hills forests in the southern Hills; Waubonsie State Park is an especially rich birding site.

Although grassland species have suffered with the decline of prairies, some of these birds have survived in agricultural fields. Grassland birds are most abundant in northern Hills.

Occasionally the special qualities of the Hills are accentuated by a researcher discovering the seemingly impossible. This occurred in 1983, when several populations of the very rare Ornate box turtle were discovered forty years after the last turtle of this type had been seen in the area. Two other rare species, the Plains pocket mouse and Southern bog lemming also were rediscovered in the early 1980s, a decade after they had been last observed here. More of these types of surprises await researchers who continue to probe the Hills, providing they are given the preservation they deserve.

Future of the Ecosystems

Your awareness of the Loess Hills may have been captured in the last few years by one of the many recently published articles on the Hills, or by the hour-long television documentary, "The Land Between Two Rivers," broadcast on Iowa Public Television in 1987. But these strikingly unusual hills have commanded attention from the beginning of their historical record, long before the recent flurry of interest. Within twenty years of the first written descriptions of the Hills in 1804 (in the Lewis and Clark expedition journals), botanists were publishing accounts of the totally new species they found among collections of Loess Hills plants. By the late 1800s, publications pointed out the similarities of these Hills to loess deposits in China. By this time the state's natural historians were theorizing about features such as the direction of migration of certain plant species, prehistoric vegetational cover, and habitation by creatures long extinct.

Although the value of the Hills' natural qualities was recognized early, scientists and conservationists showed a minimum of interest in this area through much of the twentieth century. A dramatic reawakening occurred in the late 1970s and early 1980s, in part because of efforts of the State Preserves Board, a program of the Iowa Department of Natural Resources. The board sponsored a number of studies, including a week-long Skipper foray. Experts from throughout North America toured the Hills, identifying locations where these small rare butterflies still thrive. The many studies were presented at a scientific symposium in 1984 and published in two issues of the *Proceedings of the Iowa Academy of Science* (vols. 92, no. 5 and 93, no. 3), which together provided natural historians with a definitive compilation of scientific features of this region for the first time.

Before the 1980s, you could visit some fine public parks and preserves in the Loess Hills. The state had established three large parks and the twenty-five-hundred-acre Loess Hills Wildlife Area, while county conservation boards had formed numerous smaller parks, as had Sioux City and Council Bluffs. However, even though most of these publicly owned lands preserved natural and rare features of significance, preservation of such features was not the primary criterion for the land selection.

The 1980s saw a new direction in Loess Hills preservation efforts. The Nature Conservancy, a nonprofit conservation organization dedicated to the preservation of rare species and natural ecosystems, opened an Iowa office and shortly thereafter proclaimed preservation of the Loess Hills as one of its national priorities. Following a search for high-quality prairies with rare species, the conservancy purchased the 790-acre Five-Ridge Prairie in Plymouth County (now owned by the Plymouth County Conservation Board), and the 150-acre Sioux City Prairie. If you visit the latter, note how its educational value is heightened because of its location in the heart of Sioux City, adjacent to Briar Cliff College.

The Sioux City Prairie is a tribute to the contribution that one family can make to natural area preservation. In 1979 Dianne and Bill Blankenship attended the Loess Hills Prairie Seminar for the first time. Trained in education and medicine, they knew little of natural history or of the Loess Hills. Excited by the seminar they became self-taught prairie enthusiasts and soon started to study prairies near their Sioux City home. The death of the respected local environmental educator, Carolyn Benne, prompted the Blankenships to press the conservancy to purchase the Sioux City Prairie as a memorial; the Blankenships assumed responsibility for local fund raising efforts. They have since played a major role in educational efforts on and about the Sioux City and other local prairies. Their interest in botany has developed to the point of writing newspaper columns describing local flora.

You may have read of the designation of approximately ten thousand Loess Hills acres as a National Natural Landmark. This 1986 act culminated a lengthy push for national recognition of the unique features of the Hills. This land in Monona and Harrison counties is now formally recognized as one of the nation's prominent natural features. Although designated land will remain in private ownership and use is not restricted, conservation of natural features will be encouraged.

The state also has recognized the unique value of the Hills by adding two parcels to the Iowa State Preserves System. The Five-Ridge Prairie and the Turin Loess Hills Preserve are designated as representing excellent examples of pristine natural features, which now receive the highest protection afforded by Iowa law.

One final land conservation effort promises to create the largest Loess Hills preserve in existence. The Loess Hills Pioneer State Forest in northern Harrison and southern Monona counties, now being purchased, will eventually exceed seventeen thousand acres. Some natural historians view as ironic the formation of a *forest* preserve, since invading forests are here aggressively destroying Iowa's last extensive prairies. However, management of this state forest will be focussed on multiple use, and will include prairie as well as forest preservation.

Preservation of Loess Hills forest or prairie: Which is preferred, and what is possible? Neither question can be answered perfunctorily. Certainly the expansion of forests has afforded valuable habitat to woodland animals and created a pleasant recreational resource for public use. However, ecologists agree that when managing Loess Hills natural areas, prairies are the ecosystems of choice. Iowa, once the heart of the tallgrass prairie, retains significantly large prairies only in these corrugated hills. And these prairies, with their many species in danger of local extinction and their distinctive association of western species, are too special to let disappear.

Preservation of prairies is more easily said than done. Attempts have been made to push the line of invading forests backward by physically removing woody vegetation, selective use of herbicides, and reinstating periodic fire. Forests continue to encroach in spite of these efforts. Burned areas rapidly refill with shrubs, and when burns are carried out in the wrong season or too infrequently, fire even seems to promote growth of invading sumac. This highly aggressive invasion prompts ecologists to ask whether a long-term shift toward a moister climate would be pushing Iowa's prairies back to forest even if natural processes and prairie fires still reigned.

Research into the best methods of halting forest invasion is clearly needed. This research is now being carried out on preserves throughout Iowa's northern Loess Hills, simultaneously with the use of the best prairie-maintenance techniques now known. Also necessary are efforts to reinstate forest control programs in other Hills prairies because once massive invasion of a prairie occurs, it is very difficult to set back.

Now that you have made either real or imaginary solo excursions into the Loess Hills, you may wish to explore them with others. If so, you may choose from any in a growing number of educational programs. Consider attending one of the nature talks scheduled regularly from May through September at the Sioux City Prairie (contact the Woodbury County Conservation Board for dates and times), or contact the Plymouth or Monona County conservation boards for information on their guided walks elsewhere in the Hills.

Above all else, consider spending a weekend in early June at the Loess Hills Prairie Seminar (organized by the Western Hills Area Education Agency, 1520 Morningside Ave., Sioux City,

51106). Every spring since 1977, up to three hundred participants, from infants to persons in their eighties, have gathered in the Loess Hills Wildlife Area to attend talks and nature hikes on the area's biology, ecology, and geology, and on nature appreciation. Classes are designed for the beginner, and attendance is open to all. Participants normally camp in the wildlife area, sharing meals from a "chuck wagon."

Come and enjoy the convivial, cheery spirit that permeates the weekend. Share in pleasant surprises that seem to abound when lovers of the Loess Hills convene—such as the 1982 discovery during one of the nature walks of a tiny fern never before known to science. Your appreciation of the natural treasures contained within these Hills may well expand, so that you join others across the state who make attendance at this innovative educational seminar an annual tradition. By attending seminars such as these and becoming familiar with the area in other ways, you and other concerned citizens may continue to study the forces that have molded these Loess Hills, and to take part in preserving their future.

Fig. 4.7. Amateurs of all ages getting firsthand exposure to the unique ecosystems and landforms of the Loess Hills as part of the annual Loess Hills Prairie Seminar. (Photo by Don Poggensee)

PART
III

Landscape, the Country

5

INDIAN IOWA

Robert Bunge

Ancient Iowa

When we speak of the Iowa vernacular landscape, we must realize that Iowa has been continuously inhabited and transformed by human effort for the last twelve thousand years. Paleo-Indians advanced into northeastern Iowa as the last great glacier, which covered approximately the upper third of Iowa, retreated to the north.

The earliest adaptation of these people to the environment was that of the big game hunter, who hunted the mastadon on foot, as well as a species of bison much larger than those existing today. Since the bow and arrow had not been invented yet, the spear was the principal hunting weapon. The spear thrower, perhaps a first step toward the sinew-and-wood-propelled arrow, was a kind of wooden jacket or stick that functioned as an extension of the arm and transmitted more force and accuracy to the hurled spear. Nevertheless, what a puny weapon against so massive a quarry. Other, safer tactics had to be devised to offset the prey's advantage of size and weight. Often these large animals could be stampeded over a cliff by setting the prairie aflame or by using human scare tactics, or they could be driven into a shallow marsh to become mired. The hunters could then kill their prey with spears and rocks in relative safety.

Several thousand years later, the spear thrower and the heavy, flaked spearhead were superceded by the bow and arrow, which had a much smaller arrowhead. It must have been observed by some ancient practical "physicist" that the smaller arrowhead combined with the much greater speed of an arrow would pass clear through a bison, sometimes striking another on the other side.

The hunting of big game made economic sense. After dressing out a bison, perhaps one thousand pounds of meat could be shared by the tribe; the same effort in dressing a deer resulted in only one hundred pounds of meat, hardly enough for a village of any size.

Information on these very early people is somewhat scanty, but much can be inferred from the most durable of artifacts, namely, those made of stone—such as spearpoints still stuck in the ribs of a mastadon skeleton.

With the passage of time the adaptation to the forests of northeastern Iowa became more sophisticated. The life-styles of the later periods are richer in artifacts than those of the earliest period; therefore, more can be learned of these later societies. With their woodworking tools such as the adze, the axe, and the wood gouge, these societies must have developed better dwellings and boats. To a diet of meat they added fish, fresh water mussels, wild rice, nuts, and fruits and berries.

For the antiquarian traveler today entering Iowa at Dubuque, a right turn on Iowa Highway 52 will lead through a series of picturesque towns from Guttenburg to Marquette. Then, three miles north of Marquette, an awe-inspiring world is encountered at Effigy Mounds National Monument. The traveler will find the work of a people of an age known to archeologists as Hopewellian—100 B.C. to 500 A.D. Three of these mounds are only one hundred yards from the Visitor's Center of the park, a quick lure to what lies ahead.

Unbelievably, the rest of the mounds are located on top of a three-hundred-foot cliff above the Mississippi. The path circles back and forth, following closely the original trails used by the mound builders, with an occasional railing to aid in catching your breath. During the warmest times of the year, the park service people strongly suggest that mosquito repellent is used. Otherwise, you may come down a little more distorted than when you went up.

The exertion is worth the effort. As you reach the summit, a strange hush falls over the landscape. Even the sounds of nature seem subdued as if in tribute to one of ancient Iowa's truly holy places. The path levels out between colossal "linear" mounds approximately 150 to 200 feet in length and about 3 to 3½ feet high. Curiously, the mounds are covered with a smooth grassy coating, with few trees on the mounds themselves except the mound on the right has a tree growing out of the middle section.

Some of the oldest in the Mississippi Valley, these mounds were built by a people known as the "Red Ochre Culture," who existed about twenty-five hundred years ago. In a European time frame, this would be the Greece of Socrates, Plato, and Aristotle. In the East, this would be the China of Confucious. This Red Ochre Culture is sometimes called the Red Ochre Cult, as the mounds were burial sites, hence of a religious nature. A prominent feature of these burials was the sprinkling of red ochre (iron oxide) on the body and on the floor of the burial chamber. Why red ochre? Nobody knows for certain, but it no doubt had a religious significance.

Beneath the placid surface of Iowa with its Victorian towns, its corn and soybean fields, and its landmass marked off in square mile sections, lies an elder Iowa of profound mystery. Tantalizing evidence of this older Iowa is brought to light by plowshares and bulldozers almost daily in the form of arrow- and spearheads, potsherds, tools, and jewelry (especially fresh-water pearl necklaces).

The people of the Hopewell Culture were one of the most mysterious races to inhabit this ancient land. The artifacts and jewelry found suggest an advanced and prosperous people. A community is poor from an economic standpoint if its people must devote ninety to ninety-five percent of its time in providing food for themselves. The Hopewell artisans had the time and leisure to produce articles of "conspicuous consumption" (i.e., luxury items purely for adornment and ceremonial purposes). Moreover, they established a trading network with tribes over a thousand miles away. Appalachian mica, Rocky Mountain obsidian, conch shells from the Gulf of Mexico, and copper from the Upper Great Lakes bear silent but eloquent testimony to this fact. Remember, there were no overland conveyances at the time. The little prehistoric horse no larger than a dog had vanished, and the modern horse would not be introduced to the Americas until the advent of the Spanish Conquest centuries in the future. Practically all of this culture flourished along waterways, which suggests river or coastal travel.

Indications are that it was a status-conscious, ranked society headed by powerful men capable of commanding the large labor force necessary for mound building, wherein up to seven million cubic feet of earth were moved, basketful by basketful. Both cremation and burial were practiced—the important and powerful destined for burial and the poor destined for cremation, as personal funerary attire and grave adornment testify.

Ideas, especially prejudicial ideas, are hard to kill even with scientific evidence. Early historians of Iowa and modern anthropologists have long tried to account for the rise of the Hopewell Culture about 100 B.C. and its total disappearance in 500 A.D. Answers to these questions would shed new light on social organizations, economics, and religion. Yet, despite uncertainty, nineteenth-century notions persist that the mounds were built by a strange race unrelated to and technologically superior to the tribes of Iowa. The tribes with which the white immigrants to Iowa were familiar seemed both scientifically and temperamentally incapable of constructing effigies and mounds requiring the rudiments of geometry, the knowledge of rather exact units of measurement and angles, plus the engineering skills. But the mounds show an obvious relationship to the clans and totem animals of later Iowa tribes. Beside the linear mounds mentioned earlier, there are conical mounds and then the effigy mounds themselves. Just past the linear mounds are Little Bear Mound and Big Bear Mound. The Big Bear Mound measures 70 feet across the shoulders and forelegs, 137 feet long and 3½ feet high. These mounds are so gigantic that they can be recognized in their entirety only from above. Aerial photographs alone permit the beholder to appreciate the magnitude of these works, such as the mounds of the ten marching bears and the bird mounds. Each bear effigy is 80 to 100 feet long.

Fig. 5.1.   Aerial view of bear and eagle mounds,
Effigy Mounds National Monument, with mounds
outlined in chalk. (Photo courtesy of State Historical
Society of Iowa)

Fig. 5.2. Three small, unmarked mounds near Abbe Creek, northwest of Mt. Vernon, Iowa, in 1983. The woman is standing between the first and second. Such mounds can still be found in many parts of Iowa. (Photo by Bob Campagna)

Meanwhile, speculation continues. Some archeologists regard the mounds as simply burial chambers, others as monuments to clan totems, and still others, as both. The latest and most informed theory, in my opinion, is the "integrative mechanism" theory advanced by R. Clark Mallam in an article entitled "Effigy Mounds in Iowa—Ideology from the Earth." Mallam argues that the "mounds functioned as institutional devices for maintaining unity and cohesiveness among and between territorially limited social groups of hunters and gatherers."

Mallam goes on to formulate a more comprehensive theory in which he relies heavily on native beliefs of the historic period. In addition to functioning as burial vaults, territory demarcators, and devices to ensure unity and coherence on the social level, the mounds are ritual expressions of the twin cornerstones of native thought—harmony and balance between the people and the forces of nature. Relationships were and are all important; nothing is "real" until it is ritualized. In Native America, even today, relationships are not confined to the human sphere of activity but extend to all that is in the native cosmos. The mounds represent, in a monumental and epic form, Ancient Iowa's participation in upholding and maintaining the native universe in the most meaningful way possible.

Suddenly, in the year 500 A.D., the Hopewell Culture vanished into the mists of Iowa prehistory, leaving behind abundant evidence of its power and vitality. What happened? Nobody knows . . .

The disappearance of the Hopewell Culture did not stop mound building all over Iowa, however. Around 1000 A.D. a new culture, the Oneota, developed and carried on this activity until about 1300 A.D. The later descendents of the Oneota, the Ioway, the Otoe (also spelled Oto), and Winnebago, all Chiwere Siouan—speaking folk, were living in Iowa at the time of the first contacts with the Europeans (and the beginning of what anthropologists call "historical times").

Historical Indian Iowa

The first "white eyes" to gaze upon the land now known as Iowa were two Frenchmen—Father Marquette and his companion in exploration, Joliet. With the French came writing. And so Iowa left prehistory to enter the pages of history. This was in the year 1673.

The first tribe encountered by this duo representing Church and State, was the Illini, camped on the west bank of the Mississippi. The name Illini means "men," or "we are men." This people is now extinct as a tribe. Marquette and Joliet also knew of the Mascoutin, or "Meadow Indian"—these people, too, are extinct, but their name is perpetuated in the name Muscatine, Iowa.

Many of the tribes were transient or resided in Iowa for only short periods of time. Others were native to the region or were to become long-term residents. The tribe from whom the state derives its name is one of the latter.

Iowa is one mystery after another. Probably no state name is more shrouded in linguistic fog than the word "Iowa." The tribe's name, Pahoja or Pahuja, is variously translated by authorities as "Gray Snow" or "Dusty Noses" or "Dusty Faces." There is a traditional tale in support of the name "Dusty Noses," which relates that this tribe camped near the Mississippi in the vicinity of some bare and wind-swept sandbars from whence the winds filled their nostrils and eyes with stinging mud.

Riggs, in his *Dakota-English Dictionary,* glosses the word Iowa as "something to write with." The Dakota name for this tribe is *Ayu Hba,* meaning "Sleepy Ones." There is a tale told this writer by a Yankton elder that supports this last name, in which this tribe of Iyowa, meaning "Yawners," had a very unusual business and social practice—that is, certain mores not understood by surrounding tribes. At the great trade fairs held annually up and down the Missouri, they did not seem to want to partake in the festivities that preceded trade, but would uncharacteristically want to "get down to business" and then yawn as though they were wearied of the merriment around them. They would then retire to their own camp. Tribes often acquired a nickname, which stuck forever, after a single observed incident.

Other translations of the name Iowa include "People across the River," "This Is the Place," "Crossing or Going Over," "Beautiful Land," "Here I Rest," "Curved Channel," and "Dead-Fish Eaters." The last translation is a corruption of Kiowa, which is the name of a southern plains tribe meaning "Great Medicine." The *Handbook of American Indians* by Hodges lists 102 forms of the word. Spelling includes Anjoues, Ayawas, Ihoway, Yahawa, Ayoes, Aiaouas, Hayuas, and Aiouez. In short, nobody knows for certain, but it seems to us that the Dakota term "Sleepy Ones" is the most likely meaning.

Archeological evidence seems to indicate that the Chiwere Siouan–speaking peoples, of which the Ioway were a subgroup, spread into western Iowa about 1500 A.D. and, as such, have spanned the Oneota period and historic times. Despite the fact that all the tribes settling in Iowa farmed, the Ioway were an extremely migratory people. Every explorer who mentions them has sighted them in a different location. In historical times, it seems they undertook fifteen or sixteen major migrations between the Mississippi and Missouri and then back again. The first white man to meet the Ioway was a Frenchman named Nicolas Perrot, in 1685. Although ethnologically and linguistically akin to the other tribes of Siouan stock in the area, they were the hereditary enemies of both the Sioux and the Osage.

Whatever riddle there may be about the name "Ioway," the ultimate fate of the tribe is no mystery. In the century and one-half after the encounter with Perrot, the Ioway, under the leadership of several great chiefs, including Man-Haw-Gaw (Wounding Arrow) and his son Ma-Has-Ka (White Cloud), were able to overcome their enemies and prosper in the beautiful Des Moines valley. They met defeat not at the hands of their ancient Siouan enemies, but at the hands of the powerful Sac and Fox tribes recently displaced from Wisconsin and Illinois after the Black Hawk War.

The Sac and Fox, under the leadership of Pash-E-Pa-Ho and the same Black Hawk recently defeated at the Battle of Bad Axe, utterly routed the Ioway at the seat of their power—the northwest corner of Van Buren County where the town, or rather the trading post, of Iowaville was established. Less than a decade later the Ioway were removed from the state now bearing their name, first to Nebraska and later to Oklahoma where most of them live today. The Ioway formed an alliance with the Otoe, also a formerly powerful tribe in Iowa, and are now known as the Otoe-Iowa. The languages of these two people are almost identical and are presented as a single language in language texts prepared for tribal schools today.

For the visitor to Iowa, a trip to Living History Farms in Des Moines lets him back into Iowa's yesterdays. Here, on a six-hundred-acre open-air agricultural museum, the tourist may see a reconstructed Ioway farm site, with explanations of the scenes given by live, period-costumed "interpreters."

To reach this fascinating replica of a bygone time, drive down I-80 to the west end of Des Moines, take Exit 125 (also called Hickman Road, or Highway 6) on the combined interstates of 35 and 80. It is open May 1 through the last weekend in October, and the hours are Monday through Saturday, 9:00 A.M. to 5:00 P.M.; Sunday, 11:00 A.M. to 6:00 P.M. This unique outdoor museum covers the entire history of farming in Iowa from the Ioway tribe who lived in long, bark lodges to the farmers now living in solar houses. The buildings, planting methods, and livestock are authentic to the time periods and, in the case of the Ioway site, even native grasses, trees, and plants have been successfully reintroduced. The time frame of the museum's Ioway site is given as 1700, so that numerous trade items may be shown, mainly metal utensils such as kettles, axe heads, knife blades, beads, and cloth.

The fertility of the rich soil of Iowa enabled the native populations to settle in permanent or semipermanent villages, to farm and thereby become more independent by not having to rely so heavily on hunting as a source of food. Thus the Ioway combined the farming skills of the woodlands to the east with the hunting skills of the plains to the west. Along with the metal trade utensils and tools are the traditional Ioway farm implements such as the native hoe made of the shoulder bone of a buffalo lashed to a wooden handle and the cultivator, indicating that even though European technology played an ever-increasing role in native life, the Ioway, well after the time of contact, still relied largely on their traditional tools to till the soil.

It is well known that the Indians of North America contributed a host of hitherto unknown foods to the world's larder.

Many of these foods retain their original Indian name such as succotash, hominy, and pemmican as well as corn (called "maize" by the English), the pumpkin, etc. The Ioway raised several varieties of corn and, according to the interpreter at Living History Farms, the "corn was roasted, parched in earthen pots, or ground into meal for corn bread." Other foods, samples of which are to be seen at the site, include "Hidatsa red beans, Michigan Indian beans, banquet squash, and various kinds of gourds and small, oval, Omaha pumpkins."

While agriculture was generally women's work among the Ioway, the tobacco plot was tended by the medicine man, since tobacco was believed to be an especially sacred plant. Today the Indians joke about their gift of tobacco to the white man, saying, "We gave them tobacco and they gave us whiskey. We traded them a liver for a lung."

Fig. 5.3.   (A) Na-na-wa-che standing before the traditional Mesquakie wickiup; the photo was taken around 1900. (B) Copy of a na-ha-che of the Ioways (similar to but more oval than the Mesquakie wickiup) at Living History Farms, Des Moines. Today many Mesquakie keep various adaptations of wickiups beside or behind their houses for use as sweatlodges and shelters for cooking and eating in hot weather. (Fig. 5.3A. Photo from the Ward Collection, courtesy of State Historical Society of Iowa; Fig. 5.3B. Photo by Miriam Dunlap, Living History Farms)

The Ioway lived in *na-ha-ches,* lodges, that were somewhat similar to the Mesquakie *wick-i-up* except that the *na-ha-ches* were more oval in shape. These lodges are representative of a general woodland-culture type of building. At Living History Farms, the visitor can see how this Ioway lodge was constructed of a series of tall saplings arranged in a circle and bent over and lashed to each other at the center top to form a frame. Bark slabs are placed over this frame and then fixed in place with willow poles.

To the east of this exciting, innovative, open-air museum lies Iowa City. There on Clinton Street on the University of Iowa campus is McBride Hall. Inside is Iowa Hall, where exhibits ranging from Paleo times through the archaic and woodland periods to the Mesquakie settlement of historical times are maintained. The Mesquakie exhibit and an exhibit of the first European contact with the aboriginal peoples of Iowa employ lifelike mannequins, which transport the visitor to the time and place of these events on the continuum of lived experience in Iowa.

The Sac and Fox

Related but different tribes, the Sac (Sauk) and Fox (Mesquakie) are both Algonquin-speaking people who stem from the same eastern woodland tradition. These tribes shared a common mistrust of white men in general, and of the French in particular.

Said to have their origins along the St. Lawrence Seaway, both tribes were gradually driven westward to Green Bay, Wisconsin.

The Fox were the special object of French hatred, for their interference with the French fur trade probably played a major role in the French defeat at the hands of the English in Canada. The French relentlessly conducted a war of annihilation against them over much of what was then the Northwest — namely, Michigan, Wisconsin, and Illinois. Finally the Fox, decimated by this Gallic persecution, allied themselves with a kindred people, the Sac, and moved into Iowa well within historic times — about 1800.

Fewer in number at this time than the Sac, who had suffered less at the hands of the French, the Fox were fearful of being engulfed by the Sac. Therefore, zealous of maintaining their identity, they carefully preserved their own traditions under their own chiefs and lived in villages near to but apart from the larger Sac encampments.

The early decades of the history of the Sac and Fox in Iowa were dominated by two powerful Sac chiefs — Black Hawk and Keokuk. Under pressure from the encroaching white immigrants who were backed by militia troops, Keokuk and the majority of Sac and Fox withdrew from Illinois and settled in Iowa. Black Hawk, however, chose to "lift the hatchet" on the east bank of the Mississippi and fight for his Rock Island home, starting what was known as the Black Hawk War. In it a young backwoods railsplitter named Abraham Lincoln got his first glimpse of frontier warfare.

Black Hawk, who distrusted both the French and Americans and who never was in favor with the Americans because of his loyalty to England in the War of 1812, was defeated at Bad Axe just north of Prairie du Chien, Wisconsin. In fact, the band led by Black Hawk was known as "Black Hawk's British Band."

After serving a term in a military prison and after a trip to the East, which the government gave him to impress upon him the extent of American power, Black Hawk was returned to his people, who now resided in Iowa under the leadership of Keokuk. The old warrior was deeply humiliated by being released into the custody of a man whom he remembered as a youth who had not yet earned the right to speak in council.

Which chief was right? Old Black Hawk, who went to war rather than compromise his way of life? Or young Keokuk, the orator and diplomat who realized perhaps the time for open warfare was past and negotiation was the wave of the future? Who knows? Another mystery of the region . . .

Black Hawk, in the story of his life, which he dictated to J. B. Patterson via the Indian interpreter Antoine LeClaire, gives an interesting account of the way the Sac managed their resources and their land.

> When our national dance is over . . . and our corn about knee high, all our young men would start in a direction towards sundown, to hunt deer and buffalo . . . a part of our old men and women to the lead mine to make lead . . . and the remainder of our people to start to fish and get mat stuff (reeds and rushes). Everyone leaves the village and remains about forty days. They, then, return: The hunting party bringing in dried buffalo and deer meat . . . the party from the lead mines bring lead and the others dried fish and mats for our winter lodges.

Black Hawk goes on to say that everything is shared with everyone, that

> "this is a happy season of the year—having plenty of provisions, such as beans, squash (pumpkins) and other produce, with our dried meat and fish, we continue to make feasts and visit each other until our corn is ripe. . . . When our corn is getting ripe, our young people watch with anxiety, for the signal to pull roasting ears—as none dare touch them until the proper time. When the corn is fit to use, another great ceremony takes place, with feasting and returning thanks to the Great Spirit for giving us corn.

Black Hawk did not live to see his people removed in 1845 by treaty from the well-watered fertile plains of Iowa to the bleak prairies of Kansas. This was accomplished by Keokuk. Today most of the descendants of the Sac and Fox who followed Keokuk to Kansas are living in Oklahoma.

The Mesquakie

Now for the remarkable story of the Mesquakie (Fox), a people unique in the history of Iowa and, as far as this writer knows, unique in the annals of North America.

The name "Reynard," or "Fox," was given the tribe by the French, probably because of the elusive way they had of blending into the woodlands of their original home around the St. Lawrence River. In the ancient Algonquin language that they speak to this day, their own name for their tribe is "Mesquakie," meaning "People of the Red Earth"; and naturally, this is the name they prefer. The Mesquakie are the only tribe in Iowa today who are recognizable as a tribe.

A ride down Highway 30 from Cedar Rapids will take the visitor between the towns of Tama (pronounced Tay-mah) and Toledo. A mile or two past Toledo, a sign appears on the right with the inscription "Mesquakie Indian Settlement." The settlement is an enclave consisting of some thirty-six hundred acres of the most fertile and beautiful land in Iowa. Drive in and you will leave the square section lines of most Iowa roads and find a harmonious mixed landscape of hills, forests, and smaller fields. You will also be able to participate in tribal-run bingo games or, in August or early September, to go to the annual Mesquakie Pow-Wow. But be considerate. For another remarkable and unique fact is that the land has been entirely paid for with Mesquakie money and the tribe holds title to it.

The Mesquakie prefer the word "settlement" for two reasons: 1) it is not really a reservation (even though the Bureau of Indian Affairs [BIA] is a presence there) because the land was bought and paid for by the tribe as opposed to being assigned to them by government fiat, and 2) the word "reservation" has certain punitive and undesirable overtones that settlement does not have.

Until 1856 the Mesquakie suffered the same physical and psychic abuse other tribes underwent. As noted previously, the French hounded the Red Earth People from 1701 to 1735 — a period of thirty-four years! Peace was not formally restored until 1742, according to Jonathan Buffalo, tribal historian.

In 1734, a low point in Mesquakie history, they formed an alliance with the Sac for survival. And, although to this day, they are known as the "Sac and Fox of the Mississippi of Iowa," they steadfastly maintain their separate identities, saying that "the Sac left for Kansas 135 years ago." The Fox, or Mesquakie, also had no part in the Black Hawk War.

For the Fox as well as the Sac, the Iowa interlude of the 1830s and 1840s was one of further concessions to the white man's greed. Of the more than four hundred treaties the Long Knives (Americans) made with the North American Indians, all were broken, and the history of the Sac and Fox in Iowa was no exception. Removed to Kansas in 1842, the Mesquakie languished there until 1856. At that point, a group of Mesquakie, having raised $735 by selling their ponies and by collecting donations, arrived back in Iowa with the incredible idea of *purchasing* eighty acres of land from a man named Butler. Here, true mystery takes over.

Butler asked $1,000 for the land. The Mesquakie brought the money they had to Governor James W. Grimes, who promised to buy the land for them and to act as their trustee. The record is a little vague on where the remaining $265 came from, but there are veiled references that this part of the debt was satisfied by ponies.

Remember the period. Remember the sorry history of white-Indian relations. Remember the white's hunger for land— Iowa's fertile, productive land, in particular. Remember the white feeling that Indians were better kept away from "civilized" people. And the mystery grows.

Fig. 5.4. Aerial view of the eastern portion of the Mesquakie Settlement in Tama and Toledo townships in Tama County. Much of the Mesquakie land is in trees (the result of reforestation in the 1920s), and the roads follow the contours of the bluffs along the Iowa River. (Photo by U.S. Agricultural Stabilization and Conservation Service, 1970, courtesy of Univ. of Iowa Map Collection)

Why did 152 citizens of Marion, Iowa, sign a petition for the Mesquakie in support of their remaining in Iowa? Why did Governor Grimes intercede on their behalf, acting as their trustee, apparently in good faith? Why did Iowa, in a time of darkness through the land, hold aloft the candle of enlightenment? And how did the Mesquakie leadership recognize and take advantage of the touching white belief in the sacred nature of a commercial transaction?

As far as the white population was concerned, money (in gold) had been paid, the title had been transferred; a hallowed ceremony had taken place and no one, as far as it is known, has ever again disturbed the Mesquakie in their full possession and enjoyment of their land.

Mesquakie holdings have since expanded from the original eighty acres to about thirty-six hundred acres in the heart of Iowa. They vigorously resist any white encroachment on their tribal land, whether this encroachment be political or cultural. As Jonathan Buffalo remarked in our discussion about the journey of his people, "The North is too cold; the South is too hot; the West is too barren; the East is too drenched with our blood. Iowa is where we will live." And he added softly, "We know we are not the first tribe to live here but we are and will be the last."

Urban Indian Life

Today two great myths are entrenched in the mind-set of the dominant society. The first is that Indians still live in their traditional lodges and wear the clothing of a bygone era. "Do Indians still live in tepees?" Europeans might be expected to ask that question; their Indians come from the history books or from a television show. But Americans? Even those Americans living in states with many reservations have this curious perception.

The second question is a spin-off of the first: "Are there really any Indians left?" In Europe the question is a hopeful one; they *want* to know the Indian survives. In the United States the question carries surprise. Indians are generally identified with the past century, have nothing to do with the twentieth century. And there is an uncomfortable feeling about having them survive. As one woman remarked complacently at a luncheon where the talk turned to Indian needs, "I refuse to feel guilty about the Indians. They can make it if they want to." Of course, what she meant by "making it" is a white concept that has no basis in Indian reality — but that's a whole other story.

Chicago has an Indian population of fifty thousand divided

among eighty tribes. They go unnoticed in a large city like Chicago because most deliberately keep a low profile or because they have jobs in which they are not readily visible. For example, they go out on Lake Michigan with the fishing fleet or they are "high-iron workers" on skyscrapers.

About the time of the Civil War, Iowa went "white" with a vengeance. After the Spirit Lake and Lake Okoboji skirmishes, the Dakota led by Inkpaduta retired to the Dakota Territory, where the next and last phase of the so-called Indian wars would be played out on the plains over the next thirty years. Now even Iowa college curricula are white with one notable exception in Sioux City on the far western border. Morningside College has an Indian Studies program. Sioux City itself has an Office of Indian Education, an American Indian Center at 619 6th Street, and an Indian population of about two thousand. This is the center of urban Native American life in Iowa. None of the other larger cities in the state—cities like Dubuque, Des Moines, Council Bluffs, etc.—list either centers or Indian offices as of August, 1987. Sioux City apparently stands alone for urban Native American life in Iowa as the Mesquakie Settlement at Tama does for tribal life.

A majority of the Indians living in Sioux City are members of one of the Siouan-speaking tribes of the area—namely, Santee Sioux (Dakota), Winnebago, and Omaha—all of which are located in nearby Nebraska today.

The greatest danger in urban Indian life is the loss of identity as an Indian or, in the case of third or fourth generation urban Indian dwellers, never having had an identity as a Native American. Many urban Indian children do not know for certain to which tribe they belong. A schoolchild will say, "I'm Omaha, I think." This statement by Reuben Snake, Chairman of the Winnebago tribe in Nebraska is particularly revealing: "I knew I was Winnebago; I knew I was Siouan; I knew I was Red. But in all the years I went to school—BIA schools, public schools, mission schools—no one person ever told me what I should be proud of as an Indian. If anybody called me a dirty Indian or a damned Indian, I usually punched him in the mouth because I was proud of being an Indian. But nobody ever told me what it was that I could be proud of." Reuben goes on to explain how professional education is not going to mean a thing if red people lose their identity as such.

One of the most difficult concepts for white people to understand is that unlike all other groups, many, perhaps even most Indians, *do not* desire to assimilate, acculturate, or become part of mainstream America. White people, especially if they are the children or grandchildren of immigrants, recall how those new "Americans" wanted to discard their languages and European clothes and become "Yankees" as quickly as possible. Most Indians do not want to do this, and while practically all modern Native Americans realize that certain skills are necessary to cope with the larger society, they wish to remain Indian and are reluctant to give up their values for what are perceived as the Coca Cola and juke box values of the dominant people.

Many Indians have "made it" in adjusting to urban life—though many others have not. Those who have not often fall prey to alcohol or drugs. But these problems are merely symptoms of the underlying psychological and socioeconomic causes. The transition from reservation to city life can be traumatic indeed. One of the more undesirable aspects of city life noticeable immediately to the recently arrived reservation Indian is that surroundings are impersonal and people are objectified. There is little chance for the one-on-one personal relationships to which he or she is accustomed. Combined with the hassles of city living, commuting on public transportation, finding living quarters, etc., dealing with a rigidly ranked, bureaucratic society on an impersonal level make some long for the democracy of 4th Street (Sioux City's Skid Row), a haven for derelicts both red and white. I asked a white "wino" once if he were prejudiced; he replied, "Man, when I'm drinking I can't afford to be prejudiced against nobody!"

One very valuable asset that enables Native Americans to survive incredible odds is their irrepressible sense of humor. In spite of the long entrenched image of the stoic Indian, no one has a better sense of humor. Indians joke about the white man and his foibles and also about themselves—their passivity, their adventures or misadventures in the larger society.

The story is told of an Indian woman attempting to cash a check in a local bank. She signed the check with an "X." The teller told her that she needed a witness to her signature. The woman looked back and saw a long line of *wasicus* (whites). She was too shy to ask one of them. Suddenly another Indian woman entered the bank.

"Pst!" says the first woman.

"Pst!" says the second. "I'll be right over."

After hearing the need of the first woman, the second woman agreed to be her witness. And signed the check with her own "X."

"Mah!" says the first woman. "We're relatives! We have the same last name!"

A people who have a strong identity and, moreover, an

identity they can be proud of, plus a strong sense of spiritual values coupled with a sense of humor, will go far. One *can* live in the white world and the traditional world as well. I know people who have the best of both worlds right here in Sioux City.

At Morningside College, Thelma Thomas, who holds a master's degree in educational psychology, is director of the Indian Studies Program. She and Joyce Thomas (secretary and aide) run the program. Robert Conley, former director of Indian Studies, is a member of the prestigious Western Writers Association and an author and poet of international repute; he is also a professor of English at Morningside. Pat Gordon, recently awarded the Distinguished Alumnus award from the college, was also Woman of the Year for Sertoma in 1982 at a local level, going on to win national awards. She runs summer camps for Indian children in the Black Hills and the Southwest. Her motto is "You are only young once but you are Indian forever."

The Indians learned the skills of the white man to help their own people and, yet, they retain Indian values and participate in traditional life. They guarantee that Indians will remain a presence in Iowa as long as the earth, nourished by the sun and rain, endures. For these are the descendants of the "First Nations" of Iowa—a people who were neither "noble savages" nor "skulking redskins," but rather a people who time and again made successful adjustments to their natural environment, and continue to do so.

Selected References and Reading

Alex, Lynn Marie. "Exploring Iowa's past." In *A Guide to Prehistoric Archaeology.* Iowa City: University of Iowa Press, 1980.

Bataille, G. M., D. M. Gradwohl and C. L. P. Silet. *The Worlds Between Two Rivers: Perspectives on American Indians in Iowa.* Ames: Iowa State University Press, 1978.

Black Hawk. *Life of Black Hawk.* Ed. J. B. Patterson; trans. Antoine LeClaire. Boston: 1834. Reprinted by the State Historical Society of Iowa, Iowa City, 1932.

A Brief History of the Sac & Fox of the Mississippi in Iowa. Tribal publication. Xerox, n.d.

Carlson, John B. "Hopewell: Prehistoric America's Golden Age." *Early Man Magazine,* Winter 1979.

Edmunds, R. David. *The Otoe-Missouria People.* Phoenix, Ariz.: Indian Tribal Series, 1976.

Fulton, A. R. *The Red Men of Iowa: Being a History of the Various Aboriginal Tribes.* Des Moines, Iowa: Mills & Company, 1882.

Gibbon, G. E., ed. *Oneota Studies.* Publications in Anthropology, No. 1, University of Minnesota, Minneapolis, 1982.

Hagan, William T. *The Sac and Fox Indians.* Civilization of American Indian Ser. vol. 48. Norman: University of Oklahoma Press, 1958.

Harvey, Amy E. *Oneota Culture in Northwestern Iowa.* Rep. 12. Iowa City: University of Iowa, Office of the State Archeologist, 1979.

Hassrick, Royal B. *The Sioux: Life and Customs of a Warrior Society.* Norman: University of Oklahoma Press, 1964.

Horr, D. A. *Sac, Fox and Iowa Indians.* Vols. 1 and 3. Garland Ser., New York: Garland Publishing, 1974.

McKusick, Marshall. *Men of Ancient Iowa, As Revealed by Archeological Discoveries.* Ames: Iowa State University Press, 1964.

Miner, W. H. *The Iowa.* Cedar Rapids, Iowa: The Torch Press, 1911. Reprinted from *The Indian Record,* as originally published and edited by Thomas Foster.

Riggs, S. R. 1852. *Dakota-English Dictionary.* Washington, D.C.: Smithsonian Institute (GPO). Reprinted by Ross and Haines, Inc., Minneapolis, Minn., 1968.

Vogel, Virgil J. *Iowa Place Names of Indian Origin.* Iowa City: University of Iowa Press, 1983.

Zielinski, J. M. *Mesquakie and Proud of It.* Kalona, Iowa: Photo-Art Gallery Publications, 1976.

The following articles were obtained at the Effigy Mounds Monument and carry no information other than Office of the State Archaeologist, Education Series numbers as given:

"Paleo-Indian Period," I.
"Archaic Period," 2.
"Woodland," 3.

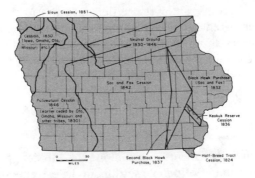

PATTERNS OF
PRAIRIE SETTLEMENT

Dorothy Schwieder

In June 1833 hundreds of settlers crossed the Mississippi River into Iowa, an event that marked the beginning of official settlement of the Hawkeye State. Over the next thirty years, thousands more pioneers would arrive, most looking for fertile prairieland to put under the plow. With each new wave of settlers the newcomers, native-born and foreign-born alike, moved further into the state, mainly from east to west. By the 1870s all of Iowa contained both town and country dwellers. Although Iowa officially had no frontier areas after 1870, migration continued; by 1900 the state contained 2,231,853 people. Throughout the nineteenth century, Iowa exhibited distinct settlement patterns, which were often closely tied to specific ethnic groups and which indicated distinct economic patterns.

Driving across the state today, visitors might be struck with the homogeneity of the land. Certainly Iowa contains some areas with pronounced hills, particularly those in the northeast, and areas with flatter land such as that in north central Iowa, but much of the state is covered with gently rolling hills where woodlands, rivers and streams, and farms and small towns blend together harmoniously. In Iowa one will find no sharp contrasts in landforms or topography such as that found in South Dakota with its Badlands and Black Hills, or Minnesota with its Iron Range Country, or Missouri with its Ozarks. Iowa, by contrast, is more moderate in its physical characteristics, and that moderation had a direct impact on the settlement patterns that evolved in the nineteenth century. Given the presence of tillable land in all parts of the state and the absence of barriers to settlement in the form of mountains or even large, timbered areas, settlement proceeded methodically and rapidly.

Federal Policies

The first settlements began along the Mississippi River with the greatest number of people settling in the extreme southeastern part of Iowa. Some people moved inland along rivers and streams, but overall settlement proceeded in a rather even fashion. By 1838, the year federal officials created the Iowa Territory, over twenty counties had been established in the eastern one-third of the territory.

The methodical, orderly settlement was also aided by the federal government in negotiating treaties with local Indian tribes. In 1832, as a result of the Black Hawk War, the government obtained a strip of land in extreme eastern Iowa, which measured fifty miles wide and extended from the Missouri border to about three-quarters of the way up Iowa's eastern border. Known as the Black Hawk Purchase, the land had previously been owned by the Sac (Sauk) and Fox (Mesquakie) Indians and had been taken from them as punishment for their part in the Black Hawk War. The following year the Black Hawk Purchase was opened for settlement. Four years later, federal authorities met again with representatives of the two tribes and signed a second treaty. This time a triangular piece of land was obtained, which in turn allowed settlers to move further into Iowa Territory. The last treaty with these two tribes was signed in 1842 and, in effect, ceded most of south central Iowa to the federal government. The Indians were allowed to remain in the area until 1845 when, assisted by soldiers at Ft. Des Moines (the site of Des Moines), they were removed from the state.

One last Indian treaty remained to be negotiated before all of Iowa could be opened for settlement. In 1851 that treaty was concluded with the Santee Sioux, who had inhabited areas along the state's northern border; Iowa's Santee Sioux were part of a much larger Sioux settlement in southern Minnesota. With the removal of the Sioux to areas north and northwest of Iowa, all of the state could be surveyed and, in turn, sold.

With the first official migration into Iowa, residents of eastern states had various ways of obtaining information about the newly opened area. Maps and guide books were available that detailed how to reach Iowa as well as what people would find there. These publications continued into the 1850s when a booklet appeared entitled *Northern Iowa: Containing Hints and Information of Value to Emigrants.* Although purportedly written "by a pioneer" the material was actually published by a local railroad company. Among the information intended to attract new settlers was the fact that proportionally Iowa had fewer paupers and criminals than did the eastern states. The publication explained that this was because of the great opportunity available in Iowa: "A man who can make more by honest labor in the day time than he can by stealing at night, will not be a thief, and the same reason accounts for the comparatively small amount of paupers, beggars and vagabonds."

Once a family decided to come to Iowa—and most settlers traveled in family units—they found several forms of transportation available. Railroads would not be built until later, but people could travel part way on canals and stagecoaches, and many travelers came by covered wagon. Steamboats began operating on the upper Mississippi in 1822 and quickly became the major means of transportation. Travelers could then travel down the Ohio River by steamboat, change boats, and travel up the Mississippi.

Fig. 6.1. The major Indian land cessions in Iowa from 1824 to 1851. (Map from Leland L. Sage, A History of Iowa, *Iowa State Univ. Press, 1974)*

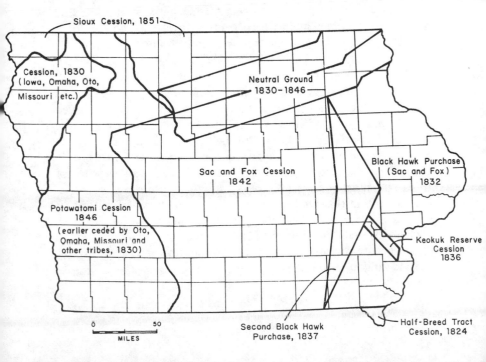

Immigrants found steamboat travel comparatively easy and cheap. For those arriving at the port of New Orleans, passage could be booked on several different lines for transportation to an Iowa river city. The trip took about three weeks. Immigrants were especially attracted to river travel for they could obtain "deck passage," which cost about one-fourth that of regular or cabin passage. Although deck passage meant living on the lowest level — which also contained the engines, boilers, and other mechanical gear as well as cargo — immigrants were willing to tolerate the hardships to realize the savings in passage fare.

Steamboating also took place on the Missouri River, but this activity did not affect Iowa to the same degree as that on the Mississippi. The Missouri River provided the means for goods to be shipped into the two major Missouri River communities, Sioux City and Kanesville (later renamed Council Bluffs), brought in military supplies for local forts, and provided goods for travelers preparing to head west on the overland trail. Much of what the Missouri River steamboats carried, however, both in passengers and cargo, was related to movement west rather than permanent settlement in Iowa.

Once under way, settlement increased rapidly. In the 1830s the eastern portion of Iowa came under settlement, by the 1850s settlers had moved into the central portion of the state, and by the 1860s and early 1870s newcomers were taking up land in northwestern Iowa, the last major part of the state to be settled. Although some land would obviously be more productive than other land, the entire state was regarded as capable of sustaining agriculture. Settlement in north central Iowa was slowed for a time because the flat terrain was often under water. Once this area had been tiled, however, it proved to be some of the most productive land in the state.

Two major considerations in determining why people settled where they did within the state were the time at which they arrived and the areas then open for settlement. In 1833 new arrivals were restricted to the Black Hawk Purchase, whereas by the time the major Danish immigration began in Iowa in the early 1870s, only two areas remained largely unsettled — southwest and northwest Iowa. In effect most newcomers, whether coming alone or in groups, found that while they usually had a choice of settling in several different counties, the general location within the state was largely determined by the federal government and its work in clearing land of Indians, carrying out surveys, and marking off individual counties.

Early Settlers

The majority of Iowa's first settlers came from Pennsylvania, Ohio, and Indiana. Up to the 1870s Iowa also contained a substantial number of southerners, particularly from Kentucky, Virginia, Tennessee, Missouri, and North Carolina. After 1870, however, the number of southern-born settlers gradually decreased. Many of these early arrivals most likely had already relocated several times before they arrived in the Hawkeye State. Historical studies also show that many settlers coming to Iowa would, after a few years, move further west.

One couple, David and Mary Nutting, who decided to make Iowa their permanent home in the 1850s, demonstrate, nevertheless, the mobility of nineteenth-century Americans. In the early 1850s David Nutting operated a foundry near Boston, Massachusetts. Due to financial reversals, he lost his business and then relocated four times within his home state. Deciding that more opportunity lay to the west, Nutting traveled to St. Louis where he worked for a time and later moved to Lexington, Missouri. He then sent for his wife and two sons who had remained behind in Massachusetts. In 1855 Nutting walked from Lexington to Warren County, Iowa, where he claimed 120 acres of land, and a short time later his family joined him.

Like David and Mary Nutting, most people coming to Iowa hoped to obtain land and take up farming. In the late 1700s the federal government had determined that all public land would be surveyed before being sold. That decision meant that landowners would quickly have in their possession a land deed that included a precise description (range, township, section, and acres) of their purchase. Land sales would be conducted through land offices, set up by the federal government.

The surveys began in 1836 in extreme eastern Iowa and proceeded westward, finishing in 1859 in the extreme western part of the state. As surveys were completed land offices were opened and land auctions held. The first two offices opened were in Burlington and Dubuque in 1838, and four years later offices were opened in Fairfield and Marion. Land agents then held auctions where they sold land for a minimum price of $1.25 an acre, in amounts of no less than eighty acres.

While many Iowans purchased land at the minimum price, land could also be obtained in other ways. Newcomers could obtain land from one of the four land-grant railroads although this land was considerably more expensive — from eight dollars to twelve dollars an acre. Railroad officials figured, however, that the land was worth the extra cost as owners then found themselves closer to the railroad and were assured of better transportation facilities. Land could also be obtained by performing military service for the federal government, which in the late 1700s had started the practice of partially compensating soldiers with land for their military duty. The new nation faced a chronic money shortage so it seemed practical indeed to use some of the vast land reserves as an inducement to enlist; this practice continued throughout the nineteenth century. Men who served in the Black Hawk War in 1832, for example, received land from the public domain. In Iowa these military bounties accounted for 39.7 percent of the state's total land disposal. Many soldiers who received the bounties were not interested in redeeming them, a situation that led to considerable land speculation. One individual who took advantage of this situation was Simeon Dow. Born in New Hampshire in 1821, Dow moved with his parents to Michigan, and following his marriage to Chloe Smith, headed west, hoping to settle in western Iowa. Dow was not an ordinary pioneer, however, as he carried along sufficient military bounties to entitle him to almost twenty-six hundred acres of land. The couple settled in Crawford County, and in 1874 they completed a substantial home on the prairie. Visitors traveling through Crawford County can now view the Dow House, which is open to the public much of the year.

Railroad Policies

While the majority of settlers traveled to Iowa by steamboat before the Civil War, after 1865 railroads provided the major means of transportation. Railroad building started in Iowa in the early 1850s, with some trackage laid by 1855. Four of Iowa's five major railroad routes were determined, not by decisions made in this state, but by the location of the major routes in Illinois. In the early 1850s when Iowans began to think seriously about building railroads, four Illinois routes were expanding westward from Chicago. These railroads—the Illinois Central, the Chicago and North Western, the Rock Island, and the Burlington—would all terminate at the Mississippi River. Enthusiastic Iowans residing in the four river cities across from these termination points (Dubuque, Clinton, Davenport, and Burlington) quickly realized the economic potential. Before long, citizens of these four communities began to plan local railroads. While all four railroad companies started construction in the 1850s, the lines were not completed across the state until after the Civil War. In time each of these routes was taken over by the major Illinois line, which lay to the east.

Once railroads began to plan their rights-of-way, towns along the potential routes began to vie for the railroad. Local boosters understood all too well that if a railroad bypassed a community, it could mean the end of that town. By the same token, towns included along the right-of-way had an excellent chance to prosper. In some cases towns that were bypassed actually picked up and relocated along the railroad line. Some towns profited even more as they were selected as administrative headquarters for a particular stretch (known as a division) of the railroad. Division points usually contained switchyards and repair facilities that further magnified the railroad's economic impact on the community. Boone, located along the Chicago and North Western Railroad, was selected as a division point. The city still retains the reputation as a railroad town. It takes pride in its Boone and Scenic Valley Railroad and puts on a railroad festival every September, "Pufferbilly Days."

Once railroads reached central Iowa, however, it was necessary to pursue a different policy for the railroads had now advanced so far that they had run out of towns. This change meant that by the end of the Civil War, railroads moved into town planning. The Illinois Central, the route extending from Dubuque to Sioux City, serves as a good example. Between 1865 and 1870 railroad officials planned and developed over twenty town sites along the projected right-of-way. Employees platted the town sites and then held auctions to sell lots. Many of these towns appeared almost overnight. Once a lot had been purchased, businessmen often pitched a tent and immediately began to sell their wares. The towns created by the Illinois Central include Manson, Fonda, Aurelia, Alta, and Remsen; most were spaced about twelve to fifteen miles apart. Other major railroads in western Iowa followed the same practice. The railroads speeded settlement, for they not only brought in settlers more quickly but also the supplies and equipment the settlers needed.

Along with creating new communities, railroads were anxious to sell the land they had received from the federal government. In 1856 the state of Iowa received a land grant of four million acres from the federal government to encourage the development of railroads. The practice had started in Illinois and the Illinois Central received the first such grant. Railroads receiving land are those presently known as the Illinois Central, the Rock Island, the Chicago and North Western, and the Burlington. Typically the land grants consisted of six alternate sections (640 acres in each section) on either side of the right-of-way. If land along the railroad route had already been claimed, the company received land in other areas. To sell land to secure revenue for continued building, the railroads advertised throughout the United States as well as in Europe. Some railroad companies kept agents stationed in eastern port cities, particularly New York, where they met immigrants as they stepped off the boats. A common practice was to sponsor trains whereby the immigrants could travel to Iowa and other midwestern states at a reduced rate to view the available land. These promotions and advertisements were successful, as people from all over Europe and the British Isles purchased railroad land in various areas of central and western Iowa. Because of the land grants and the subsequent land promotions, railroads became known as the great colonizers of the West.

Today, driving through Iowa, the landscape looks quite different with regard to railroads. Many lines of track have been abandoned, and left behind are rusty tracks with weeds growing up alongside and between the rotting railroad ties. Railroad bridges that once carried as many as a dozen trains a day are now falling into disrepair. However, some of these abandoned routes have been turned into biking and hiking trails providing yet a different kind of transportation for Iowa's citizens (see Chapter 16, "Iowa: Bicycling Heaven").

Foreign-born Settlers

By the 1850s Iowa was becoming home to an ever growing number of foreign-born people. The Germans proved to be the most numerous group throughout the nineteenth century and as early as the 1840s were visible in Iowa's Mississippi River cities. During the 1850s Dubuque was the nation's major producer of lead and attracted both Germans and Irish to work the nearby mines. The heavy concentration of German and Irish Catholics soon made Dubuque the center of Catholicism in Iowa, a reputation that the city still enjoys today. The settlement of Germans did not end at the Mississippi River, however. Throughout the nineteenth century and even into the twentieth, Germans moved into each of the ninety-nine counties, in most cases to pursue agriculture (see Chapter 7, "German and Dutch Ethnic Communities").

The Irish were the second largest foreign-born group in early Iowa, and many worked in river towns and on steamboats. Once railroads began building across the state, officials often hired Irish workers, many of whom came from cities in the northeast. Probably most continued moving west with the railroad or returned east, but some purchased land from the railroads and took up farming; often they helped organize the first Catholic church in their neighborhood. Today Irish-Americans are located in every part of the state. They are particularly evident in Emmetsburg, and on St. Patrick's Day they celebrate by drinking green beer and holding parades.

Scandinavians were also major early settlers. The first Swedish settlement was in New Sweden, in Jefferson County in 1845, and it is a good example of how a settlement could be determined both by chance and by the availability of land. Thirty-six Swedish immigrants, led by Peter Cassell, wanted to settle in one large community so they needed a large, unclaimed area for their farms. The group left Sweden intending to settle in Pine Lake, Wisconsin, where a Swedish settlement already existed. Coming through the port of New York, however, the Cassell group accidentally encountered another Swedish immigrant who told them that they should go to Iowa rather than Wisconsin. Convinced by the man's apparent knowledge of Iowa, they headed west and settled in Jefferson County. In the mid-1840s roughly the eastern one-third of Iowa had been surveyed, including Jefferson County. Much of the land to the east had already been claimed, and land in central Iowa was not yet available. So they seem to have chosen the land mainly because it was open at that date.

A second group of Swedes illustrates another kind of settlement — by mistake! In 1846 Anna Dalander and a group of over forty people left Sweden intending to join Peter Cassell at New Sweden. Following the instructions that Cassell had sent them, the group arrived in Iowa but were not certain if Cassell had intended for them to head west along the Skunk or the Des Moines River. Believing that the larger Des Moines River must be the one that Cassell had in mind, the group started their trek, traveling along the north side of the river. After a time they reached Ft. Des Moines where soldiers told them that they must have the wrong instructions, which in fact they did. The group persisted, however, determined that New Sweden must lie ahead. They wintered in Boone County, assisted by a solitary settler, Thomas Gaston. The next spring, after having learned of their mistake and having the opportunity to return to New Sweden, they decided that the Boone area looked promising and decided to purchase land there. In effect, the group had moved out ahead of settlement simply by misunderstanding instructions. They named their new community Swede Point, which was later changed to Madrid.

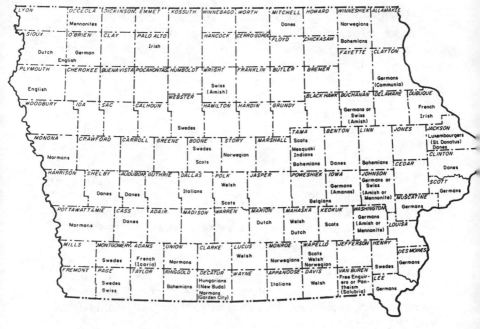

Fig. 6.2.   The principal ethnic settlements in Iowa.
(Map modified from LeRoy G. Pratt, Discovering
Historic Iowa, Iowa Dep. Public Instruction, 1975)

Rural Ethnic Neighborhoods

The Swedes were like other ethnic groups in founding what
were rural communities. Today we think of ethnic neighborhoods
primarily in terms of towns and cities, but for many years in Iowa
the rural population outnumbered the urban, and ethnic considerations were just as strong—or stronger. So as one travels
through the state today, one finds many areas that were settled by
a particular ethnic group: Norwegians settled in large numbers in
the Decorah area in Winneshiek County in the 1850s, and a short
time later, large numbers came to what is today Story City in
Story County; Czech settlers arrived a few years later, locating
first in Winneshiek County around the community of Spillville
and later redirecting their settlement toward Cedar Rapids and
rural Linn County; Danish immigrants settled in some eastern
counties such as Johnson and Black Hawk, but the great majority
continued west until they reached southwestern Iowa, particularly
Shelby and Audubon counties. For a time, that area would contain more Danish farm families than any other area in the nation;
Elk Horn and Kimballton are Danish villages. The Dutch also

settled in substantial numbers, locating first in and around Pella in Marion County in 1847 and then, about twenty years later, establishing a second major settlement in northwest Iowa, particularly in Sioux County around Orange City. There were many benefits to this rural clustering. When people in European countries decided to emigrate, they usually knew where former residents of their villages had settled in America and that provided an inducement to follow. Letters from their compatriots provided the encouragement to bring even more people to the United States. One of these immigrants, Sjoerd Sipma, immigrated from Holland in 1847 and the following year he penned a long letter to friends and relatives back home. He carefully described what was involved in obtaining land in Iowa, the matter of taxes, the problems involved with transportation, and in a somewhat different vein, a description of American women. In reading his letter it is easy to imagine countless numbers of Hollanders scrutinizing this document again and again, eagerly searching for the information they felt was necessary to make a decision. For the most part Sipma counseled others to join him in Iowa.

> [In America] we really have not been disappointed because if we remain healthy, we will be able in a few years to start our own farm, which we would never have been able to do in Friesland. And then to live on one's own land! Even now we already have a better living. We can eat the best bacon and meat three times a day, and we save money besides. What a contrast to Friesland!

Thus a further inducement for immigrants to settle in a particular location was the presence of relatives, who could also help the more recent immigrant find a job if additional money was needed to buy land.

Many of Iowa's early settlers did not possess the one hundred dollars needed to buy eighty acres of land, with the result that both men and women often took temporary employment to earn additional money. Some men worked in local mines or quarries, others worked on railroad construction, and still others taught school during the winter months. Women often worked as cooks, laundresses, and housekeepers for neighboring families. Throughout the entire process of emigrating, selecting land, and creating a new home in Iowa, the help of family members was of major importance.

During the nineteenth and early twentieth centuries, while many immigrants were still arriving in Iowa, settlements reflected the Old World origins of each group. By choice or necessity the first generation dressed in a manner suggestive of their native clothes, and each group spoke the language of the mother country, both at home and in public. Sermons preached in German Lutheran, German Catholic, Norwegian Lutheran, Swedish Baptist, and Danish Methodist churches were in the native tongues. Typically, young people married members of their own ethnic group, often through the third generation. Holiday celebrations, particularly those associated with religious holidays such as Christmas, included ethnic foods, dances, and entertainments.

Coal Mining Camps

While most nineteenth-century immigrants came to Iowa to acquire land, some were attracted by specific industries. Railroads needed vast quantities of coal, and by the 1880s Iowa's coal mining industry was well under way. The majority of early miners was from the British Isles, particularly England, Wales, and Scotland. After 1900, however, the majority of miners was from eastern and southern Europe. The largest number emigrated from Italy and Croatia, but Iowa also attracted people from Austria, Hungary, Poland, and Russia. The majority of the immigrants lived in coal camps established by the coal operators. Unlike incorporated Iowa communities, coal camps were usually small, containing around two hundred people, and were regarded as temporary. This meant that little money would be spent on either initial construction or maintenance of the homes and that no money was spent on landscaping. Although most coal camps have long since faded away, a few remnants remain. Two miles south of Madrid, several houses mark the spot where the large camp of Zookspur once stood. Nearby, the coal camp of Moran, still included on Iowa's official highway map, contains about a dozen original camp houses. Additional traces of the once significant mining industry can be seen in dozens of towns in central and southern Iowa. When the coal camps began closing down, local individuals would buy up a group of houses, often for fifty dollars each, and move them to nearby communities where they would be placed on foundations and either rented or sold. Today driving through towns like Boone, Des Moines, Ames, or Madrid one can see former camp houses identifiable by their square shape, truncated roof, and one-story design. Passing by these houses, it is intriguing to speculate on how many different families, newly arrived from Italy or Poland perhaps, experienced their first year of life in America within the walls of these dwellings.

Black Communities

The coal mining industry also played a major role in attracting blacks to Iowa. Some blacks had come into the state earlier via the Mississippi River, working as laborers aboard steamboats or at loading docks. Some blacks also worked on railroad construction in Iowa, but a far larger number found jobs as miners. At the peak of the coal industry, Iowa contained about four hundred underground mines. Although blacks sometimes encountered segregated housing in coal camps, it seems that little if any discrimination was practiced in the mines themselves. Two coal camps were particularly noted for their high black populations: Muchakinock (Mahaska County) existed from about 1868 to 1900 and blacks accounted for about half of the community's thirty-five hundred residents and Buxton (Monroe County), which after 1900 became the dominant black coal mining community with a population of just under five thousand. Blacks accounted for slightly over fifty percent of Buxton's population during the first decade of its existence, but from 1910 until 1923 when the coal company abandoned the community and moved its headquarters to Bucknell, blacks were slightly less than a majority. During Buxton's tenure an Iowa newspaper hailed it as the "Negro Athens of the Northwest."

During the same time periods that Muchakinock and Buxton existed, only a handful of blacks went into agriculture, but many more were moving into Des Moines, Iowa's largest city. By 1870 Polk County contained 303 black residents, most of whom probably resided in and around Des Moines. The black community there continued to grow with some members working in nearby coal mines as well as opening small businesses. By 1895–1896, the city directory included 517 blacks who had listed occupations that ranged from laborer to porter, barber, plasterer, and minister. In total, twenty-four different occupations were listed for the black residents. During the 1890s blacks in Des Moines also started their own newspaper, *The Iowa State Bystander,* which was published continuously until March 1987.

Blacks also settled in Sioux City, Waterloo, and other major cities in the state. By 1880 Woodbury County contained 178 black people, many of whom had opened barber shops, laundries, dance halls, and restaurants in Sioux City. According to one historian, blacks were often the first in that city to open these establishments. A few blacks had settled in Waterloo before 1900, but that number increased significantly after 1911 when the Illinois Central convinced southern black railroad employees to come north and work in the railroad shops. That year white railroad employees in the city had walked off their jobs in an effort to get company recognition of an employees' union. The railroad's actions of transferring blacks from the South to Iowa resulted in the first sizable black population in Waterloo. In time, blacks in Des Moines, Sioux City, and Waterloo would establish not only black businesses, but black churches, black lodges, and chapters of the National Association for the Advancement of Colored People.

With the settlement of the state and the creation of ethnic neighborhoods in both rural and urban areas, ethnic social and religious institutions remained intact for several generations. As these groups passed through the second and third generations, many of the ethnic practices and traditions were often forgotten. By World War I many groups had ceased speaking their native language, and the war hastened the demise of the practice. Some churches had already modified their schedules so that sermons were presented in a foreign language only once a month, and Governor William Harding's proclamation against speaking foreign languages in public prevented even that. While ethnic names of churches remained, such as the Swedish Baptist Church, after World War I these designations had increasingly less meaning.

With the lessening of ethnic solidarity, disappearance of ethnic neighborhoods, and change in language patterns, the most visible ethnic traditions have become associated with Iowa's towns and cities rather than with rural neighborhoods. Today one can visit ethnic celebrations in many parts of the state. With their tulip festivals, the Dutch in both Pella and Orange City celebrate the hardships endured by their forefathers. Norwegians in Decorah celebrate their heritage with a Nordic Fest while Norwegians in Story City sponsor Scandinavian Days. Ethnic traditions are also presented in the formal settings of museums. The Norwegian Vesterheim (meaning Western Home) in Decorah displays magnificent examples of rosemaling, hand carved furniture, and other artifacts that reflect the Norwegian past, both in Norway and in Iowa. Danish-Americans are soon to have a national Danish-American museum in Elk Horn that will bring together for protection and display the artifacts reflecting the Danish-American experience. Czech-Americans in Cedar Rapids also have a museum that highlights their national heritage.

Some communities, although lacking a specific celebration, stand themselves as testimony to a particular ethnic heritage. Holstein in Ida County is known as home to many German-Americans, Spillville in Winneshiek County has always been identified with Czechs, and towns like Stanton and Boxholm are associated with Swedish-Americans. A visit to Spillville provides an opportunity to visit the Catholic cemetery that contains many metal grave markers, reminiscent of an Old World practice still used in Europe. While some direct reminders, such as the cemetery at Spillville, still exist, for the most part these reminders have been institutionalized and are presented in the form of an annual celebration or museum.

Throughout much of the nineteenth century, Iowa was known both in this country and in many parts of Europe for its rich prairieland. That land, readily available and quickly dispensed, was the great magnet that attracted most people to the Hawkeye State. The patterns of prairie settlement that followed took many and varied forms, both socially and economically. While native-born Americans were in the majority, the most visible legacies have been left behind by the immigrants. Although most rural ethnic neighborhoods have faded away, the heritage of many different groups can be recaptured through visits to festivals or museums. In a larger sense, however, the entire state serves as a legacy to the patterns of prairie settlement. Every town, whether prospering or declining, every railroad track, whether used or abandoned, and many old farmhouses, whether inhabited or abandoned, stand as testimony to the initial hard work of nineteenth-century individuals who chose to make the prairie state their home.

7

GERMAN & DUTCH ETHNIC COMMUNITIES

Philip E. Webber

Even a casual glance at a map of Iowa reveals something of the state's German heritage. Many place-names simply *sound* German (Bettendorf, Fredericksburg, Froelich, Guttenberg, Humboldt, Oelwein), and even some others still owe their origin to German-speaking settlers. One plausible explanation for a predominantly German-American town being named El Dorado lies in the fact that in German—far more than in English—mention of that legendary city of wealth and opportunity evokes images of a veritable paradise on earth. Often enough, a town with a strong immigrant heritage bears a name reflecting a nostalgic longing by earlier residents for a particular city or region in the European homeland (Hamburg, Schleswig, Holstein).

As an aside, it might be noted that historical maps of the state reveal other vestiges of the German presence. Local history sleuths have long recognized the fact that a number of municipalities and townships with the name Liberty or Lincoln once bore identifiably German designations. Only too frequently, this changed with the anti-German frenzy of World War I that peaked in Governor William L. Harding's 1918 proclamation banning the public use of any language other than English. One town to suffer such a fate was Lincoln (in northwestern Tama County), whose original name was Berlin.

A traveler entering one of our tourist-information stations near the Iowa border might find several dozen pieces of literature promoting attractions in communities that openly advertise their German heritage (most notably Amana, though in their own ways also Kalona and the Quad Cities). In 1983, Iowa had a highly successful program "Sharing our Heritage: A Celebration of German Culture and History" at Davenport's Putnam Museum. The museum continues to offer a vivid documentation of German-American life in the Quad Cities as part of its panoramic exhibition, "River, Prairie and People." In celebration of the 1985 tricentennial of the first arrival by Germans on American soil, the Iowa State Fair chose as its theme the German legacy, expressed in a number of appealing and often refreshingly original displays and demonstrations.

Germans began arriving in Iowa as part of the group that first entered the Black Hawk Purchase in 1832. A major impetus for migration in significant numbers was the turbulence of the (often abortive) revolutions of 1848–1849 in Europe. Any serious history of Davenport, for instance, will include a major discussion of its patriarchal "forty-eighters," who brought to that city the distinctly liberal, free-thinking atmosphere that accounts for so much of its dedication to education and the arts. By 1850 Germans constituted slightly more than one-third of Iowa's foreign-born residents, or about four percent of the state's total population.

During the last half of the nineteenth century, Germans joined a much larger wave of Europeans seeking new opportunities in this country. In addition to the desire to seek greater opportunities and material security, Germans often came to avoid involvement in wars with France and Denmark. The 1890 Census recorded more than 127,000 native Germans on Iowa soil. Their followers and progeny have subsequently grown into Iowa's largest ethnic presence, with a majority of the residents in about two-thirds of the counties claiming German ancestry. The 1980 Census shows that the percentage of German-American population (forty-six percent) in Iowa ties for fourth place in the nation.

It is no wonder, in view of the pervasive German influence in Iowa, that the one word that best describes the German experience is *variety*. A field linguist could spend a lifetime here. Both German and American scholars have devoted their energies to a study of our Low German–speaking communities (in the northwest in Schleswig and Holstein, and in central Iowa in Butler and Grundy Counties). Technically speaking, the speech of these groups differs sufficiently from standard German to be considered a separate language altogether. Doctoral dissertations have been written on the German of the Amana Colonies and the language(s) of the Amish. Many German communities thrive in our agrarian heartland, where barns with banked approaches to the main entrance offer unmistakable clues to a German presence. On the other hand, Davenport was frequently the port of entry to Iowa, and to this day there is no single concentration of German-Americans in the state to match the very urban Quad Cities.

Nowhere is variety more evident than in the spiritual realm. Generally, the desire to seek out other Germans of similar religious views proved even stronger than the impulse to settle near immigrants from the same region in the European homeland, or to identify compatriots engaged in the same occupational activities (though in many instances these groups were virtually identical). The frequent presence of parochial schools in both rural and urban settings, where a child was surrounded by other young persons of the same ethnic and confessional background, tended to enforce the notion that it was natural for a good German-American to be a pious Catholic, a staunch Lutheran, a gentle Anabaptist, or a firm-standing freethinker.

Of perennial and special interest to travelers are the communities established by, or strongly associated with, the less frequently encountered religious groups. Favorite sites include the Amana Colonies, founded by the Community of True Inspiration, and the Kalona area, with its highly varied spectrum of Anabaptist adherents. Visitors to these communities should bear in mind, however, that they do not represent German-American life in Iowa in general, but rather survive as enclaves of groups with a special place in the state's cultural mosaic. No less German, for instance, are the German Catholics, whose loyal ranks formed an essential part of the Iowa envisioned by the Reverend Mathias Loras (the first bishop of the Quad Cities and for whom Loras College in Dubuque is named), as a center and stronghold of the true faith in the American Midwest.

If there are common, unifying factors of the German experience, they may be summarized by the maxim *Kinder, Küche, und Kirche* (children, kitchen, and church). Although often cited merely as a formula for the traditional German ideas about the duties of women, the maxim actually summarizes German cultural patterns and values in general, especially as perpetuated in Iowa's German-American communities. The essence of the German experience is family, food, and the church.

The Young and Young at Heart in the Quad Cities

I sometimes muse about an imaginary (but not unimaginable) German family on whose wall is a plaque bearing the familiar inscription, "The Family that Prays Together Stays Together." Next to it is another plaque, stating that "The Family that Plays Together Stays Together." In a very particular sense, these summarize the basis for cohesiveness in a major segment of Iowa's German-American population. Children are socialized early to the norms of a community in which it is important to engage in participatory activities stressing interaction with other German-Americans.

The history of Davenport (and eventually, of the Quad Cities) in the latter half of the nineteenth century is dominated by the presence of the Turner associations. While each society or *Turnverein* had its own unique character, all shared certain basic tenets, and were dedicated to the benefits of physical fitness; to social welfare of the membership; and to continuing, lifelong education, or *Bildung*. Most could thank their presence in Iowa to the arrival in Davenport of the patently liberal forty-eighters, which hence boasted a membership of unapologetic freethinkers. Typically, the *Turnverein* fostered programs in music, often in theater, and occasionally in the other arts as well. While the history of these organizations generally focuses on programs for adults, it must not be forgotten that this was a main avenue for leading the young people into active participation in the German-American community. There is perhaps a bit of historic justice in the fact that the Turner movement today is known primarily (not only in the Davenport area, but wherever it survives in areas of historically heavy German ethnic concentration) as an alternative to organizations such as the YMCA and YWCA.

Prominent in the history of the Turner movement are the lectures that they sponsored. As early as 1857 Davenport's Germans enjoyed a program on the status of women. While some topics might elicit a chuckle today ("Is Water or Beer Preferable for the Health of Human Beings?" or "How Can We Counteract the Temperance Movement?"), there was no dodging such heady issues as capital punishment, evolution, and the proper role of Congress in pension legislation.

Several times a year a lecture or debate series would focus on topics dealing with the education of the young — How should one best teach moral values, the German language, music, or physical fitness? In other words, how might children best be provided the skills and attitudes that would allow them to *play* (and therefore, if the theory held, to *stay*) together as full participants in an ethnic experience?

An indication of the importance of music is given by the fact that an entire issue of the State Historical Society's *Palimpsest* (July 1964) was dedicated to the history of music in early Davenport. Although the articles do not strive to present a vignette of German-American history per se, they do, and are well worth reading.

Within a few years of their arrival, the forty-eighters (and those who followed) established choral, band, and philharmonic ensembles, some of which survive today. Even the Americans had to admit freely that both the vocal and instrumental development in Davenport rested with the German population.

Musical festivals small and great abounded, culminating in such extravaganzas as the four-day Sängerfest of 1898, generally conceded by townsfolk of all ethnic backgrounds to have been well worth months of planning and the investments of tens of thousands of dollars. While events of such magnitude are a rarity, the record shows that the Quad Cities continue to offer a broader and richer variety of musical programs than one might find in the average Iowa community, and that musical groups dating back to the heyday of the nineteenth century, such as the *Liedertafel,* continue to thrive in the Scott County area.

Fig. 7.1.   The Turner halls attest to the German attachment to culture, fitness, and fellowship. The nineteenth-century Turner Hall in Davenport shows the German influence in its architecture. (Photo courtesy of State Historical Society of Iowa)

Occasionally in late July during the Bix Beiderbecke Memorial Festival in Davenport, as one listens to accounts of how the area's most prominent jazz artist received his inspiration from the musical idiom of a riverboat town, it is tempting to wonder whether Leon Bismarck Beiderbecke (1903–1931) was not simply a very good German-American, in the tradition of his hometown, who learned to play for a larger audience.

Those wishing to delve deeper into the tradition of the German forty-eighters and their legacy in Iowa might want to consult the lead article in the first issue of *The Iowa Journal of History and Politics* for 1946 in their local library, and then visit some of the still-active Turner facilities along the eastern flank of the state. In the Quad Cities area, there are Turner societies in Moline, Keystone, Rockford (the old Central Turners), and at two locations in Davenport. Especially worth a visit are the halls of the East Davenport Turners, at 2113 East 11th, and of the Northwest Turners, at the corner of Washington and 11th, in Davenport. Still dedicated to the ideal of a sound mind in a sound body, the societies are especially interested in providing programs for the young that complement the scheduled offerings of the school systems. For young and old alike, however, there is an overriding emphasis on group-centered social activities. Some time ago when I made my first acquaintance with the Northwest Turners, I was advised that the hall offers a gymnasium, a meeting space for rent, and a public tap. My own observation has been that these are used in the true Turner tradition.

Vestiges of *Küche und Kirche* in Traditional Amana Life

The Amana Colonies were founded by adherents of the Community of True Inspiration, a German Pietist sect with communal principles and practices. (Occasionally one encounters the misconception that *Am*ana, with its German roots, is the home of German-speaking *Am*ish. This never was the case.) In 1854 an Inspirationist scouting party from near Buffalo, New York, chose the area of the present colonies as the new and permanent site for the sect, and in the following year the first of the seven colonies was laid out. A communal form of theocratic governance and operation persisted until 1932, when it was deemed wisest, in the face of economic and social pressure, to establish a system of private enterprise under the aegis of the Amana Society, and to vest spiritual authority in the separate Amana Church Society. The communal era had ended. While the colonies have been featured in numerous popular and scholarly publications, those wishing to delve into the historical record should not bypass the rich selection of materials, at a bargain price, in Lawrence G. Rettig's *Amana Today*. Other publications, including a number of attractive photographic anthologies, are available throughout the Amana area.

Any serious tour of Amana must begin with a visit to the Historical Museum. The audio-visual presentation, offering background on the Inspirationist movement and the settlement in Iowa, will enhance one's understanding of the colonies and the role played by such inspired leaders as the visionary Christian Metz and Barbara Heinemann. After gaining some feeling for the principles of the communal life, take a walking tour and look at some of the large, freestanding communal kitchen structures, noting how even the exterior architecture suggests the coming together of many people, and a sense of cohesiveness for which the sharing of a life-sustaining meal becomes an apt metaphor.

More than merely a place to eat, the German kitchen has always been the center of family life. A great deal of unpretentious socializing goes on in the preparation and consumption of food, and it is no accident that the communal kitchen is one of the most prominent, independent (yet integral) features of the traditional Amana townscape.

The simple yet dignified interiors of the Amana church buildings with their plain blue walls, the fervor of readings of the Inspirationist texts by lay membership, and the songs with improvised accompaniment to the single melody line of the C-clef notation in the *Psalterspiel* hymnal, combine to form a powerful impression on the observer. Although some services are held in English, the traditional order of Inspirationist service and hymn singing will be found in the German services. There is some seasonal variation in scheduling and location, hence visitors should contact a representative of the Amana Church Society ahead of time.

Those who do not find it convenient to attend a service may wish to consider a visit to the former church building in High Amana, which has, as the Arts Center Gallery, become a major focal point for folklife, art, and craft exhibitions in the colonies. Although the use of a church structure for the display of art and craft realia departs from traditional colony practices, the choice of items for inclusion in the various exhibitions has shown tastefulness and a respect for traditional values. Under the aegis of the Amana Arts Guild, the gallery has offered retrospective exhibitions of works by local artists, features on individual craft traditions (tinsmithing, woodcarving, garden art, etc.), the architectural tradition, historical photographs, and much more.

Exhibitions change at a refreshingly brisk pace of about once every three to four weeks. The gallery is generally open Friday through Sunday, 11:00 A.M. to 4:00 P.M., June through September. Visitors will, however, want to verify these hours for subsequent seasons.

Equally exciting is the just-completed renovation of the *Schule* (school house) adjacent to the gallery. The first floor will be used for activities related to the teaching and preservation of Amana traditions and material culture. The second floor will be dedicated to artist-in-residence programs. The envisioned use of this facility will be to continue the Amana Arts Guild's ongoing program of seminars and instructional opportunities for individuals wishing to learn more about the use of clay, basketry, fiber techniques, and other craft areas.

The crafts of the Amana Colonies, along with those of Pella and Kalona, were featured in "Everyday Elaborations," one of the essays in *Passing Time and Traditions: Contemporary Iowa Folk Artists* (Iowa State University Press), a volume with a number of studies of interest to the traveler in Iowa.

Family and Spiritual Life in the Amish and Mennonite Communities

Another excellent way to gain an appreciation for the traditional German family life is to take one of the tours of the Kalona area sponsored by its chamber of commerce. It is necessary to schedule these tours in advance, and to guarantee participation by a minimum number of individuals. For a modest fee one receives a guided tour to a number of points of interest (with individual wishes always given special consideration). Though each tour is individually planned, what all have in common is a main noontime meal in a Kalona home, usually with a conservative Mennonite family. One senses a quiet efficiency, in the face of a busy schedule and unusual demands on energy, emanating from the kitchen and infusing the entire household and its guests with a sense of unhurried well-being. Even in the plainest homes where there may be virtually no decoration on the walls, one can expect to find a collection of fine plates or glassware, a testimony to the fact that the kitchen is seen as the source of an essential social and aesthetic experience in which all family members and guests are invited to share.

The Amish are part of the larger Mennonite tradition that runs a spectrum from the Old and New Order Amish through the Beachy Amish (or "Rubber Dutch," who allow themselves the use of some motorized vehicles) and Conservative Mennonites to branches of the faith that appear to an outsider as simply another manifestation of conservative Protestantism. What all have in common are baptism at an age that allows the candidate for membership to make an individual testimony of faith (*the* cornerstone of Anabaptist Protestantism), close adherence to Scripture, refusal to bear arms or take oaths, and an active affirmation of the plain life. (The faithful of various Mennonite persuasions, in fact, often refer to themselves as "plain people.") There were Amish in the Kalona area as early as 1845, with an established congregation in the following year. The early 1890s found Amish in Wright County, and by 1914 a settlement had been established in Buchanan County, at Littleton. In more recent years Amish have moved to the Southeastern counties of Van Buren (near Milton) and Davis (in rural Drakesville).

For anyone unfamiliar with the Mennonite tradition, there is no better place to start than Kalona. In addition to Mennonites of many persuasions, one finds the Kalona area the largest Amish settlement west of the Mississippi River. Take a day to visit the Kalona Historical Village. Peruse the local bookstore literature. Visit a craft shop such as Kalona Kountry Kreations (the proprietor, incidentally, is an Amish woman who, in contrast to popular and often misleading stereotypes about the Amish, has seen more of America and the world than will be seen by many Iowans in a lifetime). The "plain" Community Country Store northeast of town (closed on Sunday and Tuesday) affords a rare glimpse into the unpretentious yet wholesome lifestyle for which Kalona is noted.

Several excellent books are readily available on the Amish, including John A. Hostetler's *Amish Society* (3d edition, Johns Hopkins University Press), and—for those wishing to focus specifically on the Amish in our own state—Elmer and Dorothy Schwieder's *A Peculiar People: Iowa's Old Order Amish* (Iowa State University Press). Both are richly illustrated and help the visitor to locate clues from the landscape and farmscape (the "Opahaus," wireless homes, hybrid machinery, horses and buggies, etc.), all of which indicate that one is in Amish territory.

Most individuals who choose to visit an Amish service are pleasantly surprised at the warm reception given a "stranger" (cf. German *ein Fremder,* not necessarily a pejorative term). A bit of advice is in order to help smooth the pathway to contact: be curious, but not a curiosity seeker; dress modestly; speak softly; respect the fact that most Amish feel uncomfortable around a camera. Previous contact with a member of the local Amish district (as the organizational unit is called) is certainly appropriate, though not strictly necessary. Experience and observation suggest that such contact is usually more helpful in reassuring an apprehensive guest than in forewarning the hosts.

Since the Amish do not use church buildings for their fortnightly services (though they typically do maintain a separate edifice for Sunday School held on alternating Sundays), one needs to know how to locate the worship site. The plain wooden benches without any "lazyback" (backrest) used during services are kept in the so-called Bench Wagon that appears parked by the home where services will be held next. Furniture is cleared out of ground-floor rooms and the benches set up in a manner that physically separates the women and men. There may also be divisions according to age. On Sunday morning, as much as an hour may be given to very leisurely singing (one sustained note per breath) from hymnals containing texts but no musical notation. Scripture reading may be in German, and the sermon may be in Pennsylvania German. Exhortations and prayer may extend the service to three hours, after which a plain but wholesome meal is shared. Because of the demands of hosting such an event, families often maintain the Bench Wagon at their homes for two consecutive services, so that preparations already in place may serve for a second round.

Fig. 7.2. In communities with an Amish population, it is not unusual to see the customary horse and buggy. (Photo by James Hippen)

Fig. 7.3.   Amish bench wagon (rural Kalona) is parked where worship services will be held next. (Photo by Philip Webber)

One way for the nonspeaker of German to gain a feeling for traditional German Anabaptist practices is to attend services at an assembly of the Apostolic Christian Church. (Congregations of this historically German/Swiss brotherhood are located in Burlington, Elgin, Garden Grove, Lester, North Liberty, Oakville, and Pulaski.) Although the language is now entirely English, the customs and service remain much as they were in earlier years. Adult membership is based on an affirmation that confession of sins has been made; on a testimony of faith, conversion, and peace with God and man; and on baptism (normally by complete immersion). Lay ministers offer unpremeditated sermons on simultaneously chosen passages of Scripture. Men and women are seated separately, and female members wear a veil as a head covering. Prayer is offered by male members of the congregation. Music is sung in four-part harmony from printed notation, but without instrumental accompaniment. Members greet one another with the "kiss of charity." Between morning and afternoon services a light lunch is served, providing an excellent opportunity for interaction with church members.

The Traditions and Festivals of the Dutch

A higher percentage of Iowa's residents (about one in sixteen) claimed Dutch ancestry at the time of the 1980 Census than did the citizens of any other state. Concentrated primarily in south central Iowa near Pella, and in the northwest (Sioux and Lyon counties), our Dutch-American neighbors constitute one of the state's most vital and energetic ethnic groups.

Virtually all of the Dutch enclaves in Iowa were established (directly or indirectly) as offshoots of the 1847 settlement in Pella, under the visionary Reverend Hendrik Pieter Scholte. Scholte's palatial residence is open to the public, and an excellent starting place for a tour of Pella. One also ought to get some taste for the life of the common man, as documented in the exhibitions of the walk-though Historical Village. Some of the early architecture can be seen there and in the buildings of the Strawtown Complex on the west end of town. Using a reproduction of the early town map that can be purchased at the Strawtown Store, take an exploratory hike at your leisure. Those preferring a somewhat more systematic approach will want to look at the printed and slide-tape materials for an architectural walking tour prepared by the Historical Village under a grant from the Iowa Humanities Board/National Endowment for the Humanities. Also, the Pella Historical Society has published a two-volume local history consisting entirely of contributions by local residents on family history and material culture in the area. A study of the language and ethnicity in Pella is in *Pella Dutch: The Portrait of a Language and Its Use in One of Iowa's Ethnic Communities* (Iowa State University Press).

Many tourists visit Pella during the annual Tulip Time, the second Thursday through Saturday of May. There is no other time when so much historical realia appears in the windows, or when one can attend such special features as the historically reenacted service, with Dutch choir, at the First Reformed Church. Extraordinary research and craftsmanship are lavished on costumes worn almost exclusively at this time of year. Groups such as the Dutch Family Singers and Dancers show the fruits of their labors. There are several events in the area worth considering at other times of the year, however.

The summertime *Kermis,* or carnival, though not specifically ethnic in flavor, often provides the chance to meet townsfolk with strong interests in the local heritage. Touring the open grounds of the Historical Village provides an excellent opportunity to catch a bit of local color in a more relaxed setting.

In my own opinion, there is nothing more truly Dutch in

Iowa than the arrival of the Dutch Saint Nick, *Sinterklaas,* the first Saturday in December. The good saint arrives on a ship (supposedly from Spain), and with his helpers (Piets) identifies the good children who are to receive candy, while tying a few select scoundrels into bags to be taken away for punishment. The event is a perennial favorite, with more specific adherence to traditionally Dutch practices than at any other time during the year.

In the late winter months, at a date announced each year, the Christian Reformed Church in neighboring Peoria hosts an evening of Dutch Psalm singing. Bring along your C-clef Psalter, and expect an enjoyable musical experience followed by a community "coffeetime" (local parlance for snacktime) in the church basement. The older rule of one note for one breath is no longer followed; hence, the music is not quite as patently largo as in former years. This stately music is, however, still dignified, infused with sincere fervor, and provides a unique link with the traditions of an era still remembered by a few of the folks whom you will meet.

Equally intriguing is the Dutch corridor along the northwest border of our state. Here one finds colleges sponsored by both of the main branches of the Dutch Reformed tradition: Northwestern College of the Reformed Church in America in Orange City; and Dordt College, affiliated with the Christian Reformed Church in Sioux Center. There is perhaps a slightly greater conservatism in the Dutch communities of this area than in Pella; the Dutch language has been preserved and is spoken by a surprising number of residents in this area. And, for the general inquirer to get an overview of the resources available for research on the Dutch-Americans in Iowa, there is no better place than in the highly attractive and accessible Dutch Heritage Collection at Northwestern College.

Orange City has much to offer, especially if one is trying to capture some of the unruffled calm of a small town that has not yet experienced the commercial explosion witnessed by many other centers of tourism. Each year, exactly one week later than Pella, Orange City celebrates its own Tulip Festival. In addition, the windmill on the south edge of town houses unusually fine displays of the physical environment that would have been familiar to many of the Dutch immigrants who first settled Orange City. The local historical museum, though relatively compact, does an excellent job of presenting the everyday realia of both the Dutch-American and more general pioneer life on the Great Plains.

Windmills, genuine and ornamental, are common enough in

Dutch-American communities throughout this nation, but Orange City's mills can stand up (or turn around) among even the most notable. Every lover of Dutch-Americana should see the Northwestern State Bank windmill, and "The Old Mill" at Vogel Paint and Wax Company. The latter shows a blend of Dutch and American forms as unique as the community in which it is located.

To note the transformation of the European tradition (symbolized in the windmills) and the Dutch-American legacy (suggested by the exhibitions of the historical museum) is to receive a brief glimpse into the dual, if not at times schizoid, worlds of the immigrant. To realize that both the European homeland and the world of the earlier settlers are now a century away from our contemporary experience, should be reason enough to spend time in these facilities whose mission is to preserve something of the worlds whence we came.

Fig. 7.4. The first Saturday in December, Sinterklaas arrives in Pella, on a ship from Spain. (Photo by Philip Webber)

Fig. 7.5.   The Old Mill at Vogel Paint and Wax Co. Inc., Orange City. (Photo courtesy of Orange City Chamber of Commerce)

8

VIEWING
IOWA'S FARMSTEADS

Lowell Soike

Most of us today know little about farms or the farming we see going on while traveling the roads of Iowa. This is more so with our children—a generation that has little touch with the farms of our grandparents, where buildings contained the secret places of our childhood weekends and summers. And with ever-decreasing proportions of Iowans farming the land, prospects dim that Iowa citizens will have the same familiarity with farms that our parents had. Mark Twain's "How I Edited an Agricultural Paper" (1876) foretold our growing ignorance. "Have you ever edited an agricultural paper before?" inquired the old reader with the latest issue in hand. "No," Twain replied, "this is my first attempt."

"Some instinct told me so," said the old gentleman, putting on his spectacles and looking over them with asperity. . . . "I wish to read to you what made me have that instinct. Listen and see if it was you that wrote it."

"Turnips should never be pulled; it injures them. It is much better to send a boy up and let him shake the tree."

"Now what do you think of that—for I really suppose you wrote it."

"Think of it? Why, I think it is good. I think it is sense. I have no doubt that every year millions and millions of bushels of turnips are spoiled in this township by being pulled in half ripe condition, while if they had sent a boy up to shake the tree . . . ."

"Shake your grandmother! Turnips don't grow on trees!"

"Oh, they don't, don't they. Well, who said they did? The language was intended to be figurative—wholly figurative. Any-

153

body that knows anything will know that. I meant that the boy should shake the vine."

The old gentleman got up and tore his paper all into small shreds and stamped on them, . . . and said I did not know as much as a cow. . . .

Our ignorance of farms is magnified by the gradual but dramatic changes that have altered Iowa's countryside in just one generation. Those who were growing up in Iowa in 1950 now find little more than half as many farms and half as many people living on them, while the average size of farms has almost doubled. The effects are visible in driving across the state: abandoned or partially used farmsteads, clusters of trees where a farmstead once stood, fewer fence lines, fewer mailboxes, fewer people. You do see, however, more farmers driving equipment on the roads because most Iowa farms are no longer arranged in compact blocks. Rather the dense network of all-weather roads and the large modern machinery—designed for road travel and enabling one person to till more land than before—have permitted farmers to put together sizeable, but fragmented, farm operations made up of dispersed parcels that they own or rent. Commuting to them as needed, the farmer achieves an economically efficient farm size as well as the prestige that comes from operating as much as owning the farm.

With a few clues, even casual roadside observers can begin to appreciate the changing character of farming. While much is to be learned from examining specific farmhouses and farm buildings, looking at them collectively—at the mosaic formed by the individual pieces—can be even more informative. For this mosaic of barns, sheds, storage buildings, and houses, which I will call the farmstead, is the center of operations on the American farm. Its design and organization, age and condition tell a great deal about the rest of the farm activity and economy. Therefore, it is what I will focus on. I will look at the farmstead as it varies with the different farm regions of Iowa, as it reflects changing construction trends, and as its diverse buildings reveal changes in farm operations.

Farm Regions

Driving through Iowa one sees the generally prosperous look of farms compared to other states as well as different kinds of farming, although it is not easy at times to perceive what makes it so. In every Iowa county farmers devote more acres of their cropland to corn than other crops and feed most of it to

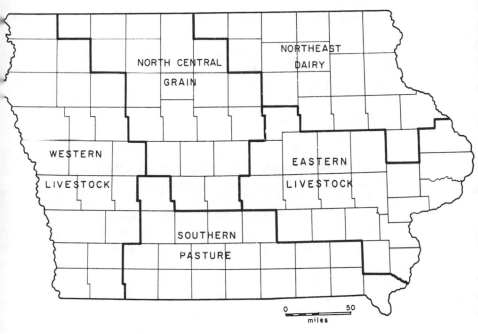

Fig. 8.1. The different kinds of agriculture most
commonly practiced in five regions of Iowa. (Map
from Leland L. Sage, A History of Iowa, *Iowa State
Univ. Press, 1974)*

hogs or cattle, but no one can say with any accuracy that corn
and hogs are what is raised on any one farm. This fact is most
noticed where certain kinds of farming are concentrated in certain regions of the state. These regions are where, because of
similarities in the lay of the land, soils, or proximity to markets,
enough farmers in an area have reached the same conclusion that
the most money can be made by raising a similar combination of
crops or livestock. The result is that their farmsteads take on a
distinct regional similarity—the clusters of farm buildings reflecting the similar activities dominating an area. In few cases would
anyone see precise boundaries of Iowa's farming regions, because
each gradually merges into the other. But in the heart of each
region perhaps twenty to fifty percent or more of the farmers
have the same kind of operation, and so make the differences
between areas distinguishable.

And what are these regions? The farming regions of today
were already so clearly discernable by the opening decades of the
twentieth century that, by 1929, C. L. Holmes could ask in *Wallaces' Farmer,* "In Which of the Iowas Is Your Farm?" Then, as
now, five basic farming areas were visible: a northeastern dairy
area, a north central cash-grain area, and three meat-producing
areas—in the western, southern, and eastern counties.

The vast numbers of travelers whisking either down Interstate 35 or across Interstate 80 unfortunately glimpse little more than two of the five farming areas. The northeastern dairy region is missed entirely by both, the southern pasture area is lost to I-80 motorists and those riding on I-35 see nothing of the eastern or western livestock regions.

Large dairy barns with their plentiful loft space for storing hay and with their adjacent milk houses or outside bulk cooling tanks along with numerous towering silos serve notice to the traveler of having entered the northeast dairy region. Hogs and cattle are raised by many in this hilly, rough terrain of Iowa, but dairying has become most prominent, primarily because land for planting row crops such as corn is limited, while hay and pastureland on which dairy cattle thrive is plentiful. Also, since winter feed for dairy cows is needed and since raising corn to maturity in the cooler north is riskier because of the chances of an early hard frost, farmers often cut the whole corn plant green, chop it up — stalk, ears, leaves, and all — and put the silage in silos as fodder to see their herds of dairy cows through the winter months.

In recent decades dairy farms have become fewer in number, with the remaining farms maintaining larger, higher-producing herds. This is partly a response to stricter health and sanitation standards imposed during the 1950s. To produce Grade A market milk, which brings the highest price, the farmer needed to install modern milking and cooling equipment throughout and keep the barn very clean and in good repair. Grade B (manufactured milk) producers also faced higher standards and added costs. Many who were unable to afford the expense of upgrading their barns went out of business, while the farmer who remained coped by building larger herds of higher-producing cows and separating the facilities where he feeds and rests the cows from where he milks them. The result is commonly seen today in small, one-story "milking parlors," where cows are milked under very sanitary conditions but not housed. The milking parlor, usually a low pole-barn, is more compact than the adjacent old stall-type dairy barn and easier to clean and cheaper to outfit with milking equipment.

Driving west out of the dairy area toward the north central counties that extend above Des Moines to the Minnesota border, the nature of the land changes. The stream-cut hills, with their high percentage of untillable pastureland, level out into longer stretches of slightly rolling and richer soils. Here increasing numbers of farms show signs of being part of the prosperous cash-grain area.

Cash-grain farmers sell a greater part of their crops (mainly corn and soybeans) rather than, as elsewhere, feeding them to livestock. Soybeans have become a major factor in Iowa's cropland use since the 1920s, when farmers in the southeastern counties first began planting them to get a home-grown, high-protein feed crop. Over the years, however, as demand for soybeans grew off the farm, the center of production shifted northwest into the central cash-grain region—especially after the 1950s—where today they alternate with corn in the crop rotation. With so much of the farm's total acreage tillable for row crops, the cash-grain farmer has less time during the busy spring and summer months to raise large numbers of hogs or cattle. The result is that livestock are scarcer in the cash-grain counties, and accordingly, fewer farm buildings are seen for sheltering or feeding farm animals. Where livestock are raised in the region, the farmer usually opts for hogs to feed out his surplus of corn, because little hay or pastureland is available on which to grow roughage crops for cattle. Large dairy barns and silos recede from view, replaced by large metal pole-barns for housing the large tractor, its implements, the combine, and the workshop for keeping them in running order. Next are the clusters of bins for corn and soybean storage and the means for receiving and conveying it. Also notice the sizeable attractive farm houses and perhaps large double corn cribs (each containing two cribs under a single roof placed on either side of a central drive, with bins overhead for shelled corn or soybeans). Generally, however, although cash-grain farm acreages may be large, the fewer and more specialized activities performed on them make for simpler, smaller farmsteads. If there is an old barn or a hog or chicken house left from the days of general "horse farming," they are most likely suffering from neglect or relegated to general storage purposes.

Journeying either west, south, or east out of the cash-grain region brings you into contact with one of the state's three meat-producing regions. And how do you know you have arrived? "Roll down the window!" the farmer might say, or "Smell all the money out there!" Unlike the cash-grain region, the livestock areas all have a larger amount of untillable pastureland, thus more hay and forage crops are raised. Also, because meat-producing farms involve a larger number of activities compared to the smaller and relatively uncomplicated farmsteads that characterize cash-grain or dairy farming, the meat-producing areas have more buildings and are consequently more extensive, even though the total farm acreage may be no bigger. They need wood-slatted or wire cribs; circular metal bins and silos to store the feed-grain, corn, and silage grown on the land; storage for store-purchased feed concentrates; and perhaps pole-framed sheds for baled hay.

Barns or open-front sheds and feeding operations are there for cattle, while hogs are raised in confinement or pasture housing. And, of course, there are the farmhouses and the machine sheds for tractors and implements. But similarities aside, each livestock farm also has its own individual look due to its particular livestock and crop emphasis.

Fig. 8.2.   This farmstead integrates the unloading, drying, elevating, storing, and transferring of grain into one efficient, on-farm process. The pole building houses equipment for the fields, while the farmhouse presides over all. (Photo by Steve Hink)

Farms in the southern pasture area, which comprises the south central and southeastern counties, differ from those in the other two meat-producing areas in that cattle are emphasized as much as hogs. Generally, less productive land also diminishes the scale and prosperity on the farmsteads. This greater preference for cattle reflects the relatively low-yielding pastureland and the smaller percentage of cropland for growing corn. The corresponding lack of concentrated feeds like corn has also discouraged the rise of commercial feed-lot operations that rely on inexpensive surplus feeds for fattening steers shipped in from western ranges.

Instead, the typical beef cattle enterprise in Iowa's southern pasture area commonly uses the available pasturage to maintain a herd of beef cows for producing calves in the spring. The calves are then put on summer pasture for sale in the fall. Or the farmer continues to feed them on hay and silage over the winter months so that, with the help of corn and high-protein concentrates such as soybean meal, they are pastured through much of the following year to reach marketable condition. The buildings reflect this local practice of raising beef over the simpler steer-fattening enterprises. Farms for fattening feeder cattle require little more than open-front sheds that face south onto a fenced lot, along with nearby storage for hay and feed concentrates. However, locally raised beef usually require more enclosed buildings to protect the breeding cows and young calves. These buildings commonly include a barn, which provides hay storage and animal shelter. The center of the barn is filled with loose or baled hay from the ground to the roof, which varies depending on the mix and amount of animal and storage space desired. The sides have sheds that contain feed racks, stalls, and pens.

In the western livestock region, however, you see open-front sheds and fenced-in feedlots for fattening large numbers of purchased steers. Except for cash-grain farms occupying a narrow strip of bottomland running alongside the Missouri River (through which Interstate 29 runs), this livestock region — several counties wide along Iowa's entire western border — is dominated by hog and cattle farming. The number of livestock is determined by the farmer striking a balance between the time spent in raising corn on tillable parts of the rolling farmland and the time spent running an efficient hog or cattle enterprise. There are more cattle where hay and pastureland occupy a large part of a farm's total acreage, while greater numbers of hogs are found where more of the acreage can be planted in corn. Hogs — being most efficient at converting corn into pounds of meat — come first, followed by cattle with their diet containing plenty of good-quality hay and pasture forages supplemented by corn.

Farmsteads in the eastern livestock region between the cities of Des Moines, Clinton, and Keokuk resemble those in the western livestock region because of the similar kinds of crops and livestock raised. This region differs from the western one mainly in having more hay and pastureland and more varied cattle operations, which use both locally raised beef and beef shipped in from the western ranges for fattening. In both the eastern and western livestock regions, however, the vast bulk of the corn crop is fed to hogs, and it is for this reason the hog has been deemed "the mortgage lifter" on corn-belt farms.

A variety of buildings for raising hogs is seen across Iowa's livestock regions, from huge sleek metal confinement houses to clusters of little A-frame sheds in the pastures. Part of the variety can be traced to farmers pursuing different kinds of hog enterprises — some raise their own pigs all the way from newborn piglets to market hogs; others with limited feed supplies for finishing pigs keep a breeding herd for producing only young feeder pigs, which are then sold and fattened elsewhere.

What you see in hog buildings is equally influenced by the method for raising pigs, ranging from keeping them completely confined in environmentally controlled buildings to pasturing them outdoors using movable shelters and rotating their pasture from year to year. Large-scale pork producers who raise six or more litters a year in full confinement have a separate farrowing unit for the sows and their piglets, another intermediate unit with pens for weaned pigs, and a finishing unit for bringing the pigs to market weight. Small-scale producers of one or two litters a year minimize their investment in buildings. They either raise sows and their litters in a central farrowing house and then move them onto clean pasture, or else move small individual farrowing houses onto fresh pasture before farrowing time for the sow to give birth and for the pigs to be fed to marketable weight.

Construction Trends

The one constant of Iowa farms and farming is that nothing has remained static. Early Iowa farms were small in scale, diverse, and geared to home consumption. Today's farms are specialized, larger-scale, heavily mechanized operations dependent on the international economy. This constantly changing order of agriculture is fast erasing Iowa's farming past — that is, the farm buildings and farmsteads designed to serve an earlier time. Still, with a few clues, travelers can glimpse features that reveal significant growth and change on the farm.

First, observe the building materials themselves. Particular construction materials achieved widespread popularity during one of three great waves of building activity that gave Iowa farmsteads most of today's buildings. By observing the number and scale of buildings made from the different materials, you can recognize the important periods in the life of each farmstead. These three agricultural construction eras might be called the wood and stone era (1880s), the masonry and concrete era (1905–1920), and the metal era (1960–1980). Each construction era coincided with a period of major agricultural expansion in Iowa and the Midwest.

The earliest and perhaps the greatest increase in building activity took place between 1880 and the Depression of 1893.

Fig. 8.3.   The wood barn and stave silo of the 1890s. Because the wood swelled when filled with the moist, chopped corn and shrunk after being emptied, the tension on the rods and hoops holding the staves together had to be adjusted frequently. (Photo from the 1973 Webster County architectural survey, courtesy of State Historical Society of Iowa)

Most of the wood barns on stone foundations seen today date from the agricultural building boom of this era, when horse farming called for sheltering horses and cattle from the wet, cold, wintry winds, and for providing enough feed under roof to see the animals safely through the winter season. Those who stuck to using their Iowa "hayshed" barns were ridiculed. "You who have no barns for you cattle," wrote a frontier Iowa farmer, "just examine your stock in the spring after one of our hard winters, and then, while their gaunt frames, rough hair, sunken eyes and shivering limbs are fresh upon your memory, go to the farm of your neighbor, who has a good barn for the protection of his stock, and compare the conditions of his plump cattle, sleek and satisfied as they are, with the condition of your own." Several hundred all-stone barns and outbuildings were also built where local stone could be easily quarried (mainly eastern Iowa), but frame buildings erected on stone foundations predominated during these years.

By the time the second agricultural building boom came into full stride in 1915, building conditions had changed. With lumber now higher in cost and lower in quality, the growing movement was toward erecting permanent buildings made of concrete and clay products. More baked, hollow, clay tile blocks were being manufactured in Iowa than in all its bordering states combined, and no plant was farther than fifty miles away. The resulting cheap availability of the tile led to the increased use of the clay products in building barns, hog houses, poultry and icehouses, round corn cribs and granaries, and silos. The round clay tile silo is the most visible widespread evidence of this masonry era.

Fig. 8.4.   The "Iowa silo" of clay tile was popular
from about 1910 to 1930. Because seepage corroded
the internal reinforcing rods until the walls cracked,
these clay tile silos gave way to concrete stave and
solid concrete ones. Today they are left standing
empty and unused mainly because of the inconven-
ience of tearing them down. (Photo from the 1973
Webster County architectural survey, courtesy of State
Historical Society of Iowa)

Another reason for the popularity of hollow tile was its promotion by the Iowa State College Agricultural Experiment Station at Ames, especially in silo construction. Working with a local manufacturer in 1906, M. L. King and J. B. Davidson of the college built a silo using curved hollow clay tiles with steel reinforcing rods embedded within the mortar joints. Soon dubbed the "Iowa silo," its popularity spread so fast that within the next nine years between three thousand and four thousand were reported to have been built in Iowa alone. "One cannot travel more than a few miles in almost any part of Iowa," wrote an observer in 1915, "without seeing some kind of farm building that has been built to last, and which will not have to be replaced within a generation." Concrete manifested its influence during these years mainly in displacing stone for foundations and in superceding the use of dirt floors. The most conspicuous uses that catch the traveler's eye today are the huge, round, concrete corn cribs and granaries made out of a special concrete block with air openings. This second era of construction began to fade when Iowa slipped into an agricultural downturn in the twenties, with the era ending during the Great Depression.

Fig. 8.5.   Three ages of farm buildings. Modern pole building on the left; a curved, gothic-roofed barn in the center; and a low, gable-roofed barn on the right. (Photo by Robert F. Sayre)

Our most recent period of farm construction, climaxing in the 1970s, brought another change in building materials. The high cost of wood or masonry, compared to the cost of buying, installing, and maintaining sheet-metal siding and roofing (mainly in the form of prefabricated buildings), brought metal to the forefront. Although metal had been used occasionally for several decades in grain bins, water tanks, a few silos, or corrugated siding for buildings, its use accelerated in the 1950s, and with the increasing cost advantages today, metal has become the leading construction material. Corrugated steel and aluminum sheets predominate on all major structures added to farms in recent years: single-story pole-barns for sheltering farm animals, machinery, or crops; circular grain bins to contain the burgeoning yields from hybrid corn; and the mechanically emptying, stove-enameled, blue Harvestore silos.

The traveler also becomes aware of the transformation of Iowa's farms by noting the buildings that have fallen into disuse. As these structures stand unpainted and in disrepair, they conjure up more than nostalgia. Some appeal to us as picturesque reminders of bygone times—the lone, rusted windmill leaning over a partially collapsed wood fence. But the collection of such ruins, buildings, and structures also offers mute but dramatic evidence of the way farms are changing.

Many buildings, once the pride of the farmyard and built to last for generations, today stand idle and neglected. The buildings made perfect sense in their day and exhibited the latest thinking of progressive agriculturalists; however, as time has shown, farm buildings built to the highest standards in one era often prove useless in the next.

Some structures became obsolete because they simply were no longer needed. When rural electric lines were extended to Iowa's farms in the 1930s, the highly productive days of the windmill were numbered. An electrically pumped supply of running water joined together with the septic tank forever closed the door of the privy, which somehow had always seemed a hundred yards too close in the summer and a hundred yards too far in the winter. Other victims of electrical power on the farms were the icehouse and the springhouse for cooling milk. The butchering shed and smokehouse need not be included here because their fate had already been sealed before the 1920s when all-weather roads and the automobile made town-processed meat accessible to farm families.

Other buildings passed into obsolescence more slowly. After World War I when the gasoline engine and farm tractor began emancipating farming from its dependence on horsepower, the small corn crib and general purpose barn began to disappear. Traditionally, the double corn crib (two cribs sharing a common roof with a central driveway running between them) was low and squat, suited to the methods of handling grain by bushel, scoop shovel, and wagons. But with engine-powered mechanical elevators (some transitional versions of which were horse-powered), there was no limit and the farmers now built the side walls of 1920s double corn cribs to heights of sixteen to twenty feet. It also became common to construct grain bins over the driveway to take full advantage of the mechanical elevator. Other types of storage structures consequently became taller as well — circular metal bins, wire mesh cribs, and wood-frame rectangular central grain storage buildings — as their low, smaller wood-slatted ancestors slipped into obsolescence.

Meanwhile, as the height increased in grain storage structures, the reverse was about to happen to the general-purpose barn. Its fortunes (and height) began to fall with the demise of horse farming. The barn doors typically proved to be a problem — they were too small to admit the horse's successor, the tractor, let alone its impressive array of implements. And the bigger tractors got, the bigger the problem. Equally important, farmers no longer needed a huge hayloft filled to the top with loose hay for feeding the workhorses and cattle. With the horses gone, even if the farmer decided to put cows inside the barn, the mechanical hay baler came along and could replace loose hay with baled hay, requiring only one-half the loft space.

If the farmer tried to fill the entire loft with the densely packed baled hay, most of the old barns could not take the weight of the load, for they had been designed to store lighter, loose hay that had been lifted into the barn by a hay fork and run down the length of the barn to be dropped in place. Many dairy farmers who keep their cows indoors much of the winter (dairy cows cannot tolerate frigid temperatures as can the hardier beef cattle) have reinforced the floors of their hay lofts in order to bear the weight of hay bales that are lifted into place by conveyors and then stacked from floor to ceiling. But most of the old general-use barns either have been abandoned to storing junk, as farmers join the trend toward one- or one-and-a-half-story buildings for handling cattle and baled hay, or have been converted to housing for hogs or the interiors have been opened up to hold huge open bins of shelled corn.

Perhaps the most common relic on Iowa's farms is the chicken house. After World War II it fell victim to improved research aimed at achieving high-volume chicken production. Consequently, poultry production shifted to a relative few large-scale, specialized producers. The change has been remarkable. In 1930 Iowa ranked first among states in chicken and egg production. Large numbers of farms (with only a few being specialized poultry operations) raised small flocks averaging one hundred to two hundred chickens. It served as a side enterprise to supplement the family income. Today a huge broiler industry (producing tens of thousands of birds per "farm" annually) has made the old type of production in small flocks uneconomical. And with little more than one Iowa farm in ten now raising chickens, the former twenty-foot square, shed-roofed chicken houses lie scattered on farms across the state—weather-beaten and empty.

In addition to farm buildings abandoned because they became outmoded or obsolete, travelers will often observe many others that appear useful but empty. This is partly because farmers no longer need them after shifting from general farming to a more efficient specialized operation. Also with fewer Iowa farms in existence—many having been absorbed into larger farms—duplicate structures are forsaken to the elements.

Individual Farm Buildings

Finally, much of the story of what has changed on the farmstead is wrapped up in the histories of the individual buildings and structures. Each kind had its time of emergence and popularity, its own variety of architectural forms and geographic distribution.

It used to be, as Henry Ward Beecher put it in 1869, that "a barn is the real headquarters of the farm. The dwelling-house represents the people; the barn, the work." It was in the barn where workday chores began and ended. But in an era of specialization and mechanized animal feeding, a building conceived to house farm animals below with a hayloft overhead for storing food is an anachronism. Some lament the passing of barns as we knew them as yet another sign of the nearly complete shift from traditional to fully commercialized farming. Others are reminded of barns built by grandfathers with the help of their neighbors, and still others mourn the loss of barns out of respect for the skills and craftsmanship embodied in their construction.

To roadside barn readers, perhaps the best single piece of visible information about barns is the shape of the roof—an indicator of its age. The oldest surviving barns, those built in Iowa from the Civil War to the 1880s, had a rectangular shape and a gable roof, where two straight slopes rise to meet at a central ridge. In the 1880s the new gambrel style made its appearance and, by the turn of the century, surpassed the gable roof in popularity. The two pitches of the gambrel offered more storage area in the loft. It reached its heyday (or hay-day) between 1900 and 1925. During the years after 1900 squarish-shaped barns appeared with either broad gable roofs or a broken gable type (shed-gable) with a central section taller than its surrounding sheds. Often filled with hay in the center, this feeder or beef cattle barn was built with considerable frequency until the 1920s. Barn building went into a general decline during the 1920s and 1930s—years of hard times for Iowa farmers. By the 1940s most of the new barns had concrete walls and a curved gothic roof. This roof, constructed of factory-made, flue-laminated, self-supporting arches, typified progressive barn thinking. Most of them, however, seem to have been built mainly as replacements for ones lost to fire or windstorm.

GENERAL PURPOSE   LATER DAIRY

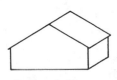   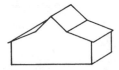   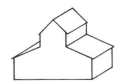

Gable (1840s-1900s)   Gambrel (1880s-1920s)   Gothic (curved/round)
                                                        (1940s)

BEEF CATTLE FEEDER BARNS

3-bay Gable   3-bay Shed-Gable   3-bay Shed-Monitor Gable
(1890s-1920s)   (1890s-1920s)   (1900s-1920s)

Fig. 8.6. Common barn and barn roof shapes, generally, are good indicators of use and age.

Where you spot a barn with a gable or gambrel roof, you also are likely to find a T- or L-shaped farmhouse or one with tall, square, boxlike outlines. This is because they shared a common period of popularity. The traditional T or L farmhouse, which dates back to the 1850s, occurs more frequently with the older gable barn form. But you will notice the strongest correlation is between the large, square, frame house and the gambrel-roofed barn because they came into greatest favor during the very same years: 1880 to 1925.

It takes little acquaintance with Iowa's countryside to recognize these two leading types of farmhouses, although they come in many sizes and variations. The T or L often combines a gable-roofed two-story main section with a one-story wing and a porch nestled in the angle of the two. The square house is most commonly a large, plain, white, two-story frame building with a hip roof and a large front porch. It was praised in *Wallaces' Farmer* for being economical to build and to heat, while many options like dormers and bay windows made it more than just a cube with a roof. Both styles were convenient and functional types of houses that were easily built by local builders and carpenters, and they easily could be adapted to the needs of rural Iowans.

Fig. 8.7.   The T- *or* L-*shaped farmhouse is found in many varieties across the Iowa countryside. This style of farmhouse was built from after the Civil War through the early 1900s. (Photo from the 1973 Webster County architectural survey, courtesy of State Historical Society of Iowa)*

Fig. 8.8. The square "corn belt" house built from
the 1880s until after World War I. (Photo by John
Langholtz for 1975 Madison County architectural
survey, courtesy of State Historical Society of Iowa)

Following close to the house and barn in visual importance
is the silo. First introduced to Iowa farms in the 1880s, the silo
serves as a container to store or "can" green field crops in order to
preserve their feeding value and succulence (juiciness) until the
farmer needs them in the feed troughs. The silo enabled the
farmer to carry larger numbers of livestock through the winter in
safe and healthy condition. The feed stored in silos — usually
chopped green corn but sometimes sorghum or hay grasses — fer-
ments to become ensilage, or silage. By the turn of the century,
round upright silos surpassed other experimental types. Built of
wood, concrete, or hollow clay tile, the upright silo became the
leading storage container for ensiling crops until the 1960s, when
more farmers began turning to trench and bunker type silos.

The upright silo attained its highest perfection in the deep-
blue Harvestore silo (introduced by A. O. Smith Company in
1949) and reached its greatest popularity during the prosperous
1960s and 1970s. Fiberglass-lined (to seal out juices from the
structure, which deteriorated mortar joints in earlier masonry silos) and virtually airtight to keep oxygen from promoting
spoilage, the Harvestore silo came with an automatic unloader.

Its high cost, however, (nearly twice that of conventional upright silos) has confined its market mainly to large-scale dairy and beef producers. Conventional silo makers recognized the advantage of the automatic unloaders and soon made their product self-emptying also. This feature thus saved farmers from the onerous daily chores of climbing to the top in order to hand-pitch down enough feed for the animals. But with corn yields increasing and the substantial cost of the upright silos, farmers turned to cheaper, horizontal trench and bunker silos. With this type the chopped corn plant — "green chops" — is piled into the horizontal silo and packed down by driving a tractor back and forth over it, which squeezes out the air. The material is then covered with a few inches of dry forage followed by sheets of black plastic weighted down by old automobile tires to protect against the winter winds. With a bunker or trench silo, however, this ease of storage and feeding (by scooping out the silage with the hydraulic loader on front of a tractor) is offset by greater losses from spoilage.

UPRIGHT (TOWER) SILOS

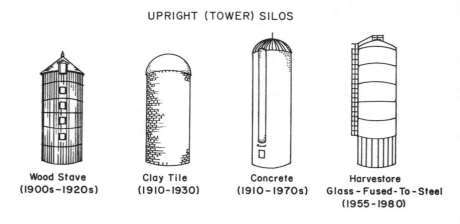

Wood Stave
(1900s–1920s)

Clay Tile
(1910–1930)

Concrete
(1910–1970s)

Harvestore
Glass–Fused–To–Steel
(1955–1980)

HORIZONTAL SILOS

Trench
(1920s–1930s; 1960s–1980s)

Bunker
(1940s; 1960s–1980s)

Fig. 8.9. Types of silos used to store silage.

Cumulatively, these changes have helped reshape the farmstead. As the tall barn passes from the scene, as trench and
bunker silos proliferate more rapidly than their upright cousins,
and as single-story, metal-covered pole buildings multiply for hog
confinement, machinery storage, and cattle shelter, many farmsteads are assuming a long and low horizontal look. This "meta-
morphosis," John Brinkerhoff Jackson foresaw in 1972, makes
the farm workplace more flexible, efficient, and effective. "Modern methods and equipment," he wrote, have "largely eliminated
[the former advantages of] gravity flow and the difficulties of
horizontal movement." Consequently, "mobile machinery and
electrical power have greatly encouraged a horizontal layout and
the consequent abandonment of many vertical installations" on
the modern farm.

Two other influences have affected the look of Iowa farmsteads: debate over the most efficient use and arrangement of
farm structures, and the growing importance of the agricultural
engineer in standardizing farm buildings. The first is a century-
old debate between devotees of a distributed system, in which a
separate building is provided for each kind of stock or particular
purpose, and devotees of a consolidated system, in which as
much as possible is placed under one roof or the buildings are
connected to one another. Until the late nineteenth century in
Iowa, farmsteads followed a distributed approach, comprising a
cluster of small rectangular buildings, pens, and sheds with each
new function bringing forth another building to accommodate it.
By the 1880s, however, advocates of consolidation were making
headway in pressing for large barns to hold all the stock, hay, and
grain. Arguing over ventilation, lighting, and the dangers of disease from housing large numbers of animals together, disputants
carried the issue over into the new century. Agricultural researchers have studied the relative merits of centralized hog houses and
community poultry houses, and gradually the burden of research
knowledge, coupled with farm specialization and mechanization,
has favored the distributed system. Separate buildings for sheltering each kind of stock, for storing forage and grain, and for
housing farm machinery now prevail.

Secondly, the farmstead today shows more the influence of
the agricultural structures engineer than it does the handiwork of
the traditional village carpenter. Since the turn of the century
farm construction has shifted away from home-built or local car-
penter-designed buildings to contractor-built facilities based on
architect-engineer designs and prepared plans. In Iowa some
building designs went out to farmers in agricultural experiment
station bulletins or farm magazines. But since the early 1930s,

more plans have emanated from the Midwest Plan Service, with headquarters in Ames, Iowa, supplemented by plans from dealers of package farm buildings and farm buildings equipment.

The alert Iowa traveler can see that farmsteads are in the grip of change. As farms increase in size and as farmers specialize, the effects of their production decisions show in which buildings they are, and are not, maintaining. Next to some gleaming new buildings stand near-obsolete ones in need of a coat of paint and repairs, while obsolete structures are torn down, radically altered, or left to disintegrate. Barns, early silos, small corn cribs, and windmills are rapidly passing from the landscape. Before all traces of these features from Iowa's past are lost, efforts must begin to identify and document them, to encourage the preservation of those that will best tell the story of Iowa agriculture, and to point out to people the history they can see around them.

PART
IV

Landscape, the Towns

9

THE EDGE OF TOWN

Jon Spayde

One Landscape or Two?

The word Iowa conjures up nineteenth-century images in American minds: the farmstead, the classic country town, a premodern pace of life. But the fact is that it has only been with the invention of twentieth-century modes of travel that certain of Iowa's most enduring images have been created and some of her greatest beauties revealed. Grant Wood's rolling landscapes, after all, are views from a moving airplane. Wood was fascinated by highways and speed, too, as well he might have been. Nineteenth-century travelers on their horses and in their pokey carriages regularly compared the windblown tallgrass prairie to the ocean; but it is only in a car humming along at 55 or 65 mph that you can really feel the oceanic undulations of the land and enjoy the gentle down-and-away motions of the Iowa horizon. No traveler on a flat railway roadbed could hope to learn the rhythms of the Iowa land so well.

Another truth about the Iowa landscape, a historical and social one, is particularly clear in a car: Iowa is as much a series of townscapes as it is a pattern of farms. On the highway, it is about twenty minutes between towns, big or small; so we are always being served up a settlement at about the time we are really ready for a change of scene from corn and bean rows, frame farmhouses, and long power lines.

This regular rhythm of town-country-town is easy to take for granted, but it is in fact one of the distinctive features of the

Iowa landscape (a feature it shares with most, but not all, mid-western states). No one driving through Iowa feels that open space is a potential enemy, as anyone can when crossing the vast empty stretches between mobile-home hamlets in Wyoming or Nevada. On the other hand, you can cross Iowa's most extensive townscape, Des Moines, in less than an hour—even if all the lights are against you—and the city fairly flies by when you take the interstate. Except for a few suburbs, Iowa has no instances of the linked towns of New England, each one announced only by a city-limits sign and a date-of-incorporation marker (a pattern of settlement that allowed the Massachusetts poet Emily Dickinson to write of "a distant town/towns on from mine"), or the center-less, linked suburbs of northern and southern California. Still less familiar to Iowans is the megalopolitan pattern of massive cities joining hands at their edges, as along the Boston-Washington corridor.

One of the oldest and still liveliest American myths is that town and country are places of refuge from one another. Fear of the "surrounding wilderness" (filled with bloodthirsty Indians and animals, according to our anscestors, or infested with boors, boobs, and bores, according to the classic New York attitude) has long sustained the idea of the American city. The suburbanization of America and the vacation industry, on the other hand, are modern footnotes to the Jeffersonian idea of the countryside as the true home of virtue and the refuge of the threatened and harried city dweller. For the Iowan, city/town and country give way to one another, gently and easily; people move readily between the two. Does this mean that Iowans don't feel the difference? One person to ask is the gentleman often met in town, the retired farmer, who has a major adjustment to make when he moves off the farm and into the upper floor of a frame house in a hamlet of two hundred people. It doesn't matter to him that a New Yorker might mistake his entire town for a turkey-processing plant; he doesn't care that his city cousin labels both small town and farm landscapes "rural." He knows that he lives "in town" and has had to get used to what he experiences as crowding and loss of privacy. Nor are small-town officials sheepish about calling their municipalities "cities"; the City of Burgville is no less a city, according to their system, with a population of eight thousand.

Two of the most important and perceptive writers of fiction about the Midwest interpreted landscapes similar to the Iowa norm, in accordance with both the city-versus-wilderness myth and the concrete experience of people—and came to opposite conclusions. The sometimes Iowan Hamlin Garland and Minnesota's unhappy son Sinclair Lewis both wrote about very small towns and their adjacent countryside as if the two were opposing realms.

In Garland's story "A Day's Pleasure" (from *Main-Travelled Roads,* 1891) Mrs. Delia Markham, a typically careworn inhabitant of Garland's rural "wilderness" of toil and disappointment, comes to town with her husband. He is bringing his wheat to market in the hamlet, which is nothing more than "a cluster of small frame houses and stores on the dry prairie beside a railway station." Not exactly Paris, or even Pierre, but to Mrs. Markham it is a disconcerting world of citified manners and dainty luxuries. "She grew bitter," Garland writes, "as she saw a couple of ladies pass, holding their demitrains in the latest city fashion."

Knowing no one except the local grocer, Mrs. Markham actually experiences a sort of urban alienation in this one-horse town, until a kind local woman befriends her. Mrs. Markham has her first glimpse of Mrs. Hall through the window of the Halls' "cottage" (Garland chooses the genteel word). "Two men and a woman were finishing a dainty luncheon. The woman was dressed in cool, white garments, and she seemed to make the day one of perfect comfort."

Fig. 9.1.   The roof-top view of Rolfe, Pocahontas County, is contemporaneous with Hamlin Garland's 1890s images of the town and country. The "small frame houses and stores" are not elegant, but compared to the bleak prairie beyond, they are snug and sociable. (Photo courtesy of State Historical Society of Iowa)

Altruistic Mrs. Hall and her husband, "a man of culture and progressive views," spot the bedraggled farm woman, and invite her in for a sit-down and a chat. The Halls' sitting room is a vision of luxury, calm, and good taste. "[Mrs. Markham] saw everything—the piano, the pictures, the curtains, the wallpaper, the little tea stand. They were almost as grateful to her as the food and the fragrant tea. . . . She was shown all the pictures and the books." Refreshed by food and human sympathy, Mrs. Markham returns to "the world of corn and stubble" with a lighter heart.

Hamlin Garland was a farm boy who perhaps never outgrew his fascination with town, and he wrote at a time when the midwestern small town was in its prime as a symbol of what was most distinctive and best about American civilization. When town-born Sinclair Lewis wrote, a generation later in the age of H. L. Mencken, the American ideal of the good life was becoming metropolitan, composed of equal parts urban sophistication and suburban nature worship. Lewis looked at the world of the small-town bourgeoisie—at the pictures, curtains, tea stands, and the "men of culture and progressive views"—and found nothing but pettiness and fraudulence. *Main Street* (1920), the tale of Carol Kennicott's wary coming to terms with Gopher Prairie, Minnesota, and its assorted prigs and pretenders to culture, also makes an absolute split between town and country, the other way. Lewis's countryside does not produce dust and sweat; here the stubble is transformed into emerald. When Carol and Will, her doctor husband, return from Will's rural rounds, the landscape through which they pass is so idyllic that it comes supplied with the gentle cattle of English pastoral poetry:

> They drove home under the sunset. Mounds of straw, and wheatstacks like bee-hives, stood out in a startling rose and gold, and the green-tufted stubble glistened. As the vast girdle of crimson darkened, the fulfilled land became autumnal in deep reds and browns. The black road before the buggy turned to a faint lavender, then was blotted to uncertain greyness. Cattle came in a long line up to the barred gates of the farmyards, and over the resting land was a dark glow.
>
> Carol had found the dignity and greatness which had failed her in Main Street.

While these writers, working generations ago for a largely metroplitan audience, cannot speak for Iowans today, they undoubtedly helped to further and create attitudes toward the midwestern landscape that still affect us today. They both understood the retired farmer's intuition that town (even a very small town) and country are different realms. No matter how familiar we may be with both realms, we probably feel both sides of the ambivalence we see in these writers. The country is a world of hard, dull work, and the town means Friday night fun; the country is open spaces, freedom to drive, and the town is a world of cops, judges, and zoning regulations. The town is where the best people live, and God knows what goes on out in the country; the country is full of honest neighbors and the town is nothing but a Peyton Place. Two forms and visions of freedom; two forms and visions of order.

These writers also understand their worlds well enough to imply that town and country rely upon one another. Mr. Markham has to bring his crop to town to market it. Gopher Prairie isn't big enough to sustain Dr. Will Kennicott's practice, so he must seek patients beyond its borders. In our own uneasy day, hard times out on the county roads have the power to close banks and implement dealerships in town, and to starve the merchants on the square who look forward to a quick influx of country cash on Friday nights, when the stores stay open and there is a game at the high school. In fact, to support the idea of town and country as distinct and mutually dependent realms, we don't have to look much further than the often tragic history of the relations between farmers and town merchants of all kinds.

Now if two realms exist, there must be a border between them. And if the two realms differ psychologically, we must be able to register a border between them in our heads, too. The enjoyment of a familiar landscape is always partly an exploration of what is out there—the clues to life and history that the land itself provides—and partly an exploration of what is inside us—what seems characteristic of a place to us and how we know what sort of place this is. A project that can teach us to look at the Iowa landscape with a keen eye, and thereby discover things we seldom look for and usually pass over completely, is the seemingly simple one of finding the line between town and country.

Looking For the Border

At first this sounds like an easy enough task. You pass the city limits sign, and you are in town. And in statutory terms, so you are. But what about the mammoth Ben Franklin store you passed before you reached the sign? And the motorcycle dealership and the ranch-style houses? Are they part of your basic image of the country? Do they "belong" to the landscape of farm and field?

Answer "yes" to this question and you will immediately be perplexed by the fact that the same kind of landscape—the auto-oriented landscape of the "strip"—continues inside the city limits until you reach the first of the tidy houses that tell you for certain that you are in an elderly, orderly, Iowa small town. We "feel" that something that is no longer the country is happening before we come to the city limit sign; the statutory boundary of the town, we begin to suspect, is not the only one.

It makes good sense, then, for us to begin our search for the real edge of town right in the middle of land that is one hundred percent rural. Classic Iowa farmland, ten miles or so from, let's say, the eastern city limit of a town of eight thousand souls. We are traveling on a two-lane U.S. highway, and what we see all around us are tall farmhouses set in windbreak groves a little way from the highway. Barns sag in many of the farmyards, their jobs taken over by pole-building machine sheds and tall grain bins. There are not many billboards out here, and very rare is the farmstead that addresses the passerby with a homemade sign touting produce or live bait. Unlike the semisuburban rural landscape, of, say, central New Jersey—where farmers' markets abound, anxious to attract the eyes of passing suburbanites and junketing city people—the rural landscape, like the Iowa farmer himself, goes about the business of the day without wasted words, releasing information about itself in small, laconic bits aimed mainly at the locals and the like-minded. The Prairie Rose Church of God invites worshippers. This is a Funk's "G" field. You are crossing Elm Creek. This is not a landscape that is selling itself.

The first solid hint we have that we are approaching a town is a green mileage sign, erected by the state, but by now so standardized across the United States that it is practically a reminder of the presence of the federal government as well. Mileage listings for towns farther on remind us that our town takes its place in the regular succession of settlements, large and small, along this highway. We are in an impersonal zone that says "a town is coming" but gives no hint of the character of that town. Farms still line both sides of the road. We pass a Highway Patrol radio relay tower, a reminder that the town is a small but vital center of information and jurisprudence. This very outer edge of town represents a change in the nature of the information that the landscape is giving us, from the private messages the countryside provides (and the countryside is the realm of the private, you are always on "somebody's land") to public messages addressed to all citizens. The town is always an outpost of a larger authority, always part of a network. The country isolates, the town brings together: in the marketplace (or, in Iowa terms, "on the square"), information, as well as goods, is exchanged, and people experience themselves as part of a community of people observing one another.

As we continue, something subtle begins to happen to the still-rural landscape. Within an evergreen windbreak we discover not a two-story frame house, many-windowed and painted white, but a trim ranch-style house of blonde brick dating from the 1960s. This is no surprise in itself, since there are a few ranch-style houses deep in the country too. But this farmstead has only one outbuilding—a steel pole-building replica of an old-fashioned stable. Near the road a wrought-iron sign reads "Green Acres." This is the home of a physician who does some farming and raises horses for a hobby. It is the first evidence we have that an Iowa small town can reproduce suburbia with some subtlety. Here at another edge of town we have the beginning of a small "gentry" zone that, in its way, corresponds not to tract-house, developers' suburbia, but to the stately, horsey, nearly rural suburbia of central New Jersey or Connecticut.

Fig. 9.2.   A "gentry" house off U.S. 63 south of Ottumwa. The white wooden fence seems imported from Kentucky blue-grass country, and it and the decorative shutters advertise the owner's superiority to the merely utilitarian values responsible for the woven-wire fence in front of the adjoining field. (Photo by Robert F. Sayre)

Across the highway another gentry house appears—this one without attached outbuildings. This architecturally ambitious, rambling, multilevel, seventies-style house is stained (not painted) dark brown, with more than one large window. Another local professional is displaying his awareness of contemporary taste.

If this really were Connecticut, or Tiburon, California, or West Des Moines, or any other place that supports extensive and exclusive residential areas, the gentry zone could easily isolate itself from less handsome, less permanent, and less imaginatively designed buildings. But not at the edge of an Iowa town. Here, as elsewhere in the small community, different classes simply cannot get out of each other's lines of sight. Just a short way up the road, within sight of our gentry families, another kind of landscape begins. At first it seems like a simple continuation of the farm-scape—white and red pole-buildings that could easily be farm machine sheds. Above them rise the struts, pipes, and chutes of an elevator/grain dealer, and as we approach we see the bright logos of a farm-implement company on one of the pole buildings. The look of these structures reminds us of the farm, but their appearance is indubitable evidence that a town is coming. These businesses are good emblems of the edge of town, of the "independent" American farmers' dependence, not only upon the rural community but upon huge business concerns far from home, the implement and fertilizer and herbicide giants. These utilitarian structures are the most important places in that part of the edge of town where town and country meet to trade, and they speak very eloquently of the postwar transformation of Iowa agriculture. Here, farmers have been meeting the future of their science for forty years.

Fig. 9.3.   *A grain elevator, like this one on the edge of Dike, Grundy County, is indubitable evidence that a town is coming. (Photo by James Hippen)*

The buildings themselves are excellent embodiments of the values of the rural culture that has grown up in this period of time. The pole structures speak to the farmers' love of understatement, functionalism, and all-round lack of nonsense (a very old trait), while they also betray the fascination with rural science, progress, and innovation. They look like laboratories and factories at the same time (as the elevator buildings do)—and they come from far away. Products of large corporations, the buildings come pretested and prerecommended, as well as prefabricated. And they are cheap and fast to put up, emblems of the replacement of the ideal of craftsmanship with the industrial ideal, way out here in the country.

Another edge-of-town building comes into view (this is one you can see again and again)—the Former Farmhouse, which once stood proudly by itself, the overlord of its adjacent land, but which now has been surrounded by edge-of-town businesses. It always stands out. It is too tall for this part of town—the size of the big houses on Main Street—but unlike them it is painted white. Often it has been subdivided into apartments or turned into a retail building with apartments on top. It is across the street from the city limit sign and the 45-mph warning, which are on the same pole.

Fig. 9.4. Another edge-of-town building—the Former Farmhouse—like this one, on the edge of Fairfield. (Photo by Robert F. Sayre)

Just inside the city limits stands the Former Farmhouse's cousin, the Former Barn. Like many, this one has been customized and converted into yet another important kind of edge-of-town business, the combination LP-gas, air-conditioning, and refrigerator dealership. This is a business with both town and country customers, like the gas stations that come in a cluster now, and the café. The 45-mph zone always brings us a more crowded landscape, cluttered with signs—a landscape that belongs to the automobile and which increasingly speaks of what town and country people share—an interest in food, fuel, hardware, motorcycles, shock absorbers, and other practical things. Here the countryman is most comfortable as a townsman, and the town dweller, as he walks through the Tractor Supply Company store in search of garden fertilizer, is closest to his country cousin.

This confusing zone is often home to some of the most exuberant edge-of-town structures, and we ought to slow down to enjoy them—the Fun Houses. They are the funkier cousins of the houses of the gentry zone. Like them, they have usually been given a name (or, we should note to be strictly accurate, the gentry-zone dweller names his *land,* while the Fun House owner names his *house*—"The Ponderosa" or "Gene's Hideout"). Unlike them, they have been decorated cheerfully and chaotically, with rickety trellises choked with vines, or with hubcaps nailed up here and there. There is half a wagon wheel on either side of the entrance. Oversize wooden cardinals (birds, not Catholic prelates), plastic flamingoes, little "colored" horse-handlers in plaster, and tractor tires turned into planters complete this pleasant and disorganized picture. The closeness of this boisterous statement of individualism to the sober, businesslike elevator and implement buildings is another surprise on the edge of town.

Fig. 9.5. Yard "ornaments" of a Fun House, one of the most exuberant edge-of-town structures. (Photo by Robert F. Sayre)

We pass a 25-mph sign, notifying us of the official beginning of a residential zone. Rows of ornamental trees often overhang the highway. The trees at the edge of town are few and far between, but these are grand old trees with good growth.

We have come into town. But where was the border? At the mileage sign? The gentry houses? The elevator?

It is easier not to decide for the moment. What we do know is that to the categories of town (stately houses, shady yards, town square) and country (clusters of buildings on a green ocean) we have to add a third that is neither, but draws its definition, like a clever opportunist, from both. It is a zone, disorganized, visually confusing, and paradoxical. It is plain and fancy. It is utilitarian and yet it tries to be impressive. It is individualistic and anonymous. It makes us aware of change more readily than permanence. We need to learn a little of its biography.

A Postwar Landscape

As we pass through town, we cannot help noticing the calm orderliness and the sense of permanence that have made "Main Street USA" an archetype. The shuttered stores and sorry-looking antique shops that have replaced the once prosperous businesses here and there testify to hard times, but they do not introduce disorder, only tension and sadness.

The landscape scholar D. W. Meinig, in an essay called "Symbolic Landscapes," (in *The Interpretation of Ordinary Landscapes,* 1980) describes the classic midwestern small town and analyzes it as an expression of permanent American ideals, while also noting in a memorable paragraph the pressures that modern times bring to bear upon it.

> Created during the canal and early railroad age of the mid-19th century such landscapes were readily adapted to accommodate the electric interurbans and street cars of the turn of the century. Early automobiles were also quickly and proudly incorporated, but in time the automobile proved much too powerful to be contained and domesticated within such a landscape. It was such a revolutionary instrument, so penetrating and pervasive in its impact on American society, that it created its own landscape, its own physical and social form of community.

Meinig uses this paragraph to introduce his discussion of another archetypal American landscape, the California automobile suburb. Yet even in the small town of the prairieland, the auto created "its own landscape" in the only place it could—the edge of town. Let's continue our imaginary journey westward through our town of eight thousand, on out to the "strip" on the west side. The first thing we notice is that there is more "action" out this way. Indeed, small towns have very uneven border zones. From the east, the zone was relatively short; but here on the west side there are many more businesses and an altogether more urban feel. One reason is that the next town on the highway is much larger and there is a well-traveled corridor between the two communities. Another is the truism that success breeds success; the west side has been a lucky location for generations — it is prosperous while the other sides remain hard-luck cases year after year.

Gas stations, which we have seen here and there all the way through town, now seem to take over. Their bright oversize signs set the tone of what we can see is the beginning of the business zone that has the motorist in mind. First come large groceries with plenty of parking space — establishments that are halfway between the little privately run convenience shops in town (often on side streets) and the mammoth supermarkets we will see farther out on the highway. These stores are not doing well in an era that favors the big and the small ends of the retail grocery business — the Hy-Vees and the Caseys. These are town businesses, of course; and as we move farther west, we re-enter that zone where the local townsman, the local farmer, the long-haul trucker, the traveling family, and the total stranger to Iowa (or America) can all feel reasonably at home. Even a Japanese can recognize the McDonald's sign out here on the strip, and the New Yorker can buy the same burger that is available at 28th Street and Eighth Avenue or Times Square. But while many of the signs are familiar, the landscape is "wilder," more open and improvisatory — a straight line west, nothing like the tight little box of the town square. The square sometimes feels like a stage set with a bandstand or courthouse. It is a place where you circulate and are seen, where you are basically on display. Here there is a rough and ready democracy of businesses and atmospheres: a sorry little well-drilling establishment sits next to the outlet of a multimillion-dollar fast-food chain. It is a landscape through which people pass in the relative safety and anonymity of their cars, usually going at brisk speeds. On the square you are practically required to stop and talk; out here, you keep going.

As early as 1929 a writer in the *American Builder* called the structures that were springing up along the American highways "a completely new architectural form." He was referring to things like tourist courts, ancestors of today's motels, that had sprung up in the West and South in the late twenties; to gasoline service stations, which by the twenties were no longer humble appendages to grocery stores and stables but had turned into elaborate and often fanciful structures, decked out in Art Deco or classical decor; and to increasingly elaborate roadside eating places.

Since it was only in the later 1930s that some of Iowa's major highways were fully paved, it wasn't until the postwar years that these "new architectural forms" made a real impact upon the state. It was part of a general transformation that saw farms expand and electrify (with an accompanying decrease in the number of farm buildings), small towns seek new industries (often through local consortiums that banded together to buy edge-of-town land for industrial parks), and Iowans travel farther and farther for employment, entertainment, and the sheer pleasure of being on the road.

The small-town strip as it existed up until the late 1960s was generally a scattering of small, independent, locally owned businesses: motels, small eateries, gas stations whose designs were standardized by oil company policy but which were owned by local entrepreneurs. Writing in 1957, John Brinkerhoff Jackson described strip merchants as the "smallest of small businessmen."

The picture is quite different today. The strip is dominated by the large and easily recognizable logos of national chains. While earlier strip businesses attracted the motorist with lively names and eye-catching architecture (the Astro Motel, complete with a star on the roof), today's rely upon name recognition and the promise of a standardized product that can be trusted. Once in a while we see a reminder of the earlier era—a garish drive in, long out of business, with weeds growing around its pink pillars. The newer chain franchises are designed with restraint—low-slung, California-suburban good taste with brown and red predominating, and the grounds nicely landscaped. Establishments like this do not promise adventure and surprise to a confident, optimistic public; they assure wary consumers that what they are getting is safe, wholesome, and predictable.

Of course this is Iowa, not just the generic strip, so we recognize a few old friends, too. Here, trapped between a Best Western and a gas station, is the Town Farmhouse. The five cars and three motorcycles parked in front show that the huge structure, once home to a big family, is now divided among young singles. Everywhere we look, pole-buildings serve a whole universe of different functions. The identical structure can house a veterinary clinic in one place, a well-drilling concern in another, and elsewhere can house, appropriately enough, the local office of a pole-building company.

A structure with the characteristic stairstep roof and white brick construction of an old feed store ("Peck's Grain" has been

painted out in white above the entrance) is now something called
"Wheels Galore"—a shop where you can buy secondhand lawn-
mowers, roto-tillers, garden tractors, boat hitches, and dirt bikes.
A big former gas station nearby is now a pest-control place.

*Fig. 9.6.   This second-hand automobile lot appears
to have taken over a former grain and seed store. But
behind the false front it is a former barn. (Photo by
Robert F. Sayre)*

To appreciate what was and what is now, you need to get
out of the car, traipse around a bit on foot, and delve into the
history of these structures. Care must be taken, of course—the
edge of town is not designed for pedestrians, and is rarely seen at
two or three miles per hour, much less on foot.

The strip's facade of newness hides layers of the past: old
buildings reemployed, the shift of business fortunes, old ideas
superseded by new ones. A failed motel has become part of an
implement dealership (combines are parked where autos used to
line up) and no one has thought to take down the old "Motel"
sign and Diner's Club shield. The two signs are ludicrously small,
almost invisible in the surrounding visual clutter—mementos of a

time, twenty-five years ago, when there was less to see along this road.

If we venture back a ways from the edge of the highway, the basic history of the strip at the edge of town becomes very clear. Behind the implement dealership is a broken concrete silo and a caved-in shed, both choked with weeds. A stump dump from the farm that this was and piles of rusty tractor parts play host to weeds so tall that each patch looks like a miniature prairie. (Graveyards and railway rights-of-way preserve first-growth prairie, while rural junkyards of all types are good places to see what happens when once-cultivated land is reclaimed by grasses, some native, some not. There is something poetic in the way that the rusty waste of the machine age protects ancient plants from modern mowers.)

If we walk or drive far enough, we come to a place where the strip thins out and the land opens up. We feel the country coming; in fact, we can see genuine farms ahead. But we are actually in another border zone — strip-becomes-country. This is the land of the county fairgrounds; the lonely trailer park, bounded on two sides by cornfields; the dirt-bike track and the industrial park lined with pole-buildings (some with brick or false stone facing on the front). These structures may beckon the motorist, but only half-heartedly. Signs grow small — the reserve of the country is taking over. Businesses are set away from the highway in the vastness that eventually turns into that impersonal final edge of town with its resume-speed signs, signs giving mileage to the next three towns, power lines that come up from underground, and lonely radio towers carrying disembodied voices far out into the country.

Living on the Edge

There are, of course, more edges to town than the ones we see from a well-traveled highway. Along the strip, whether it is modest or crowded, we get only intermittent glimpses of the residential borders of town. We have already noted the Gentry Zone and the Fun House as belonging to the complicated landscape of the main roadway, but Gentry and Fun houses abound on the quieter roads into town as well — the county roads that enter obscure quarters of town in obedience to the grid pattern in which they are laid out.

On these quieter edges we can see something that probably ought to be an anomaly in an Iowa town: suburbia. In his 1980 book *Prairie City, Iowa,* Doug Bauer, one of the most careful observers of the Iowa landscape, wrote these words about the very small town of Prairie City:

> Most of the new homes in Prairie City fill the far north end of town, a thick residential finger off the flat square palm. In the north end, low ranch houses run end to end over several blocks, a tract with all the proud banality of a genuine suburb; it could easily adjoin any city.

Any observer of the end of an Iowa town with more than two thousand people is bound to find one or more such apparent transplants from the fringes of Chicago or Cheyenne. Rising up next to corn and bean fields, decorated with immature, spindly trees, and often laid out, in defiance of the universal rural grid, with winding streets, these suburbs are never older than the 1960s, and they are still being built.

Richard Lingeman's characterization of this process in *Small-Town America* (1979) is so apt and succinct that it is worth quoting at length:

> [Typically,] development consisted of growing jigsaw-puzzle tracts around the edge of town filled with rows of ranches and split-levels built by local contractors for local people yearning for the "country," a larger plot of land, and a more modish house with a picture window and a dishwasher, instead of an old but sound frame house with a front porch in town. Small towns developed mini-suburbs, a kind of middle-age spread, while their centers decayed. Farmers discovered it was more profitable to plant houses on their acres than corn, and they roundly opposed zoning restrictions as abridgements of their freedom to use their property as they pleased. They could sell an acre of land for a house for quadruple the money they would get selling it as farmland.

By 1978, according to the Department of Agriculture, three million acres of prime farmland nationwide were being lost to suburban development every year.

The presence of suburbia in small-town America testifies to a number of things at once: first of all, to the persistence of commercial land development in the shaping of the small-town landscape; after all, railway and other commercial land companies put the majority of Iowa communities on the map in the first place. Then there is the sheer prestige of the suburban mode of land use and life. Those who choose to live in this style at the edge of town are not fleeing decaying city centers or rampant pollution; a life in the center of a small Iowa town is closer to the countryside than most "genuine" suburbanites get. Rather, the ranch-style house with the attached garage; the contrived, bosky-sounding street name ("Oak Knoll Circle"); and the "countrified" curving roadway are all parts of a national cultural complex that is very compelling. The Iowan (always touchy at being considered backward) who moves into small-town suburbia is not getting away from it all — he is getting *into* a mainstream. The small-town neighborhood never appears on television, except in period pieces; the national media are scarcely aware that people still live on the checkerboard streets of small towns and small cities. But suburbia *is* an image, in auto ads, in pitches for weed control concoctions, and in dramatic series; the Iowa suburbanite suddenly discovers that in media terms, he possesses a lifestyle. And finally, the small-town suburb testifies to the strength of the idea with which we began — that town and country really are different realms. To move seven blocks toward the cornfields is in fact to edge near another vision of life, not just to occupy another neighborhood.

Edge-of-Town Values

The young family who occupies a tract house from which it can see silos and pole buildings has made a symbolic choice as well as an economic and social one. It may be only dimly aware of the dimensions of this symbolic choice, and no wonder; they are hard to get a handle on. But where we live is generally the best possible compromise between where we can afford to live and where we want to live, and the values lie in the "want."

The suburb, even in a tiny town, is that much closer to what the townspeople may see as the freedom and health of the countryside. Does this mean that the suburbanite wants the decidedly unhealthy life of the farmer, subjected to chemical poisoning and farm-machine accidents? Or the decidedly unfree life of farm routine? No, he wants the symbolic health of the country-side, as it has been passed down to us by Romantic poets, by Henry David Thoreau, and by the traditional promotion of suburban America, in which "the country" is cheerful, wild nature, not the hard-working and sometimes hazardous rural landscape of a place like Iowa. The fact is that the edge of town provides a rural backdrop, a *visual* countryside, equally removed from the traditions of the center of town (with its old houses, its square, its gentle sense of backwardness) and the realities of farm life.

To say this brings up the whole question of the edge of town as a symbolic landscape. What does it mean to be there? To be a part of it? For many people and many businesses, it means logical, even necessary convenience. The gas station, the elevator, the implement dealership, locate themselves at the boundary of two realms to transact business with both. Other edge-of-town structures seem to have more intriguing reasons to be where they are. The pole-building nightclub, near the elevators and the welding shops, is there because it requires a certain aura of anonymity; its patrons may have good reasons for not wanting to go to their cars under the watchful eyes of center-of-town folk. The graveyard is on the edge because nineteenth-century fashions in graveyard design put it there, as a public park instead of as a small appendage to a churchyard. The owner of the Fun House has escaped the conformist atmosphere of the center of town but has not yet reached the country, where a bizarre house would come under the scrutiny of the coffee-shop crowd, who are used to judging an operation by the look of it.

Fig. 9.7.   The pole-building nightclub, whose small windows promise anonymity, while its old wagon wheels and "Home Cooked Noon Special" promise old-fashioned friendliness. (Photo by Robert F. Sayre)

In fact, all of the inhabitants of the edge of town, which we have called a zone with its own identity, sit poised between two slow-to-change landscapes: that of the town, where custom rules gently but firmly, and the country, where the ideals are (and must be) utilitarian. The edge is a place where it is all right to experiment a little because no one knows exactly what the rules are. This is a zone of transience, where strangers are most likely to be found, climbing out of big rigs or loaded station wagons. Not surprisingly, it is also a place where the larger entity called corporate America is most obviously felt. The strip businesses come and go — and their logos get bigger and more "national" as the years pass. With the American genius for adaptation and re-use, edge-of-town buildings are recycled, the changes reflecting two concurrent trends: upscaling to big franchises and downscaling to ever-more-precarious businesses such as second-hand shops and auto repair places.

The distinctiveness of the midwestern small town as well as the characteristic rural landscape of the region have made them both "classic" in the minds of Americans. The conservatism inherent in both landscapes has frustrated many, while at the same time holding off what many see as the homogenization of the American landscape at the hands of developers and corporations. The conservative powers of the two great landscapes and ways of life are at their weakest at the edge of the Iowa town — where space is open both for individuals and quite impersonal forces of change that are similar everywhere in the country. At the edge, the American desire for a sphere of personal freedom (which requires some anonymity) meets the big corporations, and we see very vividly the interaction between the two, which goes so far to account for the flavor of American life.

Finally, when we consider what is special about the Iowa landscape, it may be that the most significant contrast is not, after all, between town and country, but between the landscape of continuity (the center of town and the heart of the county) and the landscape of improvisation, change, and an unstable combination of impersonal and personal values — the edge of town.

10

FARM TOWNS
&
FACTORY TOWNS

James Hippen

The Industrial Revolution lies easy on the Iowa landscape. Tall corn and fat cows are more prominent than slag heaps and tall chimneys. Certainly there are some monumental industrial enterprises, such as the Quaker Oats plant at Cedar Rapids or the various John Deere factories scattered over eastern Iowa. And they can be dramatically visible: Quaker Oats on the banks of the Cedar River is in a grand setting, and for anyone a few decades old the scene is made more impressive by knowing that that is where the cereal was "shot from guns." This large-scale concentration of industry is limited to relatively few Iowa counties, and in them to the larger cities, and that is the way it has been throughout most of the history of the state. But most of Iowa's people are somewhere else—out in the towns and countryside. (Almost two-thirds live in places with a population of less than twenty thousand; half of Iowa's ninety-nine counties have no town as large as five thousand.) These towns, naturally, have always been service centers for agriculture; they also have been the "frontier" of the Industrial Revolution, where farms and factories have met. The results are varied and fascinating.

Evidence of past industrial activity can be found in surviving buildings and structures, in the very layout of towns, and even in the absence of parts of the landscape—quarried or mined and shipped away. Take as an example Stone City on the western edge of Jones County, a few miles west of Anamosa. Here, along both banks of the Wapsipinicon River, lies an area of yellowish limestone called by the early quarry masters the "Stratified Stone

Basin." The army used the stone for bridges in territorial days (statehood was in 1846), and the quarries supplied materials for Cornell College at Mt. Vernon in the 1850s. But a substantial market for what Stone City could produce had to await the arrival of the Dubuque Western Railroad in 1860. Each of the latter decades of the nineteenth century saw new quarries, and their names conjure up associations with gold-rush days in the far west. There was Mt. Hope, Champion No. 1 and No. 2, Crow Creek, and even Gold Hill, which, despite the name, presumably never yielded anything other than good building stone. By 1910 over 200,000 railroad carloads of stone had been shipped within Iowa and to seven other midwestern states. John A. Green, the dominant figure in the business at the time, could pronounce that "it is safe to say" that the quarries "will last for time immemorial."

It did not work out quite that way. New methods of building in steel and concrete made stone construction structurally obsolete, or at least too expensive for most projects because of labor costs. A population that was at one thousand in the 1890s has dwindled to a few score; one quarry, the Weber Stone Company, is still in operation. The railroad is gone, and trees cover many traces of the past. But a visitor can still make many connections with the great days of quarrying.

Fig. 10.1.   Weber Stone Quarry, the only Stone City quarry still operating. (Photo by James Hippen)

At first glance one is struck most by the dozen or so fine stone houses that cluster along the road, by the dramatically situated stone church and the stone hotel, and the Weber Quarry where fresh cut stone is piled for shipment. On the lawn across from the quarry entrance are several large stone letters. They face the old railroad right-of-way, perhaps so passengers could see them while the locomotive took on water from the tank (visible in Grant Wood's 1930 painting Stone City), which proclaims that this was the quarry of H. Dearborn and Sons. Crossing the Wapsipinicon, one passes a marooned Milwaukee Road caboose, marking the former site of the rails that had provided the key transportation link to the midwestern market. Farther along the road there are other stone buildings. One is engraved as part of the Champion Quarry, the enterprise started by John A. Green, who came from Ireland to Boston in 1844, cut stone for bridges for the Union Pacific Railroad in the 1860s, and in 1868 arrived at the Anamosa Quarries (renamed Stone City in 1873). Green prospered, built a mansion (stone, of course) and a hotel-opera house, and was elected to the state legislature. By the time he died in 1920 stone cutting had almost stopped in Stone City. Now his mansion is a ruin hidden by trees, and the hotel is gone. There are some buildings—the great stone barn of the Champion Quarries is one—which are still visible above the summer growth. The landscape itself is a lot greener now than in Green's day, and most of the scarred hillsides that were the signs of former prosperity are hard to see.

Fig. 10.2. Stone houses in Stone City, with new bridge over Wapsipinicon River. (Photo by James Hippen)

*Fig. 10.3.   The castlelike administration building of
the State Reformatory at Anamosa used limestone
from Stone City. (Photo by Bob Campagna)*

One abandoned quarry that is accessible is one of the earliest: the Mt. Hope at the west end of the Stratified Stone Basin, just over the county line. Started in 1852 the diggings were closed before 1900. The area is now the Mount Hope Public Use Area of the Linn County Conservation Board; the gravel road that runs past the old Champion Quarry reaches the entrance. As one drives in, the former railroad spur curves to the right along the river bank, and then the access road joins the roadbed and leads to the quarry floor. The methodical, massive, and effective efforts involved in supplying the materials for the engineering and architecture of a new country are revealed in what is not there, in what has been removed. From a remarkably flat, smooth surface of dark stone, the visitor looks up the vertical walls topped by overhanging trees. It is a sight that would satisfy a nineteenth-century tourist's hunger for the picturesque, although it never was so composed then as now. And it is also a great spot for a picnic.

Returning to the east, the newest structure in Stone City calls to mind the short-lived art school operated in the 1930s by Grant Wood and associates. Located at the road junction just south of St. Joseph's Church, it is a false-front, 1987-vintage replica of the backdrop to the dour couple in Wood's American Gothic. The wooden gothic revival facade is attached to a metal building (the original house that inspired Wood was a hundred miles away). Such is the power of art and of the hope for tourist revenue to shape the present and distort the past.

Other than the art school, Stone City's fortunes have been tied to the quarries. This economic vulnerability is usually the case with towns that depend on a single industry—and the situation is most precarious when that industry is involved in the extraction of raw materials. There are exceptions, such as Dubuque, where the famous lead mines worked since the eighteenth century provided a start for what is now the sixth largest city in Iowa. An example of the other sort, where time has snuffed out the entrepreneurial flame but left a magnificent ruin, is Hurstville, just north of Maquoketa in Jackson County.

There, in a park off Highway 61, are the nicely restored remains of the great lime kilns that were Hurstville's reason for being. Lined up against a bluff, the stone structures are a perfect example of much of the industrial effort of the last century. They are the remains of an operation that was not truly mechanized, just very well organized in the light of lessons apparent in the dominant nineteenth-century system of factory manufacture and railway transportation. Limestone was quarried in the hills above the kilns, crushed, and dumped in at the tops of the large furnaces. At the bottom, on the sides, men stoked the fires with wagonloads of wood brought in every morning by scores of farmers, while from the central, lowest door the calcined rock was dumped to be packed in barrels for shipment on the railroad. The visitor can easily follow this process at the site, and a climb up the stairs to the top of the kilns is worth it. Some of the old crusher buildings can be seen, and the internal size of the stone chimneys is impressive. The only structures missing from the complex are the wooden sheds that enclosed the processing floors at the base of the kilns. Nearby was a row of workers' houses and also a cooperage to provide the barrels, which at peak capacity were filled at the rate of one thousand per day.

Yet, just as at Stone City, the early years of this century saw a fatal decline in the works. Alfred Hurst, the founder, died in 1915, and the plant closed in 1920. Contributing factors to the ending of the business were demands for types of lime that required new and expensive machinery and the rising cost of packing materials. There also must have been a growing shortage of wood in the area, both for fuel (used at the rate of close to ten thousand cords per year) and barrels (manufactured at up to five hundred per day). At the turn of the century the enterprise had been the largest producer of lime west of Chicago, but within two decades it had lost all hope of retaining a place in the regional market. The reputation of the company died hard, though, for one finds a listing in a national builders' trade directory in 1919 for "A. Hurst, Est[ate]" as one of the three lime manufacturers in Iowa.

Fig. 10.4. The restored remains of the lime kilns in Hurstville, "a perfect example of much of the industrial effort of the last century." (Photo by James Hippen)

If the business histories of Hurstville and Stone City seem roughly parallel, so do the careers of the chief entrepreneurs, John A. Green and Alfred Hurst. Born in England in 1841, Hurst came to New Orleans in about 1850. After settling in Davenport, Iowa, he fought in the Union army, returned to Davenport after the Civil War, and learned the trade of brick and plaster mason. In 1870 he started his lime kilns north of Maquoketa and founded his town. Hurst, as did Green, even served for a time in the state legislature.

Men like these were clever and talented and in the right place at the right time. Iowa's population growth was extraordinary, although, of course, not unusual by frontier standards:

1850	192,214
1860	674,913
1870	1,194,020
1880	1,624,615
1890	1,912,297
1900	2,231,853

Two aspects of these figures are worth noting. First, the sheer rate of growth meant a rapidly increasing market for all sorts of basic building materials. In the decade before Hurst and Green (our representative entrepreneurs) opened their businesses, the population of the state almost doubled, and in the next ten years it increased by thirty-six percent. The second point is that even though the percentage increase declined in each decade, the actual increase in numbers of people was still in the hundreds of thousands. (1870–1880: 430,595; 1880–1890: 287,682; 1890–1900: 319,556.) So the markets were not only increasing rapidly, the markets were large. And the surrounding states, not just Iowa, consumed the products of quarry and kiln.

The railroad was essential to any selling area much larger than a county, and facilities were soon available. Stone City had a line by the early 1860s, and nearby Anamosa was reached by a second company in 1870. Maquoketa had service from one railroad in 1870 and a second by 1872; in 1889 a spur was built directly to Hurstville. This opened the midwestern regional market to the Iowa producers, but the corresponding expansion of the rail system all over the Midwest made that market available to competing firms as well. Stone City declined not as a result of competition in quarrying stone, but from the competition of a new building technology. The demise of the Hurstville kilns was a direct result of the inability to compete in a regional market.

Hurstville, like Stone City, survives today in greatly diminished form. Only two miles from Maquoketa, it is now a suburb without an industry of its own, and it is the site of one of the finest industrial artifacts in the state. Yet, regardless of the solidity of the great stone kilns, the visitor standing before them is haunted by an inescapable awareness of the vulnerability of towns founded on a single extractive industry.

The classic case for this kind of rise and fall in America is coal mining; who has not seen photographs of desolate Appalachia with barefoot kids shuffling through coal slack, the only remains of departed prosperity! Iowa, too, has its coal counties and mining towns. Two of these towns, Mystic and Centerville, are in Appanoose County, one of the southern tier counties along the Missouri line. The fortunes of both were tied to coal, and both shared in the decline of the mines. However, their paths to the present diverged, so that today we find them in quite different circumstances indeed.

Centerville, the county seat, was founded in 1846–1847. Development was slow at first, but in 1871 the first railroad reached town, which then made it possible to sell coal to more than a local market. By 1880 the population (2,475) had doubled from what it was only five years before. The coal boom in Appanoose County began in earnest in the 1890s. In 1900 the production of 645,000 tons was twice that of a decade before and from 1906 to 1920 coal production in the county was well over a million tons annually. The Centerville population of 5,256 in 1900 climbed to some 8,500 in the early 1920s—the 1980 figure was 6,558.

So much for the statistics (a necessary evil that accompanies the history of the Industrial Revolution). Clearly coal mining was the major shaping influence during the growth years of Centerville. Yet today's visitor is hard put to find any physical evidence of this at all. Even though mine shafts were inside the city limits and were numerous to the west of town, the minehead buildings are all gone, the entrances closed or hidden, and the heaps of refuse coal and shale not to be found. An explanation of this latter circumstance is not out of order. The dumps were all over the county in the early twentieth century, usually smouldering away with fires fueled by the wasted coal, and smelling awful. The ever increasing numbers of automobiles were churning the local roads into mudholes. Then the two problems were mated into happy resolution in 1926 by using the dump shale, which had been baked into little chunks of brick, as road surfacing material. By the end of the 1960s the unsightly mounds were gone.

If the mines and their jobs, most of the railroads, and even the shale dumps have disappeared, what, one must ask, accounts for Centerville's survival? In common with all county seats, courthouse business is important economically. And supplying feed, seed, implements, and fertilizer to farmers is a constant of the Iowa economy, even if subject to the vicissitudes of hard times. But Centerville also has had, and still has, its factories. In the first decades after settlement these were mainly small providers of basic services in the immediate vicinity — flour and gristmills, sawmills, blacksmiths, wagon makers, etc. By the turn of the century Centerville's industry included foundries and others catering to the necessities of the mines. Then, in 1900, Miles Bateman and B. A. Fuller, two enterprising and inventive foundry workers, started to manufacture the Hercules Stump Puller. An improved steel version was patented in 1907, and orders came in from all over the United States and the world (including Russia, where the stump pullers were triumphant over all challengers in a government test). This prosperity and fame resulted in not only the need for a larger factory but offers from many larger Iowa cities for a new location. A "booster" committee of local bankers and businessmen was formed, and more than enough stock was subscribed to incorporate a new company, build a fine new plant in 1912, and keep the business in Centerville. After World War I the clearing of new land and the need for Hercules stump pullers declined, and then the Great Depression of the 1930s hit. Surviving until World War II, Hercules experienced a new prosperity, followed by a postwar sale to new owners, bankruptcy, and closure. The factory buildings are still there, deserted and forlorn, near the brand new engine house of the Appanoose County Community Railroad.

Centerville is a good example of a farm town, which has also been a mining town and a factory town. Although the mines are closed, the factories are still a part of economic and civic life. In the four decades since World War II many firms have come and gone, including a steel mill that lasted scarcely a year and a factory that made five thousand toasters a day. Efforts to encourage new industrial enterprises are a continuing necessity. For instance, the town has met the abandonment of local railroad lines by the major companies with the formation of its own connecting short line made up of fragments of the Burlington Northern and the Rock Island. An industrial park of seventy-two acres has been set aside, and today Centerville boasts of seven manufacturing plants with over a thousand employees.

Six miles away, to the northwest, is Mystic. It is a coal town, pure and simple.

The existence of a rich coal seam in the area between Walnut Creek and Little Walnut Creek was proved by the small mines in the 1850s, but it was not until 1886–1887 when the Chicago, Milwaukee, and St. Paul Railway built its extension to Kansas City on this route that large-scale exploitation was profitable. Mystic was platted in 1887; a map shows nine mines actually within the town in 1898, and by 1920 some twenty mines were in the immediate vicinity (seventy-four mines, employing 3,312, were in the whole county). There were slope mines, with a long inclined entrance tunnel; shaft mines, with a vertical shaft and a "mine cage"; and drift mines, entering a hillside seam close under the surface and requiring much timber support. All workings were best sited if they could be a "railroad" mine, that is, served directly by rail. Mine names ranged from the exotic, such as Egypt Block or Lady Mary, to the simple numbers of the Lodwick Brothers Coal Company.

To search for these mines today is amazingly difficult. The old railroad roadbeds are visible in town, but the mine entrances are not, at least in summer. (The interior of the mines would be most dangerous anyway, and none are open to the public.) But the town is there, and some of the miners and their wives and contemporaries still survive.

A few of their stories are collected in the *History of Mystic, Iowa, 1887–1987*, published by the Mystic Centennial Committee. Of twenty-four persons whose brief biographies are printed (sixteen women, eight men), eleven were born in or within three miles of Mystic and eight were born outside the United States. Eva Quist, a school teacher for fifty years and a writer, included a few pages of text as "a tribute to the miners." Her objectivity is noteworthy:

> Miners were sometimes killed by coal falling, and their crushed bodies brought home to grief-stricken families. My father was brought home to die after such an accident.

There is no way to tell what could accurately be called a typical miner's story, but let Charlie Bozwick be representative:

> I was born September 11, 1899 in . . . Iowa. I have lived in Mystic all my life. I was a coal miner and operated a mine for 42 years. Then I operated a tavern, the Friendly Tavern, in Mystic for 32 years. I married Fanny Kauzlarich and we had two children, Carl and Louise. Carl was killed in 1944 during World War II. I have 2 grandchildren, 4 great-grandchildren, and 2 great-great-grandchildren. I now reside at the Centerville Care Center.

It was, after all, the people even more than the coal and the railroad that made Mystic. When Eva Quist and Charlie Bozwick and Marcel Gerard and Rocco Nobile and Amelie Van Elst Van Vlassalaer and all the others (*all* their names deserve a place on history's roll) were in their twenties, Mystic was a booming place. Having had the town's frame business district destroyed rather completely in two fires (in 1910 and 1911), by the 1920s the residents enjoyed several blocks of new brick commercial buildings, plus Miners Hall at the west end of Main Street, where the United Mine Workers union met. (John L. Lewis was born in an adjoining county and worked in mines only a few miles from Mystic.) An interurban electric railway, built in 1910, connected Mystic with Centerville and ran seventeen round trips per day. The Milwaukee Road provided connections with the wider world, via Kansas City or Chicago, four times a day. The population of Mystic reached 2,816, its peak, in 1925. Then the Depression, the use of oil fuel in diesel locomotives, and the environmentally unacceptable nature of Iowa coal ruined the market and closed the mines. The interurban was put out of business by the automobile by 1933, and the population continued to diminish to 665 in 1980.

Fig. 10.5.   Old Miners Hall, Mystic, Appanoose County. "When you stand before it, think of working for fifty years in a coal seam two and one-half feet high, digging it out for a dollar a ton . . ." (Photo by James Hippen)

Yet Mystic, like many of its hardy older residents, is still there. There are the neat brick business blocks and Miners Hall. (When you stand before it, think of working for fifty years in a coal seam two and one-half feet high, digging it out for a dollar a ton, and in your prime years, getting out fifty tons a week.) There are the neat blocks of houses up the hill to the north of town, the feel of pressure from encroaching wilderness to the west and south, and the graceful sweeping curve of the railroad, the "Kansas City Extension," which carries only freight nowadays. A water tank, put there decades ago to serve the coal burners, survives as a lone reminder of the bustling yard that once gathered thirty or forty carloads of coal per day.

The railroad keeps cropping up as an important element in the story of these towns, for the simple reason that what a factory makes or a mine digs up has to be shipped, and shipped a long way if you are in the middle of Iowa. In the nineteenth century when the stories of nearly all of Iowa's farm and factory towns begin, shipping meant the railroads (save for the Mississippi or the Missouri). But we have been considering the railroad always as a partner in the business of a town being involved in a spreading industrial society. Could the railroad itself be an industry, a factory manufacturing transportation?

Donnan, in Fayette County, is an example. It has the distinction of being the smallest incorporated town in Iowa in the 1980 census, population ten. Perhaps never larger than the fifty-two persons, as shown in the 1925 census, Donnan seems to have had little reason for existence other than a school and the railroads. But the railroads were, in their time, a compelling reason, which may be hard to grasp today. The first right-of-way through the site of Donnan was what later became a part of the Rock Island system, built in 1872. This was crossed by a line, eventually part of the Milwaukee Road, put down in 1880. Both lines ran north from Cedar Rapids to the northeastern corner of the state, and they were surprisingly busy. In 1917 every day except Sunday (counting both lines) Donnan had *ten* passenger trains. By 1948 there were still six, although four of these were mixed freight and passenger. In 1976 both lines, by then freight only, were abandoned.

The junction was the nucleus for the town, a real town. Not everyone worked for the railroad. A score or two persons lived there, perhaps serving passengers, working on nearby farms, teaching at the school. Small though Donnan was, the residents had the benefit of being at what could be called an interface with the national culture. The whole nation was accessible to them, just as accessible as it was from Centerville or Mystic or anywhere else. Perhaps one can compare Donnan in its heyday to the cluster of filling stations and cafés found at most exits from Iowa's interstate highways. Here are today's single-purpose "towns," totally tied to transportation. They are commuter towns, thus not quite what Donnan was, for it was residential and almost totally dependent on the railroad for communication (they now have TV in addition to the road). These exit places may evolve, and like everything else connected with the interstate, they are worth observing.

At Donnan a good portion of the physical evidence is still present. The roadbeds can be traced by embankments or rows of trees; there are still marks in the highway pavement where the tracks crossed, and in the fields inside the triangle made by the junction are grass-covered culverts that once carried the other streets of Donnan. Apparently there are no railroad structures left, just houses and a school converted to another use. Yet there is one house, which although freshly sided, looks a lot like the standard Rock Island depot in eastern Iowa. Donnan is not yet gone; there are still a few people there, but it is not unfair to judge that it is no longer a town in any viable sense. It has suffered the fate of a truly "one factory" town.

In Tama County there are twin towns, which, because they are separated by about two miles, clarify certain of the elements in the farm town–factory town picture. Tama, to the south, is shaped by its location at what was the junction of the mainlines of two major trunk railroads, once competitors for the heavy east-west traffic across Iowa. Toledo, to the north, is the county seat. Both are farm towns; both, to an extent, are factory towns.

Tama, however, seems to have always had the edge on industry. The earliest rail line, now part of the Chicago and North Western, reached the site of Tama in 1862, which resulted in the founding of the town. Toledo, although bypassed by the rails, had been platted and established as the county seat nine years before. But shippers naturally favored Tama, and Toledo took ten years to accomplish the simple feat of a three-mile branch line. Meanwhile the business interests of Tama had moved ahead with a plan to bring waterpower from the Iowa River some three-and-one-half miles upstream. This project was completed in 1874; thus factories built in Tama could drive their machinery with water turbines or wheels rather than coal-fired boilers and steam engines. These advantages, plus the abundant water available for processing, led to the formation of the Tama Paper Company in 1878–1879. As if to seal the advantage of the southern town, when the Milwaukee Road built across the state in 1882 it paralleled the North Western through Tama. So Tama has remained the more "industrial" (and has always had a population advantage of at least a few hundred), Toledo the more "governmental" of the twins.

The visual evidence for the differences between the two is interesting to trace. Some of the continuities are remarkable. There is still a paper-packaging plant on the banks of the water-power reservoir. At least as far back as 1917 the North Western maintained shops for car repairs at Tama; today there is still such a facility a few blocks east of downtown. The buildings are not the same, but the basic function is. Of particular interest is the layout of the Tama business district. The Milwaukee came into town from the east running about three city blocks north of the North Western tracks, then turning south and crossing them at the west edge of town. This constricted the business district to the area in between the two railroads; thus downtown Tama has a linear arrangement, quite unlike Toledo, which like Centerville and most other county seat towns, is arranged around the court-house square. Even though the Milwaukee Road was abandoned in 1980, the roadbed through Tama is still apparent, as is its shaping influence on the town plan.

Toledo has not been without some industry, but, with one exception, it would seem always to have been small units, directed more toward the support of the local community than toward manufacturing for distribution to a wider market. When the connecting rail line was extended along Deer Creek from Tama in 1872, it ran along the west edge of Toledo, which established that part of town as the industrial district. Today it is a curious mixture of remains of past activity, and one very modern factory— the Pioneer Seed plant (being, of course, the exception noted above). The rail line was abandoned in 1981, but trucks can now supply all the services that were rendered by railroad branches in the past. Searching along the vicinity of the old roadbed, one comes across what looks like a miniature Stonehenge. The "megaliths" are the concrete supports for now absent oil tanks in a deserted petroleum distributor's yard. This artifact, in the placement of supply tanks and the arrangement of pipes and fittings, indicates in a simplified example the method and planning that is necessary for any industrialized activity. It also reminds us that another function of the town as it interfaces with the national culture is to provide an outlet for supplies and services from all the other factories in the system.

Standing apart from the industries, and standing on the next hill west of Toledo alongside Highway 30, one sees a truly fine panorama of the Iowa town. On the distant hill is the court-house surrounded by several churches and scores of houses. In the valley are the buildings of industry, past and present, with a trace of the railroad. Over Deer Creek stands a truss bridge, no longer carrying the main road, but once the almost miraculous engineering gateway to the town. Here one can appreciate how very alone the rural town is in the landscape, and how highly valued the cultural linkages provided by rail must have been in the days before the automobile and electronic communications.

After reflecting on the view of Toledo and perhaps taking a closer look at the iron bridge, one can find in the adjoining county to the southwest probably the best known factory town in Iowa, Newton, in Jasper County. Newton is the home of the Maytag washing machine company, and throughout the twentieth century Maytag has been a leading manufacturer, with their plant on West 4th Street North providing a sort of palimpsest of American industrial architecture. Viewing the north side of the complex from the vicinity of the Iowa Interstate Railroad tracks, two red brick buildings illustrate typical nineteenth-century mill architecture, with load-bearing walls and relatively small windows. Moving to the south of the plant and across the street from the main factory building, one can get a close-up view of the construction techniques common to these brick mill buildings. Note the framing of doors and windows, and any cornice trim. A full block to the east is a feed store at the northeast corner of West 3rd Street North and North 3rd Avenue West. Here is a rather scruffy but easily studied example of ceramic hollow tile, in vogue in the early years of the twentieth century. Also note the rails in the paving and the loading dock. Finally, turn again for a view of the Maytag plant. The main building in the southeast corner, several stories high with large window areas, is typical of reinforced concrete frame construction, with curtain walls or windows between. All of these structures fit into the main sequence of American factory buildings, although ceramic tile may be more common in areas where many silos were sold.

Most Iowa towns with factories do not look like their eastern counterparts. In New England, for example, the great textile mill complexes seem fixed in place, rooted to the bank of some cascading river or dark mill pond. The eastern mill town looks permanent, even when decayed. The Iowa farm town or factory town could become just plain farm without continued planning and nurturing of desired industries. What, after all, defines a town? It is not just some specific number of people concentrated in one spot. They have to be concentrated for a purpose. Farm towns are towns that serve farmers and are in close proximity to the farms. Nearly every nonsuburban town in Iowa fits this description. A town is also a factory town if it produces something for a larger market, from quarried stone to washing machines, paper to breakfast cereal. And here is where the ingenuity comes in. Iowans have never wanted to be only farmers. Like other Americans, they have been quite ingenious in finding other sources of income and ways of getting ahead; and looking for industrial artifacts in small towns will turn up the evidence.

Fig. 10.6. Pediment sculpture on the First Newton National Bank, in Newton, showing industry and agriculture coming together beside the goddess of plenty: an emblem of the hopes of the Iowa farm town–factory town. (Photo by James Hippen)

11

MISSISSIPPI
RIVER TOWNS

Loren N. Horton and Robert F. Sayre

We should start with a warning. Today drivers of the "Great River Road" along the Mississippi River may be in for a disappointment, for it is not a continuous highway but a composition of various county, state, and national roads. And what you see is Iowa farmland—only in towns, usually, do you see the great river. The fabulous Mississippi of Marquette and Joliet, Zebulon Pike, and Mark Twain, with its great bluffs and palisades, its sloughs and flood plains and shifting shores sometimes two miles apart, its Bald eagles fishing in the winter and its trees so dense and green in the summer that it seems almost tropical—the river eludes you. The Mother of Waters goes her own way, turning and flowing past bluffs too steep for and lowlands too wet for roads. So the Great River Road may seem like a tourist-business con, inadvertently recalling Herman Melville's book about the Mississippi, *The Confidence Man.*

The Great River Road is the Mississippi itself, and the best way to travel it is still by boat. Charter a houseboat if you can and have the time or take an excursion on one of the replicas of old steamboats that now sail from Dubuque, Davenport, and other towns. Only then do you really see this wonder of North America. And only then do you see how the Iowa towns along the river are like diverse beads on its winding length: Keokuk, Fort Madison, Burlington, Muscatine, Davenport, Clinton, and Dubuque being the major ones—"express boat" stops, so to speak—with a dozen or more small towns like Montrose, Buffalo, Le Claire, Sabula, Bellevue, Guttenburg, Clayton, McGregor, Marquette, Harpers Ferry, and Lansing being the "request stops."

Yet the Mississippi was not only the bearer of early commerce and culture in nineteenth-century America (as it had been for thousands of years before), it was also a barrier to the east-west movement of later settlement, and since then east-west has been the dominant axis of American travel. A small town might have sprung up in the 1830s or 1840s at a ferry landing, where there were gently sloping banks on each side and a narrow, reasonably calm stretch of river between, and such a town became a kind of beachhead in the American western invasion. Once the age of railroads had really begun, after the Civil War, they too ran east-west, although collectively the companies developed routes running north-south almost the entire length of the Iowa shore. (Someday they might make a remarkable "Great River Railroad," for they go much closer to the river than highways can.) From then on, the only towns with an economic future were the ones at bridges. Eventually there were nine railroad bridges, which thereby spread travel of people and freight so widely that none of the towns monopolized it. Like other Iowa towns, they had to compete for eminence. None of the Iowa river towns became nearly as large as St. Louis or Minneapolis–St. Paul. Today cars can quickly drive across the river at sixteen different points, which are also spread fairly evenly north to south, though five are in the Quad Cities of Davenport, Bettendorf, Rock Island, and Moline.

The Mississippi River towns of Iowa therefore have a common culture and history somewhat apart from the rest of the state: they are the oldest; they have many common geographical features, because of their proximity to the river and its great bluffs and lowlands; they have undergone the same transitions in communication from steamboats to railroads to automobiles and trucks; they have risen and fallen with different industries like mining, fishing and shellfishing, lumber milling, railroading, and farm equipment. And their age, topography, and past and present wealth give them a rich variety of both vernacular and high-style architecture.

But they are also different enough from each other to make them fascinating to contrast, because they have different ethnic and religious populations and some different industrial bases. South to north, they also have great differences in climate and topography, which may surprise any one who thinks that Iowa is all alike.

Keokuk, in the southeast corner of Iowa, has been shaped historically and geographically by being on the lowland (the low-

est in the state), where the Des Moines River meets the Mississippi. Since the Des Moines was the biggest and most navigable
Iowa river, Keokuk was a departure point for early white settlers,
and before them, a home for the mixed-bloods who settled in
1824 in the so-called Halfbreed Tract.

Keokuk also lies at the base of what were once the Des
Moines Rapids of the Mississippi, an eleven-mile stretch from
Montrose to Keokuk in which the Mississippi fell twenty-four
feet. Robert E. Lee, who surveyed the rapids for the U.S. Army
in 1835–1837, called them and the Rock Rapids near Davenport
"the only two serious obstacles to the navigation of the Mississippi from the mouth of the Ohio to the falls of St. Anthony."
The early Mormons, who began settling in Nauvoo, Illinois, in
1838–1839, near the head of the rapids, were among the first to
propose using them for power. But the steamboat interests and
later lumber interests did not want the Mississippi dammed.

Between 1910 and 1913, with the nation hungering for electric power, the dam was finally built, with Hugh L. Cooper as
chief engineer. (Cooper later worked on the TVA dam at Muscle
Shoals and the Dnieperstroy dam in Russia.) Its 119 concrete
arches, with spillways beneath, stretch forty-five hundred feet to
the huge powerhouse near the navigation lock on the Iowa shore,
and look like a long, low, incomplete bridge.

*Fig. 11.1. Dam and powerhouse at Keokuk, which
never became the "Power City" that was promised.
(Photo courtesy of State Historical Society of Iowa)*

The Keokuk generators had a capacity of 310,000 electrical horsepower, seven percent of all the hydroelectric power available in the United States in 1913. The impoundment upstream from the dam, Lake Cooper or Lake Keokuk, reached nearly to Burlington, sixty-five miles, and its promoters proclaimed that it would become a great center for recreation and commercial fishing. They also renamed Keokuk "Power City." (As the gateway to Iowa, it had been "Gate City.") Provided with cheap electricity, the region between Burlington and St. Louis was to become a future industrial wonder, the "Power Zone," and excursion trains and boats brought in sightseers to watch the dam being built. But disappointment followed. The utility companies kept rates high; and silt, pollution, and other problems soon destroyed the commercial fishing.

So today Keokuk is a soberer and wiser city than in the days when two thousand workers were building its great dam, and the Lee County Historical Society, at 318 N. Fifth St., in the Italianate home of Samuel Freeman Miller, whom Lincoln appointed to the Supreme Court, is a good place to learn more about its past. In 1856 Mark Twain worked at his brother Orion Clemens's jobprinting shop in Keokuk. Mrs. Annie Wittenmeyer, founder of the Civil War Sanitary Commission (precursor of the Red Cross) also lived here. During the Civil War thousands of Iowa soldiers headed south from Keokuk, and many of the wounded returned to its army hospital. In the 1860s Keokuk was also the site of the first Iowa medical college. Civil War dead were buried in the National Cemetery at the west end of Cedar St.

Facing the Mississippi, in Rand Park, is a statue of the Sac chief, Keokuk. He died in Kansas in 1848, but was later reburied here. The statue and pedestal are by Iowa artist Nellie Verne Walker.

The C. M. Rich house at 1229 Grand Avenue overlooking the Mississippi was designed in 1916 by the Prairie School architect Barry Byrne. Its magnificence and California-Spanish features give a sense of the confident pretensions of that era.

Also interesting to note as one looks around Keokuk are the different angles of the streets, in which the different grids try to accommodate the curves of the two rivers and locations of the bluffs. The suburban-type shopping center near the downtown is interesting, too, as an experiment in accommodating automobile shoppers close to the old business district.

Montrose, twelve miles upstream from Keokuk, lies at the head of what were the Des Moines Rapids. Because of the rapids steamboat cargo had to be transshipped overland from Keokuk

*Fig. 11.2.   The glory of Fort Madison is its old
houses and commercial buildings. This brick house is
at 421 Avenue E, just two blocks from the main shopping street. (Photo by Robert F. Sayre)*

and reloaded here. Montrose is also the point at which the Mormon refugees from Nauvoo reached Iowa during the winter of
1846, before beginning their monumental trek to Utah. Crossing
the Mississippi in February by ferry, by raft, and on the ice when
it froze solid enough, the trek was one of the great migrations on
the American frontier. Stand on the bank and look across at
Nauvoo and try to envision the act of almost twenty thousand
people who left their homes and property between 1846 and 1852.

Fort Madison is known throughout Iowa for the State Peni-
tentiary and the Sheaffer Pen factory. The pen. (period) was located there and built by prisoners in 1839, possibly because the
town had been the site of a U.S. fort and trading post established
in 1808 and burned in 1813 after a siege by Indians, one of whom
was Black Hawk. The Sheaffer pen (no period) was invented by a
local jeweller in 1908. The factory is an example of the kind of
local business many small towns would do anything to have,
though it is now owned by Gefinor U.S.A., a subsidiary of a

Swiss corporation, having previously been owned by Textron. Remains of the old army fort were dug up in 1965 during construction of an underground reservoir in the company parking lot.

But the glory of Fort Madison, in our opinion, is its old houses and commercial buildings along avenues E, F, G, and H between 4th and 12th streets. Among them is the Lee County Courthouse at 7th and F, built in 1842 in Greek Revival style. The twenty or thirty others are a wonderful hodge-podge of Victorian styles, from simple cottages with Gothic Revival details to massive Italianate and Queen Anne. Most are of brick with wood and iron decoration, and most are well preserved without fussy gentrification. Perhaps the stability of Fort Madison's economy has kept these buildings in long-term ownership and good repair.

Another Fort Madison asset is that the old riverfront has been widened with landfill and made into a park, with the Santa Fe Railroad tracks running beside it and U.S. 61 paralleling them. River, railroad, and highway thus pass through town together, like a historical paradigm, and in the park is a fine old steam locomotive that every visitor wants to stop and see. The nearby Santa Fe station, built in 1917, is now a museum and information center where you can get directions to the old buildings. Construction of a new fort, a copy of the old, is also going on in Riverview Park. The whole town, while not looking wealthy, seems to have pride in its appearance and history.

Burlington, a much larger, more elegant town than Fort Madison, also parallels the Mississippi and used to have thriving lumber mills. From the 1850s through the 1880s, the white pine of Wisconsin and Minnesota was rafted down the Mississippi and milled in Iowa into lumber for the houses and barns of the expanding western United States. Burlington had mills that could cut up to fifty-seven million board-feet a year, and towns further north, like Davenport and Clinton, had even greater capacity. Such mills were the first great industry of the upper Mississippi valley, from Hannibal, Missouri, to St. Paul, Minnesota, and these towns on the west side of the river were better located than those in Illinois and Wisconsin. The finished lumber and ready-made doors and windows mostly went west. The lumber mill prosperity did not decline until the depression of 1893. By then the best timber had been cut — or lost to forest fires and waste.

Burlington also had furniture factories, railroad yards and repair shops, brickyards, grain elevators, carriage factories, and food processors and wholesalers. James G. Edwards, a New York newspaperman who moved to Burlington in 1838 from Fort Madison, named his newspaper the *Hawk-Eye* in 1843 and promoted

"Hawk-Eyes" as a nickname for Iowans. During the 1840s and 1850s Burlington became the largest city in Iowa (surpassing Dubuque), which is perhaps why its name was included in the names of so many railroad lines and trains like Chicago, Burlington, and Quincy (which absorbed the Burlington and Missouri River) or the Burlington Zephyr. The name seems to echo the roar of locomotives and the cry of whistles down the track.

A danger in lumber milling was fire, and Burlington had a holocaust in 1873 that destroyed five blocks of the business district (a predecessor of the grain mill explosion of 1986 that literally shook the city). Editors and civic beautifiers therefore regularly promoted brick and stone buildings as being safer and more permanent and attractive. Wood made money, but was rude, for the west, for newer towns. Towns like Burlington wished to seem refined and established.

One can see this preference in the mansions along High and Court streets from 5th Street west. Other examples can be found further south off Main Street, in the Clay Street area. Today N. 6th Street between Washington and Columbia, "Snake Alley," is a gentrified serpentine street that is a Burlington landmark.

The fine art deco auditorium downtown and Crapo Park, between Madison Avenue and the Mississippi south of town, are further signs of Burlington's old elegance. The park has the curved walkways and drives, exotic trees and plantings, and picturesque settings that were favored in the late nineteenth century. The question Burlington asks, however, is whether this graciousness can be maintained. Much of the new prosperity is around suburban shopping centers—not in the downtown—and one of the largest employers is the Army Ordnance Plant west of town. The older, local industries do not appear so healthy. Burlington looks like an aging lady and gentleman who have hidden most of the signs of their rough past but have also lost most of their fortune.

Toolesboro, near the mouth of the Iowa River, is worth a detour off of U.S. 61 because of the Toolesboro Mounds National Historic Landmark, where the ceremonial mounds from the Hopewell Culture are preserved (see "Indian Iowa"). There is a modern visitor center with displays and dioramas that also tell about Marquette and Joliet. More adventurous gunkholers may want to look for the site of Burris City, just north of the junction of the Iowa and Mississippi rivers, where in the summer of 1858 the promoter V. W. Burris started a "great metropolis" that was to be on the "Air Line Railroad" between Philadelphia, Pennsylvania, and the Platte River, in Nebraska (an "Air Line" that never touched down). The town was destroyed by a fall flood and never rebuilt.

Muscatine, another great lumber milling town, found a second industrial goldmine in the 1890s. The story is that in the early 1880s near Hamburg, Germany, a German button worker named John Boepple experimented with some freshwater mussel shells that had come, a friend told him, from a river about two hundred miles southwest of Chicago. Buttons at that time were either made from marine shells, which were very expensive to cut and finish, or from wood, metal, glass, and other materials that broke or rusted. In 1887 Boepple went to the United States and started hunting for the shells, finally cutting his foot on the right shell in the Sangamon River in Illinois. He soon found even better beds in the Mississippi near Muscatine. "Mein buddons vill make you all rich," he assured skeptical investors, who were put off by his immigrant accents. Two Muscatine men finally backed him, and in 1891 they began making Boepple's buttons in the basement of a cooper's shop. Other men followed, up and down the Mississippi, and by 1900 Muscatine was "the Pearl Button Capital of the World." In 1910 it produced seventeen million gross of buttons.

There were other factors in this success, such as the McKinley Tariff of 1890, which raised the duty on imported buttons, and the simultaneous growth of the garment industry in New York. With such demand the thousands of shellfishermen on the Mississippi (and other rivers) overfished the beds. No means of control, whether by government, fishermen, or manufacturers, ever succeeded. River pollution and silt also destroyed the mussels, none of which, apparently, were ever taken as food. By the 1930s this boom, too, was over. But it had perpetuated Muscatine's fame as a tough little manufacturing center—a reputation it still holds today as the headquarters of Hon Industries (office furniture) and Bandag Inc. (world's largest maker of material and equipment for retreading tires).

What one sees in Muscatine is a palimpsest of this history. On the bluff in the south part of town are many old, large and small houses, built between 1850 and 1900. The Musser House, 606 W. 3rd Street, is a very imposing Anglo-Italianate mansion built in 1852 by George Stone, founder of the first bank in Muscatine. The house was sold in 1870 to Richard Musser of the Musser Lumber Co. The Couch House, 411 W. 2nd, built in 1846, has the broad second-floor porch fashionable then in the South. On the peak of the bluff overlooking the river and directly across Cherry Street from each other are "The Eyrie" and the Blackwell House. "The Eyrie," an 1852 structure, is being restored to its Classical Revival grandeur. The Blackwell House, built in 1880 for Captain W. A. Clark, is Queen Anne style and made of thin, smooth brick that required very little mortar. You can also see where more recent houses have been squeezed onto the grounds of the old mansions, so as to eke out more of the great view of the river.

Downtown there are fine old churches, stores, and public buildings. Two remaining button factory buildings are the J & K Button Co., on Mississippi River Drive, and the McKee Button Co., 1000 Hershey Road. At one time the downtown was hillier, but flash floods on the creeks between the bluffs wiped out whole blocks, so the city graded the bluffs within town and filled in the ravines and creek beds. Just north of the business district one can find the factory buildings and loading docks of Hon Industries. This area also has some good Mexican restaurants, run by members of Muscatine's Mexican-American community.

In a park along the riverfront, where Walnut Street intersects E. Mississippi Drive, is a pylon from the High Bridge erected in 1891. Not many cities would save a part of a demolished bridge. But consider what a Mississippi River bridge has meant to Muscatine — and to all Americans!

Fig. 11.3.   The James Weed house in Muscatine, built between 1853 and 1855, is still a private residence, across from the city park that was once Weed's "Pomological Gardens." (Photo courtesy of State Historical Society of Iowa)

The Peter Musser House, 501 E. Mississippi Drive, and "The Gables," built between 1853 and 1855 for Dr. James Weed, are in the northeast part of Muscatine. Weed cultivated "Pomological Gardens," which he left to the city as a park. "The Gables," in Gothic Revival style, was his farmhouse.

Finally, on the northern outskirts of Muscatine, are modern shopping centers and the Bandag headquarters. Someone on the way to Davenport, however, might prefer to take state Highway 22, because it runs close to the river, and there are many tiny settlements of fishing cabins built on stilts along the flood plain.

Fairport is where Robert E. Coker, director of the U.S. Bureau of Fisheries Biological Station in 1913, made important studies of Mississippi River ecology.

Buffalo was the site of early ferries across the Mississippi, and steamboat captains built houses here. Later it was a shellfishers' port and had a few button factories.

Davenport, today the biggest of Iowa's river towns, has a lot in common with the other river towns. As Keokuk was at the base of the Des Moines Rapids, Davenport was at the base of the Rock, or Upper, Rapids (until the building of the locks and dams by the Corps of Engineers). It too was a major lumber port and did some button making.

A historic event that separates Davenport from the rest of the river towns is that is was the first city in Iowa to get a railroad, completing one to Iowa City Jan. 1, 1856 and hooking it to a bridge across the river that April.

Throughout the nineteenth century German immigrants brought in culture and music (see "German and Dutch Ethnic Communities"), and at the beginning of the twentieth century it had more than its share of talented and rebellious young artists: Alice French, Arthur Davison Ficke, George Cram Cook, Susan Glaspell, Bix Beiderbecke, to name a few. Today one will find the Putnam Museum (a fine museum of history and natural history), a lovely Municipal Art Museum, opened in 1925, and a modern public library designed by Edward Durrell Stone.

Davenport has preserved signs of its past. The lumber barons James Renwick and John Davies built two mansions at 10th and Tremont streets on the brow of the bluffs, where they could see the rafts of logs arrive at their mills on the riverfront. These homes were later used as classrooms and dormitories by St. Katharine's School. Antoine LeClaire, the first white man to own land in Davenport (a whole square mile), built a home at 630 E.

7th Street, which has been restored to its 1856 appearance. This
new brick house was actually his second home for he had donated
his first home to the new railroad as a depot.

*Fig. 11.4.   Antoine LeClaire mansion, 630 E. 7th
St., Davenport, while undergoing restoration to its
1856 appearance. (Photo courtesy of State Historical
Society of Iowa)*

LeClaire and his contemporaries promoted Davenport as a
summer health resort. Daniel A. Curtiss in *Western Portraiture
and Emigrant's Guide,* in 1852, wrote that "the healthfulness and
beauty of [its] situation, together with the facilities for hunting
and fishing in its neighborhood, have made this place the fashionable resort, during the summer months, of large numbers of people, from St. Louis and other Southern cities." To some degree, of
course, that was standard midcentury puffery. The same was op-
timistically written of dozens of muddy western cities. Davenport
did later become world famous as the home of D. D. Palmer
(discoverer of Chiropractic), who with his son "B. J." Palmer
developed the Palmer School of Chiropractic, on Brady Street
between 8th and 11th streets in 1898. In the 1920s the institution
had three thousand students. B. J. also started WOC, the first
radio station west of the Mississippi. The third Palmer, David D.,
expanded the family's media interest to include TV stations in
Davenport, Florida, and California, and added Palmer Junior
College.

When Davenport was platted, three complete blocks were set aside as public space, as well as a broad stretch of land along the riverfront, which was soon taken over by flour mills and lumber mills. However, when they were later torn down the land was returned to public use with the creation of LeClaire Park, where the Bix Beiderbecke Jazz Festival is held every summer. The three blocks are where the Scott County Courthouse, the YM-YWCA, and the park on the north side of 4th Street west of Gaines Street are now located. Farther west are several blocks of fine houses constructed by German immigrants to Davenport in the mid-nineteenth century. Of special note is the Schick Building at 310 Gaines Street, and the Fuch house at 600 W. 6th Street.

Davenport became a business center, more like the rest of urban America—an industrial hub, a small Cleveland. The old and new industrial areas of Davenport and the other Quad Cities of Bettendorf and Moline and Rock Island, Illinois, have or once had big payrolls from Alcoa, John Deere, Farmall, Caterpillar Tractor, and the Rock Island Army Arsenal.

Clinton was once the biggest lumber port in Iowa. In 1871 it had four mills with a capacity of 113 million board-feet a year, over twice the capacity of the mills of Davenport. Its bluffs are lower and farther back than those in other towns, which left plenty of room for the mills, railroads, and broad, straight streets. *Lyons,* just to the north and now a part of Clinton, had three more mills with a capacity of 41 million board-feet.

Downtown Clinton today has many signs of the civic pride of its early citizens: River Front Park, with a gigantic public swimming pool built in the 1890s, and an art deco baseball stadium built by the WPA; big handsome churches; a large YMCA; and a good library. It also has the old Van Allen Department Store building (1912–1915) at 5th Avenue South and 2nd Street, designed by Louis Sullivan. Several other stores, like the Webster Building, have decoration by Sullivan or his school. However, the current vacancy of the Van Allen store is a depressing sign that business in Clinton is not what it was. Outside of town, gases pour from chemical plants, power plants, various paper mills, and rendering plants as wood smoke must once have poured from the chimneys of sawmills—but if you look you see that most are not locally owned. Clinton seems exploited, a reminder that a town needs not only jobs but employers who live there too and care about the town and their own reputations. If that happens again, Clinton may have the rebirth it deserves.

Sabula is on a long, low, narrow island in the river, making it, as a sign says at the end of the earth causeway that runs out to it, "Iowa's Island City." Situated at the north end of the big, broad impoundment behind lock and dam number 13, it is a perfect spot for boating. In the summer it is alive with flotillas of the shallow-draft motorized houseboats (the Mississippi's yachts) tied up in its marina. Water skiers buzz over the river and "lake" between the island and the Iowa mainland, and shell-hunting SCUBA divers search for pearls. Campers and picnickers gather on the beaches and at Sabula Lakes Park. In the winter, boats are parked in the driveways and backyards of the old brick houses — Sabula shivers and sleeps. It seems, however, to belong to the river and to Chicagoans and other outsiders who keep their boats there; Iowans ought to reclaim it.

Bellevue is beginning to discover its potential as a place for tourists coming by car and bicycle as well as by boat. It has a wild local history from its days of frontier horse thieves and lumber milling, a state park, and nearby clay pits that yield clay used for pottery. It also has nice homes on the main street with gorgeous views of the river. But the ancient stone buildings right on the river still face the street, like village loafers staring at passing cars, too lazy to even turn around.

Were some magical promoter to come along and blow a golden horn, Bellevue might wake up and build riverview restaurants and resorts. Already there is a good restaurant in Potter's Mill at the south edge of town and an elegant bed-and-breakfast house, Mont Rest, on the northern bluff. In the meantime Bellevue seems to like Bellevue as it is . . . and visitors should too.

St. Donatus, though not immediately on the Mississippi, is right on U.S. 52 between Bellevue and Dubuque, one of the prettiest roads in Iowa. It was founded by immigrants from Luxembourg, and anyone familiar with the vernacular buildings of villages and farms in Luxembourg, Belgium, or northern France will immediately see the influences. There are stone barns, not wooden ones, and stone houses stuccoed over, with heavy stone lintels, no cellars or eaves, and close to the street, not set back, as in most Iowa towns. St. Donatus is waking up to its potential as a tourist attraction, and in the summer there is a lively town festival. Another striking coincidence is the way the Catholic church in town and the large, red brick Lutheran church across the valley face each other like fortresses from the 100 Years War. Between them flows a little creek named the Tetes des Morts. *Heads of the Dead* indeed!

Dubuque might be called Iowa's rust belt. It is old. In places it looks so rundown and redbrick that parts of movies about union organizing have been shot here, while in Manhattan, Dubuque is a by-word for provinciality. But when word reached it that the *New Yorker* was not edited "for the little old lady in Dubuque," Dubuque found her — she was a subscriber. And so it fights back, clearing parts of its downtown with urban renewal, establishing others as historic places, and building new attractions as different as a ski run and a dog track. The rest of Iowa may be rural and spacious and mostly white frame houses; but Dubuque is urban and close and brick red; and no one wants to change it.

The primary reason why Dubuque's old houses are so close to each other and right next to its streets is that the bluffs are high and steep and there wasn't much room between them and the flood plain of the river. What is today the large factory and railroad district between the commercial district and the river was once marshland. Steamboat traffic was heavy in early Dubuque, with one thousand landings recorded in 1857, and the town tried to dredge a channel through these marshes and sloughs. When that failed, they were filled in.

The bluffs directed further expansion of Dubuque in three directions, each a transportation route: to the northeast along the river to Eagle Point and Wisconsin; to the northwest, through Couler Village (the French word *couler* was adopted in early Dubuque to mean a deep ravine or gully, and eventually pronounced "coulee"); and to the west up a coulee. Rhomberg Avenue follows the first direction, U.S. 52 the second, and U.S. 20 the third. Present routes into town from the south were unknown in early days. Still another way of dealing with the bluffs, however, was to go straight up them, and so in 1882 the Fenelon Place Elevator, or Cable Car, to the residential district above the city was built.

In the bluffs was Dubuque's first source of wealth, lead, which had long been known to the Indians in the area. Nicholas Perrot, a French trader, obtained their permission and assistance to mine it in 1690, and he and others continued mining and refining it through the eighteenth century. In 1788 Julien Dubuque, a French Canadian, obtained the right to mine on Catfish Creek from the Mesquakie Indians. In 1796, having had his claim certified by the Spanish government, he named the claim "The Mines of Spain." (The name has the whiff of El Dorado, and it is currently being revived as the name of a new state preserve, but prospectors mostly called the area the Mines of Dubuque or the Dubuque Mines.)

Lead rushes of the early nineteenth century brought miners

from Swaledale, Yorkshire, and by 1836 one smelter alone was producing seventy thousand pounds of lead per week. Some remnants of the lead era are the Shot Tower at Commercial and River Front streets, the Octagon House at 1095 W. 3rd Street (built by Edward Longworthy, one of the five children of James Longworthy, a miner, smelter, and real estate owner), and the mine shafts and tunnels that contractors still find in excavating for new buildings. Sink holes even open up in backyards!

Fig. 11.5.   The Octagon House at 1095 W. 3rd Street in Dubuque, designed by John Francis Rague and built in 1858 for Edward Langworthy; it is still a private home. (Photo courtesy of State Historical Society of Iowa)

From the 1840s on, Dubuque received thousands of immigrants from Germany and Ireland. The Irish settled in the southside, "Dublin," the Germans in the north, "Germany," and older Americans from the eastern states in the center, "Babel." Some typical frame houses occupied by Irish working-class families are at 37–39 and 41–47 Locust Street. German shopkeepers along Central Avenue from 15th Street north typically occupied three-story brick buildings, with shops on the first floor. For an idea of the middle-class row houses built in the 1850s and after, look at 167–169 Locust Street, 54–60 Bluff Street, and 1100–1134 Locust Street.

But these few locations only begin to suggest what remains in Dubuque from its nineteenth-century status as Iowa's first and, for a time, biggest and most prosperous town. Lead, lumber, steamboats and steamboat building, railroads, shells and buttons, wagon works, farm implements, wholesale produce, brewing, and retailing—Dubuque did it all. And it has the pretentious mansions, old breweries, warehouses, churches, jails, theaters, and hotels to prove it. A survey in the 1970s by the office of the State Archaeologist, before improvements to the Great River Road, identified eighty-five important historic sites in Dubuque—and those were just on the highway route. Had the surveyors done a comprehensive report, the number would have been in the hundreds. Dubuque is one of the best-preserved nineteenth-century cities in the whole United States. It is slowly being gentrified, with restaurants and bed-and-breakfast places in old homes, but you don't yet have to be rich to enjoy Dubuque. It is still a working town, with bowling alleys and gas stations, good beer, and cheap motels. Even Sundown, the ski development with chairlifts and three-quarter-mile trails, is so close to town that it is just beyond the suburban bowling alleys.

Dubuquers grumble that they have no interstate highway and only so-so airline service—and they have a right to. If Dubuque were on a major tourist corridor, like Charleston, South Carolina, it would be one of the best-known historic cities in America.

Guttenberg was originally named Prairie La Porte, but was then settled in the 1840s by German intellectuals escaping military service. Johann Gutenberg, the printer, was an appropriate ancestor to honor, but the first surveyor apparently spelled the name with two t's, and today Iowans pronounce it accordingly (to rhyme with buttonberg). The stone and brick buildings along the streets parallel to the river are well maintained. Guttenberg had sawmills and button factories in its early history, but its principal business has always been service to the farms west of it.

McGregor, another old steamboat port, took on a new life in the 1960s as a tourist and vacation town. This role was enhanced by its being near Pike's Peak State Park (with its glorious view of the junction of the Wisconsin and Mississippi rivers) and Effigy Mounds National Monument. "Leafers" come from all over Iowa and surrounding states to see the autumn colors. Hippies—or young outsiders so suspected—moved in and opened what first seemed to be head shops but which became craft and antique shops. As a result McGregor was one of the first towns in Iowa to begin restoring its old storefronts and discovering its history.

Fig. 11.6. Looking up the Mississippi from Pike's Peak State Park, with Prairie du Chien, Wisconsin, in the background. (Photo by George Schrimper, Museum of Natural History, Univ. of Iowa)

Seven early residents who later became famous were the Ringling brothers, whose father August Ringling was a harness maker here between 1860 and 1872. Their first show, reportedly, was in a thirty-five-foot tent held up by clothes lines in a back lot, with Al Ringling entertaining the locals by balancing a plow on his chin.

Froelich, the town nine miles west, was the home of John Froelich, inventor of the first gasoline tractor. Froelich owned a steam-powered threshing operation, and in 1892 he built the tractor to haul water to it. But being much lighter and more maneuverable than steam tractors, it could be adapted to drawing plows and other equipment. Froelich's tractor was manufactured by the Waterloo Gasoline Tractor Engine Co., later bought out by the John Deere Co.

The circus and the tractor: two great institutions of rural America! Ringling entertained by balancing a plow on his chin, Froelich found a better way to pull it.

But visitors to McGregor and towns farther north, such as *Marquette, Harper's Ferry,* and *Lansing,* have just as much reason to honor Will Dilg, the Chicago advertising man who in the 1920s and 1930s was the leader of efforts that established the Upper Mississippi River Wildlife and Fish Refuge. In January 1922, Dilg and fifty-three other Chicagoans founded the Izaak Walton League of America, which grew into the most successful conservation group of that time. Dilg's flamboyant and messianic style gained the attention of businessmen, professors, politicians, women's organizations, and national officials, and in 1923–1924 he successfully fought developers who wanted to drain approximately 28,000 acres of marshland along the Mississippi known as the Winneshiek Bottoms (15,000 acres were in Iowa, north of Lansing, and 13,000 acres were in Wisconsin, south of Lansing) and convert it to farmland. The bill that established the refuge was signed by Calvin Coolidge in 1924; the refuge eventually included more than 195,000 acres. Later a great deal of the land was flooded when the Army Corps of Engineers built the locks and dams on the river, but the Izaak Walton League still remains, and all through Iowa one comes upon signs leading to its private campgrounds and refuges.

Thus while the Mississippi River towns are some of the oldest and most industrialized, the land between them is some of the wildest in Iowa. Indeed, visitors who have tired of visiting towns deserve to go hiking in Yellow River State Forest, north of Marquette. Then, in dreams or in some later year, they might board a boat and head downstream, enjoying the *real* Great River Road. Or, if Iowa revives its railroads, they might someday be able to take an excursion train along the Mississippi to see both towns and river and to recover a sense of the railroad era, when all the way from Marquette to Keokuk these towns were among the most vigorous in the country. We all know of the Wild West and the eastern capitalists, the cowboys and the yankees, but who knows of these Mississippi River towns that milled the lumber that built the West, that smelted the lead and made the wagons and plows, and that even made the buttons on the cowboy's shirt?

Selected Readings

Blair, Walter A. *A Raft Pilot's Log: A History of the Great Rafting Industry on the Upper Mississippi, 1840–1915.* Cleveland: The Arthur H. Clark Co., 1930.

Federal Writers' Project. *Iowa: A Guide to the Hawkeye State.* New York: The Viking Press, 1938; Ames: Iowa State Univ. Press, 1986.

Hotopp, John, Margaret Hotopp, and Elka Grisham. *Iowa's Great River Road, Cultural and Natural Resources.* 2 vols. Iowa City: Office of the State Archaeologist, 1977.

Scarpino, Philip V. *Great River: An Environmental History of the Upper Mississippi, 1890–1950.* Columbia: Univ. of Missouri Press, 1985.

Treasures of Iowa. Des Moines: The Iowan Magazine, 1987.

Wilson, Richard Guy, and Sidney K. Robinson. *The Prairie School in Iowa.* Ames: Iowa State Univ. Press, 1977.

12

GHOST TOWNS IN THE CENTRAL DES MOINES RIVER VALLEY

Harriet Heusinkveld

Sweet Auburn! loveliest village of the plain;
Where health and plenty cheered the neighboring swain . . .
How often have I paused on every charm,
The sheltered cot, the cultivated farm,
The never failing brook, the busy mill,
The decent church that topped the neighboring hill.

Goldsmith, *The Deserted Village*

Iowa is dotted with places that, like England's Auburn, once throbbed with life—where people toiled and played, laughed and cried, married and had children, dreamed dreams, and worshipped their God—and now a cemetery is perhaps all that marks their one-time existence.

The towns declined and disappeared for a variety of reasons: changes in technology, political maneuvering, a new appraisal of resources, even quirks of nature and fate. Gradually, as better transportation became available, small villages gave way to larger ones, especially to Des Moines, because of the city's greater advantages of employment and trade. Interestingly, these towns still live in the minds of former residents, who come together with friends and neighbors in annual reunions, where they renew relationships and exchange nostalgia.

Four historically important towns, now disappeared, are described in some detail, and eight others more briefly. All are on or near the Des Moines River or its tributaries. Apple Grove is on Camp Creek, Buxton on Bluff Creek; Homer is three miles from

229

Boone Forks. These towns boasted blacksmith shops, ice houses, creameries, one-room schoolhouses, millinery shops, saw and gristmills, livery stables, hitching posts, river ferries, stagecoach inns, and later railroad depots, and some of them coal company camp houses.

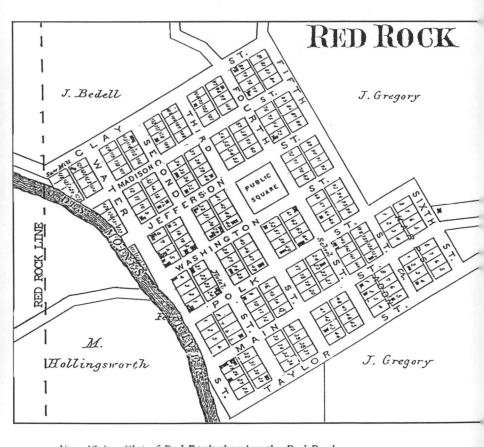

Fig. 12.1. *Plat of Red Rock showing the Red Rock Line, which was the white-Indian boundary in 1843.* (*Map from* Atlas of Marion County, *1875)*

Red Rock (Marion County), 1843–1969, the first town in central Iowa, was situated on the Indian frontier in 1843. The riverlands were the only practical location for the first settlers; they had to depend entirely on its resources. Their descendants clung doggedly to their riverlands, until 1969, when the river in its new form, Lake Red Rock, swallowed them up beneath its waters.

Indians called this little paradise Painted Rocks. For them the sixty-foot red sandstone bluffs laid down by the ancient seas were especially beautiful, as was the Des Moines River flowing serenely below. The heavy forests sheltered wild turkey and deer and were dotted by wild fruit trees. Indian trails from Red Rock led to all points of the compass and extended as far as Raccoon Forks (present-day Des Moines).

One summer day in 1835 the Indians beheld a long line of white men on horseback. They were U.S. Dragoons, a cavalry unit sent out to explore the Sac and Fox lands preparatory to buying them, which was finally done in 1842. By May 1, 1843, the Indians would have to vacate the lands east of a line drawn through Painted Rocks. By October 11, 1845, they would also have to give up the land immediately west of this line, the Red Rock line, as the whites called it. And on March 20, 1843, J. D. Bedell, a twenty-six-year-old Kentuckian and a French friend stood on the bluffs viewing the landscape. Though it was before the legal date permitting white men to enter the territory, they decided to plat a town on this beautiful spot and to open a trading post.

Red Rock, the boundary between whites and Indians, was an ideal place for Bedell's trading post. Others, including the American Fur Company, also opened posts to buy furs, skins, and maple sugar from the Indians in exchange for blankets, whiskey, and guns.

Red Rock was a rough town — debauchery and thievery were rampant — for the Indians were ready to give up almost any possession in exchange for whiskey. The Indians became destitute because they spent their government payments for whiskey, and they were depressed because they would soon have to give up their beloved lands. An early settler describes their departure:

> The Red Man's farewell occurred in May, 1845. At that time, the entire body of Indians were assembled at Red Rock, preparatory to evacuating their ancient domains. This was done in a dual manner. The braves rode their war steeds across the country to a point on the river known as Council Bluffs. All the rest, the aged warriors, squaws, papooses, took passage in canoes, some 300 or more in number and going down the Des Moines River to its mouth, they were transferred to steamboats and carried to the same point (Council Bluffs).
>
> It was a pathetic event but colorful. The Indians gave their war whoops, chanted their war songs, ran boat races, and splashed in the water like aquatic birds.
>
> No proper tribute can ever be paid that vanished people. They were ever the friends of the white and yielded to him without

parley or dispute and for a mere pittance, all their holdings. Never
did they show revenge or shed a drop of innocent blood.

W. H. H. Barker, *Knoxville Journal,*
Jubilee Edition, September 25, 1930

At midnight, October 10, 1845, white settlers in wagons and
on horseback were lined up at the Red Rock line awaiting the
shooting of guns to be fired by the Dragoons to announce that
they could go in and claim the land.

And so, a new race of people, a new philosophy of land use
began for Red Rock. People continued to come, some of whom
decided to settle in the town and set up business there. Stores, a
hotel, a schoolhouse, a church, four water-powered sawmills, and
a flour mill soon became part of the scene. A ferry to take people
and goods from one side of the river to the other was also started.
By 1880 the population was 125.

Red Rock's most pressing problem was obtaining transportation, and in this effort they were to suffer many disappoint-
ments. Congress's announced Des Moines River Navigation Plan
to make the river navigable from its mouth to the Raccoon River
by building dams and canals was abandoned because of corruption and mismanagement on the part of the company contracted
to do the job. However, after the flood of 1851 and the resulting
high waters, the steamboats came. Their loud puffing noise
stirred up commotion for miles as people lined the banks to see
them. They came loaded with goods and passengers. What a blow
it was for Red Rock when the steamboats stopped at Bellefountaine and Coalport, presumably better ports, rather than at Red
Rock.

The most bitter disappointment was the routing of two expected railroads, the Rock Island (1867), six miles away through
Otley, and the Wabash (1887), one mile away through Cordova.
People and businesses moved to Otley, and those who stayed
hauled their produce to the railroad depot at Cordova for shipping.

However, the 1890s were good for Red Rock. A bridge was
finally built to span the river, eliminating the need for a ferry, and
the Wabash built a spur to their sandstone bluffs! A boom resulted as sandstone was quarried and shipped to many parts of
the country, but it was brief. The sandstone proved to be too soft
for most building purposes.

"Red Rock against the world," they used to say. They had
no thought of disappearing from the map. In 1910 Red Rock had
a population of 693. In 1945 they built a new schoolhouse. Sense
of community was strong; people helped each other to clean up

after floods and to drive hogs to the railroad station. During the Great Depression, when they could not afford to travel very far, people of all faiths—Methodists, Latter-day Saints, Catholics—all worshipped together in the Methodist Church. Schoolhouses were centers for square dances and basket dinners.

Fig. 12.2.   Half-size replica of a Red Rock house, built in Monroe, Jasper County. (Photo by Harriet Heusinkveld)

Every few years, spring floods, exacerbated by cutting of timber upriver, plagued Red Rock. In 1947 a flood hit Red Rock, described as the worst it had ever had—businesses and houses were destroyed, animals drowned. And the bridge for which they had waited so many years washed out! Families began to move away; the prospect of rebuilding seemed too overwhelming. In the 1960s, Red Rock lost its school by consolidation with Knoxville, and the population dropped to about one hundred.

Damming the river to prevent further flooding had been discussed for years. As a result of the flood of 1947 action was taken to prevent such disaster in the future. The original government plans called for a dam and a reservoir above the town of Red Rock, which would save it from further destruction. Ultimately, however, the government decided that Howell Station, a site below Red Rock, was more appropriate, and after acrimonious hearings, it was decided that the town of Red Rock must be sacrificed for the most efficient flood control for the whole area. The inhabitants were forced to sell their properties to the government, and the buildings were sold or demolished.

Fig. 12.3.   Red Rock Church during 1947 flood.
People lived in it while their homes were flooded.
(Photographer unknown)

Red Rock's demise was sudden and complete. In 1969 the dam was closed, and in the matter of a few days, Lake Red Rock covered the old town.

All physical evidence is gone now except the old cemetery on a hill. However, memories remain, and each June a Red Rock reunion is held somewhere along the lake. Old residents reminisce, and perhaps when the water is low, they peer down to try to locate some of the old foundations, fences, and streets, visible from a spot near the north end of the Mile Long Bridge on State Highway 14. (Take Highway 14 south from Monroe for six miles, then at the sign to Painted Rock go west on a gravel road for two miles to the cemetery)

Coalport, 1857–1903, was an early Marion County farming community, but it was also a steamboat coaling station. When the steamboats stopped coming, and particularly when the river changed its course, leaving Coalport "high and dry," the town started to die.

Coalport lay in the bottomlands on a very large meander of the Des Moines River. In the bluff across the river was an outcropping of coal six to eight feet thick. Coalport pioneers dug out coal to fuel the little steamboats that plied the Des Moines River in the 1860s. In fact Coalport was the most important coaling station between Eddyville and Des Moines.

The long, hoarse whistles of the steamboats used to echo over the countryside, and boys and girls ran from the schoolhouse, passing the pottery on the way, to the boat landing below to participate in the excitement.

Of interest, too, was the little grocery store in the home of William Welch, founder of Coalport. It was stocked with groceries, which had come by boat from Keokuk. Because most people ate homemade corn dodgers and bacon and made their clothing from their own sheep's wool, Billy Welch limited his stock to salt, saleratus (baking powder), chewing tobacco, coffee, and rope.

Coalport's sawmill-gristmill furnished clapboard for building and, very importantly, flour from which "white bread" could be made. What a welcome change from hominy and corn pone three times a day!

The blacksmith put on a splendid spectacle as, in his leather apron, he worked the lever to work the big bellows. Flames and sparks shot high from the forge—the heat was almost too much to bear. Then with tongs, hammer, and anvil, the miracle of the horseshoe appeared!

In addition to his grocery store, Billy Welch ran a pottery and supplied high-quality jugs, butter churns, crocks, plates, and cups for the neighborhoods all around. He had been a potter in his native North Carolina, and in Coalport he devised his own equipment—the tank with paddles in which the clay and water were mixed, the potter's wheel, the drying shed, and the brick kiln with a fire box inside.

On Coal Ridge, a hill overlooking Coalport, stood the one-room schoolhouse, where spelldowns, singing sessions, and literary society meetings were held in the evenings for the community's enjoyment. The Coal Ridge Baptist Church was "the decent church that topped the neighboring hill."

One Coalport resident recalled the many types of pastors they had: one walked miles to minister to those in need; one

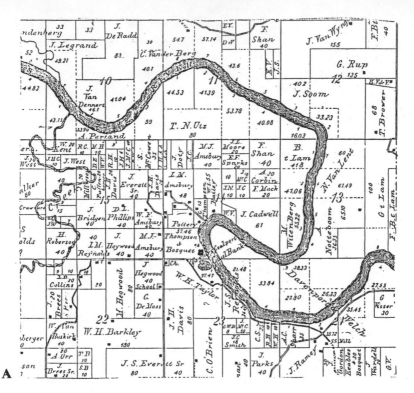

A

Fig. 12.4A, B.   Coalport's days were numbered.
Maps of Coalport before (A) and after (B) the river
straightened its course in the June flood, 1903;
Coalport was no longer a port. (Maps from Atlas of
Marion County, 1875 and 1903 editions)

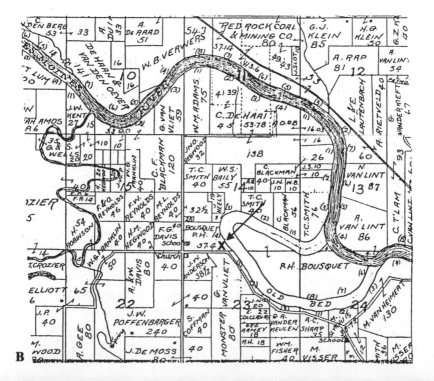

B

shouted and prayed as if God were deaf; one cut a hole in the river ice in midwinter and led converts in for baptism; and one itinerant shepherd was "seeking the lost sheep of Israel and as many yellow-legged chickens as he could devour."

But Coalport's days were numbered. Steamboats gave way to railroads, and Coalport's coal was no longer in demand. The population, at its high point of 879 in 1875, declined as people started moving away. The final blow came in June 1903, when the highest flood ever known swept through Coalport. After the waters had receded, the townspeople were amazed and dismayed to find that they were no longer on the river on which they had depended for their commercial existence! The river had straightened its course by cutting through the neck of the big meander, and the main channel was now three-quarters of a mile away.

Only the Coal Ridge Baptist Church remains today. Nearby farmers, as well as visitors to the recently developed Lake Red Rock recreational facilities, worship there now.

The old Coalport lives on in the memories of those one hundred or so former residents who come in May for the annual reunion. They recall the privations they suffered, the young ones and the parents they laid to rest in the churchyard cemetery, and the richness of the life they shared in those days of long ago. (Go nine miles southwest from Pella on Road T-15 to its junction with S-71, then three miles north)

Homer, 1852–1915. During horse-and-buggy days, any town that could obtain the county seat was assured of growth and prosperity. Commissioners appointed by the state legislature decided the location for a county seat. However, rival towns often took matters into their own hands (and got away with it), as happened in the case of Homer.

Homer, built on a lovely prairie site about three miles from the confluence of the Boone and Des Moines rivers, was in 1853 the largest (population of 150) and most favorably known town in northwest Iowa. It had been named as the county seat of Webster County (then comprised of what is now both Webster and Hamilton counties).

Settlers from the East went to the U.S. Land Office in Homer to inquire about buying land somewhere to the west. Struck by the beauty of the luxuriant prairie grasses and the fertile soil, many decided to stay. Relatives from back home were contacted and convinced to join them at Homer.

The first road surveyed by the state in 1855 passed through Homer; though it was but a furrow path plowed by the surveyor, the stagecoach traveled it between Des Moines and Homer via

Boone. The Our House Hotel was built to accommodate the stagecoach passengers as well as the hundreds of westward-traveling landseekers. To provide groceries for the swelling population, the storekeeper hauled merchandise from Davenport in an ox-drawn wagon.

Businesses included a blacksmith, livery stables, and various stores, which mushroomed in the next few years. District court and religious services were held in the newly built schoolhouse.

Meanwhile, Fort Dodge, nineteen miles to the northwest and practically abandoned after the removal of its military installations in 1853, experienced a revival—landowners there were determined to make it an important center. Before the Homerites knew what was happening, Fort Dodge staged and won a political battle to acquire the U.S. Land Office. When it was removed from Homer in 1855, a number of citizens followed.

Fort Dodge then proposed that the county seat be relocated to their town as well. The proposal was preposterous to the Homerites for the location had already been established by the legislature. Nevertheless, Fort Dodge conspired with Newcastle (Webster City) in a plan to get the Webster county seat changed to Fort Dodge and to lobby the legislature to divide Webster in two, with Newcastle the county seat of Hamilton, the newly formed county.

Fort Dodge managed to take a tier of four townships from Humboldt County to the north and add them to Webster County, thus placing Fort Dodge nearer the center of the county, a prime consideration for county seat location. (Humboldt County was never able to get these townships back and, as a result, is smaller than its neighbors by one tier of townships.)

Fort Dodge's victory (with Newcastle's help) in the election held to decide whether Fort Dodge should get the county seat was contested by Homer. It was obvious from the large number of votes that the ballot boxes had been stuffed (though likely Homer was equally guilty of this offense). When Attorney John D. Maxwell of Homer accused Fort Dodge of corrupt election practices, John F. Duncombe, a Fort Dodge booster and an accomplished wrestler, proposed a wrestling match to settle the issue. Maxwell accepted the challenge, and in the hard-fought, one-hour match that followed in Homer's public square, Duncombe won. Fort Dodge became the new county seat in 1856.

It is said that to make victory doubly sure, several Fort Dodge men with ox teams stole into Homer one dark night, mounted the makeshift courthouse on skids, and proceeded to pull it away. When they got stuck in a slough, they left the building but took the records. Whether or not this story is true, Fort Dodge did become the county seat.

It had been one of the bitterest county seat battles in Iowa. When the legislature divided Webster County, and Webster City became the county seat of the new Hamilton County, ironically, Homer was no longer in Webster County but just across the border in Hamilton County.

Another catastrophe for Homer, doubtlessly related to the loss of its status as the county seat, was that the railroad was routed from Webster City to Fort Dodge, thereby missing Homer by about ten miles. Homer continued to put up a valiant fight for existence, and for a time grew and flourished as a leading merchandising center for a large area. The goods were hauled by wagon the ten miles from the railroad station. A new Methodist Church was built in 1866, as were three other churches within the decade. Business continued to grow until 1875, but after that it was gradually eclipsed by Fort Dodge.

The Homer post office was discontinued in 1915 (official pronouncement of death), the drug store was closed in 1920, the Christian Church was razed in the 1930s, and the schoolhouse was partially damaged by a tornado and then dismantled in 1944.

The Methodist Church, with its tastefully decorated interior, survives today (1989) and is beautifully kept up. Services are held each Sunday morning at 8:15; the fifty or so members come from Stratford and share a minister with the Stratford church. The Women's Society is especially active, sponsoring ice cream and box socials, making quilts to sell, and sponsoring a fall bazaar and auction to support the church.

The only business establishment in Homer today is Lamb's Small Engine Shop, which sells and services lawn and garden equipment. Don Lamb, a native of the area, opened the business in the 1970s in one of the deserted old buildings in Homer, and he does a good business over a very wide area. His home and two other houses stand nearby.

Fig. 12.5. Lamb's Small Engine Shop, the only business establishment today in Homer. (Photo by Harriet Heusinkveld)

The rest is memories and nostalgic stories, told by former residents, the majority of whom now live in Stratford, about eight miles away. (Located eight miles north of Stratford on R-21)

Buxton, 1900–1927. During the late nineteenth and early twentieth centuries, coal mining thrived in the Des Moines River valley. Coal mining and the railroads, also at their height during this period, formed something of a symbiotic relationship, each one needing the other. Buxton, a coal mining camp in Monroe County, became a new type of community—an "instant town" that leaped into being, full-grown. It lived vibrantly and boisterously, became the largest of all the mining camps in Iowa, and died as suddenly as it was born.

Buxton was established in 1900 as the successor to Muchakinock, a mining camp in Mahaska County where the coal was practically exhausted. The owner, the Consolidation Coal Company, a subsidiary of the Chicago and North Western Railroad, bought ten thousand acres of land in Monroe County, extended the railroad tracks southward, and proceeded to build a new camp.

Consolidation's manager, Mr. Ben Buxton, took his miners, many of whom were blacks he had recruited from the South, by train to the new town of Buxton, twelve miles north of Albia.

Buxton laid out the town with a one-mile-square area in the center for the business district with lots for houses around the square. Company homes were moved in from Muchakinock, and new ones were built, to make a total of one thousand homes. By 1910 the population had swelled to six thousand people.

The homes were five- or six-room, two-story frame structures, each placed on a quarter-acre of land so that every miner could have a cow, chickens, pigs, and a small garden. The streets were irregular, following the lay of the hilly land. The company dug numerous wells for household water, but there was no sewage system.

As in the case of the dwellings, the business buildings, which included a company store, meat market, and bakery, were built with every expectation of permanence. There were even private stores as well, some in the luxury category. The company store known as The Monroe Mercantile Company was the most modern store for miles around. It was huge—half a block long, three stories high, and it had a twenty-railroad-car capacity storage warehouse as well. It was ahead of its time with electric lights, electric elevator, and a pneumatic automatic cash system. Its merchandise included millinery, wedding gowns, clothing, hardware, furniture, carpets, stoves, and coffins. The store operated ten delivery wagons. The farmers around Buxton began to plant vegetables to supply the Buxton market.

The miners were paid good wages and ate and dressed well. They placed a high premium on good social and cultural activities. The Company built a $20,000, three-story Y.M.C.A. building for the blacks, which contained a library; rooms for chess, checkers, billiards, and pool playing; classrooms for night school; a music room; and a gym on the first floor. On the second floor was the "Opera House," with a stage, dressing room, and seats for a thousand people. Motion pictures were shown almost every night, and road shows were presented frequently. Among the Negro lecturers and entertainers who performed were Booker T. Washington, Hallie I. Brown, and Blind Boone. The third floor contained lodge rooms. This was a period when secret societies were popular in Iowa, especially among the blacks.

Buxton had its own concert band, which traveled over the state giving concerts, and its own baseball team, which played with surrounding town teams on Sunday afternoons. But it also was reputed to have been a rowdy town with frequent knifings and brawls. Because it was unincorporated, and so had no city government or police, order was maintained by the county sheriff. A small vaultlike jail kept offenders overnight until they could be moved to the jail at Albia. Saloons were forbidden in Buxton, but it was not difficult to find alcoholic beverages out of town. The *Oskaloosa Herald,* March 19, 1920, carried this headline on Buxton: "Sheriff Seizes 1152 Bottles of Beer in a Wagon Between Eddyville and Buxton. Second Seizure of Contraband in a Short Time." Despite this notoriety, the majority of Buxtonites were law abiding, attended church services regularly, and were ambitious for the education and future of their children.

The Consolidation Coal Company was perhaps the most progressive in Iowa as to wages paid and safety measures provided. The workers belonged to the United Mine Workers Union, with headquarters in Albia, and joined in the strikes although they were usually of short duration. The big day of the year was Labor Day, when they joined other miners in parades, bands, and baseball games.

Although a measure of segregation existed between whites and blacks, there seemingly was no animosity. One reason why they got along well probably was that they received equal pay for equal work. The Swedes lived in the areas of town known as East Swede Town and West Swede Town, the Hungarians in their section, and the blacks in their part of town. The churches included the Colored Methodist, Swedish Lutheran, Colored Baptist, and White Methodist.

Buxton was cleaner than most coal mining camps because the mines were out of town. Some two thousand men were transported to and from the mines by train. Children met their daddies as they arrived at the depot late in the afternoon, carried their dinnerpails for them as they walked homeward together, and then the family waited while the man of the house bathed before the family sat down for the big meal of the day.

The coal was so abundant, the mining so modern and efficient, and the market for railroad coal so great that it seemed as if the Buxton "Utopia" would never end. During World War I, Consolidation had to work its mines overtime.

After the war, however, disaster struck. Other fuels entered the picture, and railroad transportation declined. Consolidation survived longer than some companies, but on March 25, 1927, they closed the big No. 18; then the miners went on strike, and No. 19 was shut down. Years later more than a hundred cars of coal were still standing at the bottom of No. 19, waiting to be hoisted up.

The *Oskaloosa Times,* October 29, 1929, said of Buxton that

> The four winds called to the population and last year it literally melted away. The banking and business houses began closing. School opened in the fine new high school this year with only a few pupils, and one school building entirely unused. . . . Six months from now, Nature will reclaim its own, and only a few foundations, a ramshackle store or two will mark the glory that once was Buxton's.

Today Buxton is a pasture thick with cockleburs and grasshoppers. The railroad tracks have long since been removed, and the grade is a gentle bank winding past the old town. Crumbled foundations of the old stores are all but lost in the weeds. The once lively town is no more. (Located five miles east of Lovilia, Monroe County; Bluff Creek Twp., Sec. 4)

Bellefountaine, 1846, existed because of its smooth shallow ford that was easily passable when the river was low. Talley's ferry carried passengers and freight across the stream in times of higher water.

When the steamboats came after the flood of 1851, Bellefountaine became a principal Des Moines River port; a boat landing was constructed, as was a warehouse for storing goods to be transported by land to other places. It was a stagecoach stop where they provided meals and lodging in a well-equipped inn and stables for the horses. Bellefountaine became so well known that it is said that on the first ballot for relocating the state capital, it lost by only one vote.

Ironically, when the railroad came in 1874, it missed this important transportation center by one mile. The population thereupon moved to Tracy, the new railroad town.

After a century of abandonment, Bellefountaine now shows new signs of life as houses and cottages are being built on its waterfront. (Located one mile east of Tracy)

Amsterdam, 1848, "the port of Pella" was platted by Dominie H. P. Scholte, leader of the Pella Hollanders, with 490 lots, a public square, and a site for a city market. Scholte sent circulars to eastern cities describing the "emporium of trade" Amsterdam was to be. A few people settled here and a brick and tile factory was in operation.

However, when steamboating on the river ceased, so did Amsterdam. (Travel four miles south of Pella on T-15, then right on T-17)

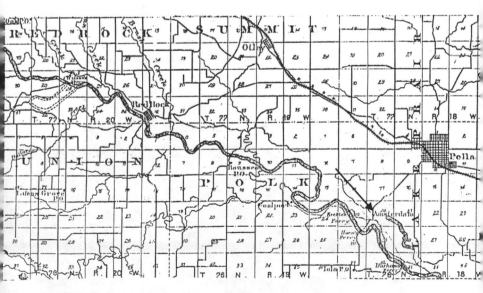

Fig. 12.6. Amsterdam, "the port of Pella," as of 1875. The map also shows Coalport and Red Rock further upstream. (Map from Atlas of Marion County, *1875)*

Morgan Valley, 1880–1903, occupied a beautiful spot along the Des Moines River in the northwest corner of Marion County. In the 1880s it was a bustling coal town, with the Wabash running railroad spurs to its various mines. When the mines gave out, the population moved away. A charming, white frame Christian church remains, and worship services are held each Sunday. (Go one-half mile north and two and one-half miles east of Runnells; ask at Runnells for Morgan Valley Church)

Apple Grove, 1844, was the creation of Thomas Mitchell, sutler for Fort Des Moines. The fort commander allowed him to register the land before it was legal to do so on condition that he build a bridge over Camp Creek, lodge and feed the public who might be traveling to and from the fort (army men, government officials), and keep a post office in his house to receive and distribute mail for the fort. His home, Mitchell's Tavern, was a popular station on the stagecoach line between Iowa City and Fort Des Moines, a voting place, and a place for school classes and religious services.

When Fort Des Moines was abandoned, the stagecoach discontinued, and the promised railroad line laid two miles to the east, Apple Grove was abandoned in favor of Mitchellville.

A plaque in Thomas Mitchell Park shows the location of Mitchell's famous cabin, the site of Apple Grove. (Located three miles southwest of Mitchellville)

Fig. 12.7.   Old school house, Elk Rapids. (Photo by Harriet Heusinkveld)

Elk Rapids, 1850, was so named because the settlers often saw elk crossing the river rapids at this place. It was one of Iowa's many early mill towns. By 1855 it had, in addition to the gristmill, a sawmill, a post office, three stores, and homes for 150 people. Most of Iowa's early mills burned, due to dust combustion. Elk Rapids mill, however, was washed out by a flood in 1857, after which the town began to decline. (Located about two miles west of Madrid; ask at Madrid)

Xenia, 1850s, was a thriving town on the bluffs overlooking the Des Moines River. When the railroad came through, it decided it could not build a depot at Xenia because the train would get stuck going up the hills out of town. Instead, it built the depot at Woodward.

A large sign marks the site of Xenia, and a well-kept cemetery nearby indicates that it once had a considerable population. (Located about one mile east of Woodward on unmarked road; ask at Woodward)

Fig. 12.8.   The replica of the Moingona depot, a railroad car, and a parklike area all honor Kate Shelley, a local hero. (Photo by Harriet Heusinkveld)

Moingona, 1866, thought to be the Indian word for the Des Moines River, had coal mines and excellent potteries and brick works, all prosperous because the railroad had routed its line through their town rather than Boonesboro. The railroad, however, was rerouted a few years later, missing Moingona by just a few miles, and this was the beginning of the end.

Moingona became famous in 1881 when fifteen-year-old Kate Shelley of rural Moingona risked her life by crawling over a railroad bridge during a severe rainstorm to warn the station agent at Moingona that the Honey Creek bridge had washed out. The agent was able to flag down the approaching midnight passenger train, thus saving many lives. A delightful museum in Moingona with a replica of the depot, a railroad car, and a parklike area commemorates her heroic act.

Moingona is staging a comeback, this time as a minor bedroom town for Boone. (Located five miles west of Boone on Highway 30; then south on R-18, follow signs)

Kalo comes from the Greek word *kalos,* which means beautiful. The town was located at a spot where the Des Moines River cuts through red and buff sandstone cliffs down to its canyon, 150 feet below. The cliffs are topped with a heavy growth of oak trees.

Kalo mined coal from the 1880s to the end of the century. Then coal deposits were almost exhausted, the railroad abandoned its line through Kalo, and the population for the most part turned to agriculture. The Congregational Church is the principal reminder of this once flourishing town. (Located about eight miles north of Lehigh on P-59)

Among other ghost towns on the central Des Moines River are Fifield, Rousseau, Dunreath, Cordova, and Percy in Marion County, all covered by Lake Red Rock; Phalanx, a Fourier Association (socialist community) town in Mahaska County; Ford, a transport center and coal mining town in Warren County; Zookspur, Scandia, and High Bridge near Madrid, and Coal Valley and Incline near Boone, all coal mining camps in Boone County; Coalville and Hardscrabble, coal mining towns in Webster County; Dudley, a once important town in Polk County, washed out by the river in 1852, as well as many early towns absorbed by the city of Des Moines.

Silence now reigns in all these places instead of the sounds of many voices. Nature is quietly reclaiming her own, as weeds and tangled vines grow among old foundations. The ghosts of the past beckon us to come to see these places, to muse about how men, women, and children once lived in these now deserted spots.

Interviews

James and Blanche Templeton, rural Red Rock; Mrs. G. Franklin, Coalport; Mary Jo and Marvin D. Johnson, Stratford; Don Lamb, Homer; Avis Van Zomeren, Pella; Audrey McVay, Madrid; Wendell and Wilma Sandell, Dayton; Mrs. Libera Axen, Lehigh.

Selected References

Andreas, A. T. *Illustrated Historical Atlas of the State of Iowa.* Chicago: Andreas Atlas Co., 1875.

Atlas of Marion County, Iowa. Philadelphia: Harrison and Werner, 1875.

Atlas of Marion County, Iowa. Chicago: Arthur M. Hovey, 1901.

Atlas of Marion County. Knoxville, Iowa: Midland Map Co., 1909.

Donnel, W. M. *Pioneers of Marion County.* Philadelphia: Republican Steam Printing House, 1872.

Gradwohl, David M., and Nancy M. Osborn. *Exploring Buried Buxton.* Ames: Iowa State Univ. Press, 1984.

Hamilton Historical Society. *History of Hamilton County, Iowa.* Dallas: Curtis Media Corp., 1986.

Knoxville Journal, Jubilee Edition, Knoxville, Iowa, Sept. 25, 1930.

Lyon, Bessie L. "The Passing of Homer," *Palimpsest,* 1922 (Dec.): 381–89.

Madrid Centennial Committee. *A Proud Community, Madrid, Iowa, Centennial 1883–1983.* No publisher listed, 1983.

Mahaska County Historical Society. *Mahaska County History.* Dallas: Curtis Media Corp., 1984.

McCown, Alfred B. *Down on the Ridge.* No publisher listed. Des Moines, 1909.

Mott, D. C. *Abandoned Towns, Villages, and Post Offices of Iowa,* compiled from back issues of *Annals of Iowa,* Iowa State Dep. of History and Archives, Des Moines, 1932.

Schroeder, Allen Lee. "The Stoneware Industry at Moingona, Iowa." Master's thesis, Dep. of Anthropology, Iowa State Univ., Ames, 1979.

Webster County Bicentennial Commission. *Webster's Prairies.* No publisher listed, 1976.

PART

V

On the Road

THEATERS OF IOWA:
THE HISTORIC &
THE UNUSUAL

John B. Harper

Prowl around the center, or what used to be the center, of many Iowa towns, and one of the larger buildings you are likely to find (besides the courthouse, the banks, and the churches) is an imposing old brick storefront with "Opera House" still visible over its main entrance. Often it is rundown and vacant, a former lodge hall or garage or antique store. Or its front has been covered by the now broken marquee of a movie house. But in some towns it is now restored, a monument to community pride and to the century-old identification of Iowans with theater.

The seating capacity of these buildings is often larger than the population of the community, and the many levels once contained ballrooms, meeting rooms, and restaurants. Early descriptions indicate that such buildings functioned very much as community social centers, the places where nearly everyone came to be entertained, to show off their finest new clothes, and to exchange notes on the latest town scandal.

Although the architectural design of these nineteenth-century theaters tended to be rather plain and simple on the exterior, the interiors were invariably plush: winding staircases, ornate moldings, and enormous chandeliers were common focal points.

The presence of a theater or opera house in the community offered an opportunity for it to be included on the touring circuits of all of the most distinguished traveling theater and opera companies. One week's fare might consist of a Shakespearean play, while the next week would bring a popular melodrama. It was not until well into the twentieth century that locally generated pro-

251

ductions became common in any of these theaters.

Iowans of the late nineteenth century took great pride in being regarded as "cultured." Indeed, it might be assumed that the average resident of an Iowa county seat had greater exposure to major theater and opera productions than the average New Yorker. And the typical pattern of productions offered would strongly disprove any stereotype that early Iowans were overly conservative or puritanical in their tastes and outlooks.

This Iowa tradition of interest and support for quality theater companies and productions, then, has a solid history dating back well over one hundred years. It was probably a combination of geographic isolation and strong community pride that led so many Iowa towns, both small and large, to invest in the design and construction of glamorous theaters and opera houses. Dozens were built in the 1880s and 1890s, and a surprising number survive today.

Fig. 13.1.   The plush interior of the Capitol Theater, Davenport, as it appeared in 1930. (Photo courtesy of State Historical Society of Iowa)

One result of this nineteenth-century love of theater was that Iowans played a key role in the beginning of the "new" American theater of the early twentieth century. Susan Glaspell was a playwright, a native of Davenport, and a student at Drake University. Her husband George Cook had come to Iowa from Harvard to teach classics. After their marriage in 1913, they moved from Iowa to Provincetown, Massachussets, where they began to implement a dream that had originated in Iowa. They gathered around them a group of the best young, aspiring playwrights in the nation and developed a theater company to nurture, discuss, and produce new, experimental works. Eugene O'Neill was to become the most famous and distinguished member of this group, and its influence on the new course of American theater was indeed profound.

By the 1920s virtually every population center in Iowa contained a legitimate theater that generally served a wide variety of purposes — shows ranging from the classics to melodrama, musical concerts of all types, and often regular showings of silent movies. Most could boast of touring productions featuring one or more of the Barrymores, Sarah Bernhardt, Al Jolson, or Eddie Cantor. Almost all these theaters had been constructed between 1880 and the outbreak of World War I, and almost without exception, their architectural design and construction was as great a source of pride to the community as the productions that were presented within them.

The 1920s were also the decade in which Professor E. C. Mabie began to build a nationally distinguished theater department at the (then-called) State University of Iowa in Iowa City. His program, with its strong emphasis on the training of new playwrights and the production of their work, soon became a serious rival to programs developed earlier in the century at Yale and Harvard. Mabie's best-known student was Tennessee Williams, who came to Iowa to study with Mabie during the 1937–1938 school year.

As Iowa moved into the thirties and into the worst years of the Depression, many of the great theater houses in the state were closed and abandoned for economic reasons. Those that survived generally were converted into movie houses for "talking pictures." In the late thirties and into the forties, some of them became performance sites for the big band concerts — Tommy and Jimmy Dorsey, Glenn Miller, Louis Armstrong, Guy Lombardo.

However, live theater productions went into a period of dormancy. Only college theater programs and a handful of large, long-established community theaters survived. Here and there, programs of the Federal Theatre Project would appear for brief periods and then die out again. Only in the late fifties and early sixties did a strong theater tradition begin to revive, often with a group performing in the local high school auditorium or the back room of a restaurant, until sufficiently well-established to begin looking for a more suitable performance site.

By the end of the sixties major developments were beginning to occur. A new performing arts complex was completed at Iowa State University in Ames, to be followed a few years later by a similar complex at the University of Iowa in Iowa City. As federal funding became available for such projects and as historic preservation gained strength as an organized activity, theater of the highest quality once again became accessible to every part of the state.

It was not until the late seventies and early eighties, however, that widespread restoration of the old theaters and development of new ones began. At first glance, this period of rapid growth and vigor would seem to defy explanation, for the state was losing population and was being increasingly hit by economic recession. Funding for the arts from state revenues generally ranked Iowa in forty-ninth or fiftieth place in per capita appropriations.

A more careful look at this question provides evidence that economic adversity and population declines, especially in smaller communities, have undoubtedly provided a major impetus for a growth in theater activity. Iowans still take immense pride in the preservation of their communities and in their heritage. Theater is an activity that brings a community together, creating a product that can be a tangible expression of civic pride.

Over the past decade Iowa has experienced considerable growth in theatrical activity, both with respect to numbers and to artistic quality. Active community theaters now number well over one hundred, and college and university theater programs are among the best and most imaginative in the nation. Modern performing arts centers in Des Moines, Cedar Rapids, and Ames regularly feature the finest of Broadway touring productions, as well as programs of such companies as the Guthrie Theater, the American Players Theater, and the Milwaukee Repertory Company. Productions of both college and community theaters routinely win top honors in regional and national play competitions.

No phenomenon in theater in the past decade has been as prevalent as the restoration of the old theater houses — abandoned legitimate theaters, vaudeville and burlesque houses, opera houses, and defunct movie theaters. All of them have special meaning and memories to the towns and cities in which they are located.

A rather typical example of this century-long historical cycle is to be found in the What Cheer Opera House. What Cheer is a quiet little community (population eight hundred) in southeast Iowa, some distance from any major population center. Its opera house was constructed in 1893, under the supervision of an Omaha contractor who had received a presidential appointment to oversee such projects in Iowa.

The opera house had an orchestra and dress circle with a seating capacity of 383 and a horseshoe balcony that seated an additional 217. The top floor of the building was an ornate ballroom area, the site of an opening Grand Ball on February 7, 1894; a schedule of regular theatrical productions began at the end of the month with "Pete Peterson and his Repertoire Group." Ticket prices ranged from $.50 to $2.50, and patrons were brought in on special excursion trains from surrounding communities. Residents of Belle Plaine, South English, or Montezuma could take an afternoon train to the opera house and return home in the evening after the performance.

Fig. 13.2. The What Cheer Opera House, What Cheer, Iowa, is the current home of The Main Street Players. Built by the Masons in 1893, restoration began in 1965; it was named to the National Register of Historic Places in 1973. (Photo courtesy of Oskaloosa Herald Shopper*)*

For the next fifty years or more, the What Cheer Opera
House presented plays, vaudeville shows, silent movies, and big
band concerts. The house became especially well known for its
bands: Guy Lombardo was the first to be booked, followed by
Glenn Miller, Bob Crosby, Jan Garber, Wayne King, Stan Kenton,
and Sammy Kaye. Groups such as Fred Waring and the Pennsy-
lvanians often came, as did popular and country-western vocal-
ists.

The opera house went into a period of serious decline in the
years following World War II and was closed down through most
of the fifties. By the early sixties, the old opera house was slated
for demolition.

The What Cheer centennial in 1965 was the occasion for
generating local interest in saving the opera house. After a centennial variety show, a group of local citizens bought the building
back from the demolition contractor, and plans for restoration
began. The opera house reopened in 1966, with a return engage-
ment of Guy Lombardo and his Royal Canadians. In 1973 the
opera house was placed on the National Register of Historic
Places.

In more recent years a theater group, the Main Street Players, was formed to present regular seasons of plays at the opera
house. After the completion of restoration on the third floor
ballroom, the group will present dinner theater productions. Today the Main Street Players shares the opera house with touring
productions of other theaters and a wide variety of musical performers.

It should be noted that the restoration and reopening of any
nineteenth-century theater or opera house is not the essence of
economic sanity. As they were built before the advent of fire and
safety codes, and as most of them had fallen into a state of
considerable disrepair, renovation and remodeling costs are often
astronomical. Beyond that, there is the consideration of maintenance and energy costs for buildings that generally are not in
daily use. Such decisions must be accompanied by a deep community commitment with long-term implications, and often the
structure must be shared by several local groups in order to come
close to being economically self-sustaining.

A more recent example of the restoration of a theater dating
back to the 1880s is to be found in the Grand Opera House of
Dubuque, recently acquired by the Barn Community Theater.
This house, the oldest theater in Dubuque, was constructed in
1889–1890 by a group of civic leaders at a cost of sixty-five thousand dollars.

The Grand Opera House officially opened on August 14,
1890, with a production of *Carmen* by the Hess Opera Company.

Given the special nature of the occasion, the house was filled, in spite of the five dollar ticket price.

The original facade of the Grand was a St. Louis brick facing with red sandstone trim, later covered by metal enamel plating. The seating capacity was eleven hundred. For thirty-eight years the Grand Opera House was a major center for live performances of opera, theater, music, and dance, with visiting stars such as Sarah Bernhardt, George M. Cohan, and Lillian Russell.

Fig. 13.3.   Cover of an early "Bill of the Play" for the Grand Opera House, Dubuque, which opened August 14, 1890, with a performance of Carmen. *It was modified in 1928 to serve as a movie house. It continued as a movie theater until August 15, 1986, when it opened again as the home of the Barn Community Theater. (Courtesy of the Barn Community Theater)*

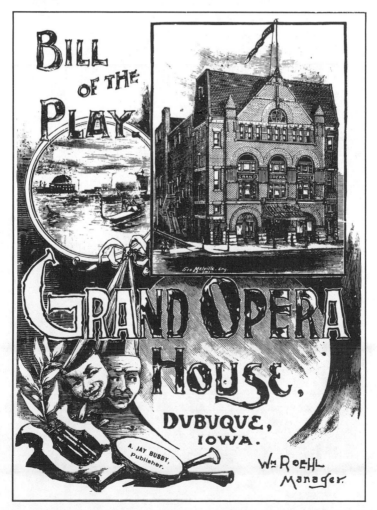

Major stage performances continued through 1928, and then the theater proceeded to adapt to changing times. By 1930 the building had been substantially modified for use as a movie theater—the third balcony and box seats were removed, the orchestra pit was covered over, and projection equipment was installed.

The Grand continued to operate as a movie theater until 1986, when a fifteen-year-old community theater organization, the Barn Community Theater, purchased the building and proceeded to remodel it as a permanent home for live theater productions. A new era of theater in the Grand was inaugurated in August 1986 with a production of *Tintypes*. The theater now has in place a year-round season of productions, children's theater performances, and an extensive program of classes, workshops, and outreach activities.

In north central Iowa, another Grand Theater has recently come back to life through the auspices of a local community theater. This theater, in Story City (population twenty-eight hundred), was constructed in 1913 as part of a larger complex, which also included the Grand Hotel. At the time of its opening the theater boasted the second largest stage west of the Mississippi, and was fully equipped for both stage productions and silent movies.

Fig. 13.4.   Story Theater, 512 Broad St., Story City. In 1988 it celebrated seventy-five years of continuous service, having never closed since its opening December 18, 1913. (Photo by Todd Thorson)

Story City's Grand, later renamed the Story Theater, opened in December 1913 with a production of a melodrama, *The Two Orphans.* Tickets were three dollars, and patrons sat in four hundred thin-backed opera chairs with hat racks underneath. *Birth of a Nation* was the first silent film to be shown there in 1917. Tickets were fifty cents, and a full pit orchestra provided the background music.

The Story Theater had been used exclusively as a movie theater from 1947 on, until the local community theater began to examine its potential for renovation in the eighties. The group, Judge Story's Theatrical Troupe, was formed in 1982, specializing in Broadway musicals and light comedies. The reopening of the Story Theater as a live performance house coincided with its Diamond Jubilee in 1988.

One final "Grand Theater" is found in Keokuk, in the southeastern corner of the state. The original Grand Theater of Keokuk was a turn-of-the-century creation, presenting everything from Shakespeare to melodramas to music recitals. In December 1923 the original building burned to the ground during a play performance.

A new, larger theater building was constructed on the same site, and opened in January 1925. This 1,050-seat house was a most impressive sight, with its purple tapestries, ornate gold medallions and chandeliers, its balconies and boxes, and its ornamental plaster and marble. It opened by importing the stage hit of the year from Chicago, *Lollipop,* starring Ada May Weeks. In the several years following the opening, major stage shows included *The Rivals, The Student Prince, George White's Scandals,* and *The Merchant of Venice.* All of the Barrymore family appeared there, as did Richard Carle, Mae Robson, and Al Jolson.

Keokuk's Grand Theater had been substantially converted into a movie house by 1929, and continued in that mode until it closed in 1957. It was completely remodeled and opened again as a movie house in 1965, receiving yet another major facelift in 1978.

In March 1987 the Grand was offered to the city of Keokuk as a gift, to be used as a municipal performance center. A long-standing community theater group, the Great River Players, is now in the process of moving its performance season to this facility, which it will share with band concerts, dance recitals, and other community activities.

Examples of restorations of historic theater houses are comparatively rare in the largest population centers of Iowa. In Des Moines, the magnificent old downtown performance houses — the Paramount, the Orpheum, and the Des Moines — were all leveled to make room for office buildings and parking lots. In Iowa City the interior of the historic Englert Theater was substantially destroyed in its conversion into two smaller movie houses in 1984. But Cedar Rapids can boast of having preserved two major downtown theaters. The largest, the Paramount, has become the home of the Cedar Rapids Symphony and hosts annual performances of major Broadway musicals. Its neighbor, and the smaller of the two, is the Iowa Theater, recently restored as the home of the Cedar Rapids Community Theater.

The Iowa Theater was originally a fourteen-hundred-seat house, opened in 1928 for movies, stage productions, and vaudeville shows. Performers over the years included Katherine Hepburn, Dan Duryea, Ethel Barrymore, and Dan Dailey, and it was used as a live-performance hall until a final concert by Nat King Cole in 1953.

In 1982 the building that housed the Iowa Theater was purchased by local businessman David Linge, who in turn gave the theater portion of the building to the Cedar Rapids Community Theater. Restoration of the space cost over one million dollars, an amount raised through a major community fund drive.

The remodeling plans called for scaling down the size of the original house to 528 seats, using some of the excess space to construct a smaller studio theater. Even with substantial modification, most of the interesting facets of the original interior have been preserved: original moldings are intact and the orchestra pit still contains the original Barton organ, the largest theater pipe organ in the state.

The Cedar Rapids Community Theater is well over fifty years old, and one of the most imaginative and respected organizations in Iowa. It presents a highly ambitious and varied program annually, with main-stage and studio shows, touring productions, and a full season of shows for young people. A typical recent main-stage season featured *Camelot, The Belle of Amherst,* and *Amadeus.*

Other fine examples of live theater in historic opera houses or legitimate theaters can be found from Akron on the western border, to Albia in south central Iowa, to Elkader and Davenport in the eastern end of the state. These converted or preserved theaters, however, are only one kind of example of the structures in which one may find regular performances of high-quality theater.

Iowa's major ongoing professional theater company, for example, is located in a most unlikely setting. In 1971 Thomas Johnson of Iowa State University and a group of nine colleagues took over a farmer co-op dairy in Garrison (population four hundred) and transformed it into the Old Creamery Theater. Activities in the imposing old brick structure gradually expanded throughout the first ten years of operation. To the original theater space was added a second studio theater and full-service restaurant. A large patio beer garden area was constructed adjacent to all three parts of the building.

Old Creamery, located within easy driving distance of Waterloo and Cedar Rapids, has become a statewide institution. In addition to its resident performing season, the company tours throughout Iowa and other midwestern states and conducts a full range of workshops and other educational activities.

A typical recent main-stage season at Old Creamery featured productions of *Noises Off, A Midsummer Night's Dream,* and *The Foreigner.* The studio theater is frequently used as a space for introducing works of new playwrights and for guest directors and performers.

Another unusual match of professional talent and unlikely performance space is to be found at Okoboji, in the northwest corner of the state. The Okoboji Summer Theater, located in the middle of the "Iowa Great Lakes" recreation area, has been housed since 1953 in an airplane hangar that was constructed in the 1930s as a WPA project.

Fig. 13.5. The Okoboji Summer Theater on opening day in 1962. It still plays where it began in 1953, in an airplane hangar built by the WPA. (Photo courtesy of Okoboji Summer Theater)

Okoboji Summer Theater has been operated by Stephens College of Columbia, Missouri, since 1958. A nine-show season from June through August is generally a balance of comedy, drama, and musicals. Professional actors and directors join forces with theater students from Stephens in mounting the season. The hangar has been expanded and remodeled a number of times through the years, and an adjacent space for the performance of children's theater was completed in 1963. Surrounding barns, trailers, and other buildings serve as dormitories, classrooms, and shops.

A professional group, the Riverside Theater Company of Iowa City, performs in one of the community's oldest (1865) and most architecturally interesting churches. Originally the First Presbyterian Church, the building is now named Old Brick and sits near the center of the University of Iowa campus. It was preserved by a nonprofit group of community leaders in the early seventies; its sanctuary has become a regular venue for theater, art exhibits, public lectures, and church services of student religious groups.

The Riverside Theater was established in 1981 by two University of Iowa theater graduates, Jody Hovland and Ron Clark, to fill a void between the programming of the local university and community theaters. The group specializes in small-cast productions, often one-man or one-woman shows, which are generally contemporary in origin. Their repertoire combines performances of Beckett and Brecht with premieres of new scripts, some by Iowa playwrights. Old Brick church presents a variety of staging possibilities to the Riverside company, which performs a full season of productions there. The company also tours extensively around the state presenting workshops.

The list goes on and on. In Sioux City, a long-established community theater makes its home in the old Shore Acres Ballroom on the banks of the Big Sioux River. Nearby in LeMars, the town's original post office has become the performance center for the local theater group, now named the Postal Players.

Summer performances can be seen in Fort Dodge in the Stark White Barn, which was converted into the home of the Hawkeye Community Theater. And summer visitors to Clinton will be treated to productions by the Showboat Theater on a Mississippi riverboat.

The vast majority of theaters in the state are members of the Iowa Community Theater Association (ICTA), one of the most active state theater groups in the nation. In a typical year, perhaps seventy-five communities will be represented in its activities. In a given year an average of four or five newly formed theater groups will join its ranks. Member theaters range in size from Waterloo Community Playhouse, with a professional staff of eleven and several thousand subscribers, to new theaters with only ten members and a few hundred dollars in the bank to buy lumber and costume materials for their very first show.

From its inception the ICTA has concentrated its attention on providing guidance and information for theater groups in smaller communities. The long-time leader of the state organization, L. K. Boutin of Des Moines, routinely traveled throughout the state to attend openings of new theaters and to meet with newly formed theater boards to render advice. Upon his death in 1985, ICTA discovered that a major portion of his estate had been set aside to carry on this work—a grant program established with these funds is now in operation. In 1988 one grant award will provide support for the Keokuk group as they continue their move into the Grand Theater.

Members of ICTA congregate at various locations around the state several times each year to attend workshops, to see each other's productions, and to informally swap information about interesting scripts or recruit volunteers. Increasingly these information exchanges are concerned with questions of locating, financing, and remodeling old buildings.

A major event sponsored by ICTA is the biennial play festival contest. At the 1987 festival in Pella eleven groups presented eleven different fully staged productions on the same stage in a two-day period. The selections ranged from an Ibsen classic to a Sondheim musical revue to a new, experimental script.

As might be expected, most theaters in smaller communities are not in positions to take major economic and artistic risks. The staple commodities of these groups are generally big-name Broadway musicals, light comedies, and farces.

Only a handful of community theaters, including Waterloo, Cedar Rapids, and Des Moines, have substantial budgets and professional directors and staff members. These groups are much more likely to present a broader range of programming and educational activities. The community theaters of Waterloo and Des Moines, as well as the Drama Workshop of Des Moines, are especially well known for their presentations of new scripts and the works of new playwrights.

Good theater can be found nearly everywhere in Iowa—from an old airplane hangar at Okoboji to a Mississippi riverboat in Clinton, from a riverfront ballroom in Sioux City to a creamery in Garrison, and from a turn-of-the-century post office in LeMars to a remodeled barn in Fort Dodge. Live theater is flourishing in Iowa, and it ranges from frequent productions of the classics in old warehouses to the latest Neil Simon comedy in old opera houses.

The majority of Iowa counties contain at least one theater that is well worth a visit. Attending a performance is an ideal way to get acquainted with a theater, in both its functional and its architectural dimensions. But even if schedules don't allow attendance at a performance, a visit to many of these historic structures will enable one to glean a sense of their past and present roles in their respective communities. As they were once the focal point of community life, so many of them are moving in the direction of recapturing that status a century later.

IOWA FOR COLLECTORS

Amy Godine

Say it starts with buttons. Or before the buttons, with a freshwater mussel from the Mississippi River around Muscatine. And say it is the kind of mussel you don't see much anymore—a fawnfoot, a pink heelsplitter, a snuffbox—and that the pair of buttons fashioned from this mussel in a factory along the river's edge somehow finds its way to a department store in Council Bluffs in 1894, the same year the good citizens of that uneasy, hopeful city greeted Charles T. Kelly's eastward-marching Army of the Unemployed with one thousand home-baked pies.

Then, say the buttons journey to a farmhouse near Red Oak where a small girl sews them on a doll for eyes. And that the doll is loved as fixedly and blindly as it will one day be abandoned on a stiff bed of sheet music ("I'm Just A Vagabond Lover," "Paddlin' Madeleine Home") in the bottom drawer of an attic dresser, where marauding mice and mildew reduce the doll to rags—but the button eyes endure.

A while later. It is 1917, late May, a dark and stormy night, and we are at war. The farmwife sits with her back to the stove and reads a postcard, her third that week, from Fort Dodge. Everybody's an insomniac tonight. The kids come in, yawning, restless. She tells the boy, "go get some putty and that big old fruit jar from the hoosier." And she tells the girl, "that box of geegaws I've been saving for no reason, you know which, go bring it."

It is something she read about in the papers—one of those silk-purse-out-of-a-sow's-ear schemes the ladies' page is full of. You take a jar (or box, or bottle) and you plaster it with glue or

putty, then cover it right up to the mouth with, well, with . . .
whatever. Indian head pennies. Bottlecaps. Old keys. Broken
china. Jacks. Charms. Thimbles. A presidential campaign badge.
A tiny glass bottle of *Evening in Paris.* A pair of pearly buttons
you salvaged from the trash. And if it doesn't turn out like anything you see in stores, at least it's . . . *different.* And you can
keep lilacs in it. And look at it and laugh. It has to be the ugliest
darn thing you ever saw.

1934. A drought year. Half of Iowa's farms are in trouble.
Foreclosures are commonplace; the "penny sale" saves a few
farms, but not enough. And the souped-up jar with the coat of
charms passes into other, more indifferent hands.

As for the box, for a little while a high school student from
Des Moines keeps a diary in it. Or a garage mechanic uses it for
receipts. Or a war hero back from Korea stashes medals in it, then
leaves it underneath the porch. Then in 1977 a farmer picks it up
for next to nothing at the first annual flea market in What Cheer
and takes it to his wife.

"That has got to be the ugliest darn thing I ever saw," she
says. "Except those two buttons. I could use those. They're
sweet."

"Never mind the buttons," he says. "Let's just hold on to it
awhile. The kind of stuff these collectors are starting to go in for,
you never know."

So far, so much conjecture. But this part is true. In West
Branch, mere yards from Herbert Hoover's birthplace, this jar is
yours for the buying. "Memoryware," the dealer calls it. And if
you think $250 is a lot of money for a jar all plastered over with
old buttons and bagatelles, think of this: back East (and very
likely it will be an East Coast dealer who picks it up), this
tarnished time capsule turned inside out could bring in twice as
much again.

Because it is not just a matter of a fruit jar stuck with junk.
It is an honest piece of handmade, homegrown folk art — a sure-
fire collectible and to some even an antique. And antiques in
Iowa are big business. From Davenport to Council Bluffs, dealers
and buyers are in accord — this state is *hot!*

Antique stores are located on an average of one per every
five and a half miles of paved road here. Antique newspapers are
published in Vinton, Dubuque, and Grundy Center. The Dubu-
que-based *Antique Trader* is the most widely read trade magazine
in the country. And the summer listings in the *Collectors Journal*
for antique shows, auctions, flea markets, and lawn sales in Iowa

alone fill pages, single-spaced.

Ten years ago when Larry Nicholson hosted the first annual flea market in What Cheer, twenty dealers showed. In May 1987 there were 350, many from out of state.

Ten years ago the town of Walnut was another two-block, down-at-the-heels farm town, empty buildings giving way to corn fields on all sides. In 1987 Governor Branstad proclaimed Walnut "Iowa's Antique City." Ten antique shops crowd the storefronts. Soon a bed-and-breakfast will open, and in the old opera house, a museum of traditional country music. Similar antique revivals have occurred in many other towns, among them Bentonsport, Bellevue, West Branch, Kalona, and McGregor.

Ten years ago a "mall rat" was a kid with stringy hair and a boom box who hung out in shopping plazas playing video games. But malls have changed. With the coming of the mall devoted strictly to antiques—a kind of nonstop, upscale garage sale as it were, representing anywhere from five to forty dealers—the Iowa mall rat is just as apt to be a businessman, a college teacher, or a retired farmer looking for a cast iron lawn sprinkler to dress up his backyard. What Iowa city *doesn't* have an antique mall today packed to the joists with Fiesta plates the colors of Crayolas, porcelain doorknobs, or Bakalite radios with Studebaker knobs that seem to pick up only country music or revival meetings? Or better than a mall, an entire antique district? West Des Moines and Davenport, Fort Dodge and Dubuque . . .

Fig. 14.1. From a two-block, down-at-the-heels farm town, Walnut became "Iowa's Antique City." A Main Street spring antique show. (Photo by Eldon Ranney)

Cynics say, "so what? All the *bargains* got discovered a zillion years ago." And they'll bend your ear about the corner cupboard they picked up for a song in 1966, and how the other day they saw one like it for the kind of money you could go to college on, and isn't it a crime.

It is not a crime. It is the market. So the golden age of the "all-out, kickass *steal*" is gone. Is that a reason to give up? Things aren't getting any cheaper, folks. There may be dips and slips in this or that (boy, let's *hope* so), but if past trends have taught us anything, it's that the value of most anything of more than strictly voguish interest has only one way to go, and that is up. Moreover, even the pricier antiques often cost less than the new stuff. "Just go compare it," urges Iowa City collector Jim Blecha. "For what you pay for an antique oak table, even up to five hundred dollars, you could never get brand-new. People get excited about the high prices of antiques, but it's still a savings when you compare."

As far as Iowa antiques, specifically? Mary Cline of the Melon City Mall in Muscatine says, "We just don't know how lucky we are. We have a great resource here. Barns filled to the brim with antiques. The furniture's just sitting there. And nobody seems to know it."

Well, not quite. Some non-Iowans know very well. An amateur Iowa collector gives a bus tour of the antique district in West Des Moines especially for Californians. At a 1987 graniteware auction in Cedar Rapids the highest bidders were from Pennsylvania and Tennessee. Out West the fastest-selling pressed-back chairs are from Iowa. An Ohio woman sweeps into a shop in Muscatine and cleans out every corn dryer on the rack. "I haven't seen these in Ohio for two or three years," she raves.

"There are people who plan their whole vacations around auctions and flea markets in Iowa," says a writer for the Vinton-based *Collectors Journal*. "They're coming from the West, the South. They can get things here. They come with *vans*."

Lou Picek, a folk and primitive antique dealer of Main Street Antiques in West Branch, in whose six-room shop the Memoryware jar may still be found, confesses, "If I had to rely on Iowans I'd never make it. Seventy-five percent of my business I do mail-order, and most of that is with people out of state."

What is it about Iowa antiques that has collectors so worked up? It is simple, really. They are still plentiful (furniture, in particular), and comparatively speaking, they are still cheap. Blecha, whose Iowa City home is chock-a-block with furniture and collectibles from auctions and flea markets all around, says, "I go into these antique shops in New Orleans and I just laugh at these people. New York City — they're *insane*."

Though dealers all lament the demise of the bedrock bargain (when *didn't* they, I'd like to know), they still agree that dollar for dollar there are great deals to be had. Farm tools, Victorian furniture, country primitives, kitchen collectibles and glass; these are the classic family heirlooms of the nineteenth- and early twentieth-century Iowa homestead, the bread and butter of antique trading in this state.

What you will not see in Iowa, unless by chance or in the finest shops, is the older stuff. The eastern stuff. The Chippendales. The early silver. The hard paste porcelain. The silky oriental rugs. And it's no wonder. Iowa City dealer Bob Swedberg explains, "If somebody was rich enough to own the really good stuff, he wouldn't have needed to move to Iowa in the first place." As far as those few good pieces that made it here in the early crossings, they were claimed a long time ago by local museums or private estates.

You may also have a hard time finding instances of local folk art, that slippery eclectic class of antique, which may be broadly defined as art by artists who do not recognize themselves as artists but whose work nonetheless reflects some kind of discrete aesthetic sensibility. Lou Picek thinks he's about the only dealer "crazy enough" to look for the stuff in the whole *state*. And when you remember that Iowa was once a hotbed of ethnic immigrant activity, this is very strange indeed.

Yet understandable. Folk art represents a risk. As the work of nonprofessionals and often, therefore, somewhat crude and childlike, even ungainly, its market is not assured. Dealers readily concede it is "out there"—but will anybody buy it? Your typical Iowa antique buff is not renowned for his pathbreaking bravura. He is conservative, a traditionalist, and he likes to play it safe. After all, this is not Massachusetts where decoys sell for $319,000. Or New Hampshire where so many antique weather vanes have been stolen from barn roofs that there is a state trooper assigned specially to chase down thieves. Iowans are more interested in what is inside the barns than in jazzing up the roofs, and they are not about to take a chance on woodchopper whirligigs from Dubuque or Minnesota-made toy birchbark canoes when they can pay a comparable amount for something they can *use*—a chest of drawers, a bedstead, a nice chair.

Small wonder, then, as has been noted, Picck draws the bulk of his clientele from dealers out of state. Not that he's complaining. The fewer tourists in his store, the more time he has to paint—large acrylic canvases of such fabled small-town icons as "The World's Largest Tiger Muskie," "The Pella Tulip Queen," and "The Man Who Thought He Was A Chicken." Which suggests another reason why Iowa is a good place to get out and hunt around. Antiques aside, you see things. You meet interesting people. The retired coal miner at the Chief Mahaska restaurant in Oskaloosa who can remember back when one thousand black migrants worked the mines in the long-gone mining town of Buxton, and who knows the way to ghost towns that are not on any map. The counter girl in Albia who makes about the finest chocolate soda in the state. Lou Picek with his store basement full of unsold paintings . . .

And then there is what you *learn*. Where the coffee shop in Chelsea gets its donuts (from "donut seeds," of course — tiny Cheerios pasted to a poster above the grill). How the volunteer firemen of Hills, Mt. Vernon, and other towns stay in form: they have "shoot-outs" with rival teams from towns around behind the fire station, aiming their respective hoses at a battered beer keg suspended from a long wire that runs high between two poles — and whoever forces it down the wire to the far end first, wins.

Fig. 14.2. "And then there is what you learn." On the road antique-hunting in Iowa, you run into things like this contest between women volunteer fire fighters. It happens annually in Mt. Vernon on Kolache Day (the first Saturday after the Fourth of July). (Photo by Bob Campagna)

Some reflections on the history of antiques here.

Most settlers who rode the crests of those early restless waves to the Midwest traveled sensibly and light. Aspiring homesteaders, tradesmen, woodsmen, immigrant entrepreneurs: the furniture they built reflects the meagerness of their resources as clearly as the versatility of their skills. They made do with what was handy. Used the wood from local fruit trees for utensils — soft maples for bowls, pines and poplars for cobblers' benches, chairs, and chests . . .

These were Iowa's own "Early American Antiques." Plain, solid pieces, comfortably proportioned, strong. But so in thrall was midwestern taste to a more elaborate, formal, presumably legitimate idea of antiquity, it was years — really, a century or more — before Iowans began to take the local handmade early stuff as seriously as it deserved. Farm-type country was so *corny*. Clumsy. Unrefined. Too, for a long time, midwesterners associated those plainspun heirlooms in the attic with hard times and failure. The successful farmer did not hang onto the old; he bought new. Cast-iron lawn furniture from out of catalogs. Hitchcock fancy chairs. Sleepy Hollow rockers. Amazing, really, how much factory-made nineteenth-century furniture wound up in Iowa considering this state was never any kind of manufacturing center on the order of St. Louis, Chicago, and especially, Grand Rapids, Michigan. But Iowans were close enough to take their pick.

Today, the prejudice against "country" in favor of more fussy, worked Victoriana has lost its grip. Whether because the endangered status of Iowa farms has roused local self-consciousness about an agricultural heritage or, as some dealers suggest, because it is simply the new look — the "country" decorative arts are *in*. Not quite folk art, but still a long way from the factories of Chicago and Grand Rapids, these tools and harnesses, hand-painted ice fishing lures, Amish quilts, Amana baskets, pie safes, butter paddles, and tin bins are the popular successors to the decade-long infatuation with brass beds and canopies, Empire sofas, and simulated bamboo. It starts with the tastemakers: a photo spread in *Country Living* or *Better Homes and Gardens*. From there the dealers take their cue and spread the word at the antique shows, where smaller dealers and just plain citizen-collectors get the message and take it to the malls and fleas. "Got any wire egg baskets? How about fishing creels? Cast-iron doorstops? Bucksaws? Bowls?"

Sometimes the process backfires. A thing can get too hot, too tony, and price itself right out of the market. Then the merchant is stuck with a shelf full of mixing bowls, painted wood checkerboards (*"Dead,"* one dealer mourns), butcher blocks, or iron banks. Mary Cline from the Melon City Mall in Muscatine remarks, "Two, three years ago everybody had to have a camel-backed trunk. Also fruit jars, and those colored glass insulators from the top of phone poles. Then people got smart and started going up to the attic."

Which takes us back to our working composite of the Iowa collector. He won't pay the inflated prices that dealers ask out East. He knows his budget and he holds fast. The impulse purchase is fine and dandy for the odd collectible, but when it comes to, say, late nineteenth-century furniture, mill made and shipped here in bulk, he is going to shop around.

And why shouldn't he? As Hills dealer Judy Ball explains, "In Iowa, you can compare. The stuff is all right here. The commodes, the bedroom sets . . ." In *her* store the furniture is heaped so thick you can't even get *into* it, it's like hacking through a rain forest — you come out gasping for breath. Better, maybe, to visit the old barn for farm machinery where she keeps the overflow. Rows and rows of Indiana hoosiers and their older cousins the Iowa hawkeyes. (A funny story behind Ball's passion for these homey farm cupboards with the built-in flour bins and the broad shelves: she started out in business selling candles at flea markets, using the hoosiers as display cases for her wares, but when the hoosiers sold like hotcakes and she was still stuck with all the candles, she knew it was time to get into antiques.)

Sally Robinson from Iowa City who furnished her home with Mission Oak, likens browsing the antique district in West Des Moines to "going to a department store. Prices are still fairly competitive because there's still so much there."

Out near Maquoketa, three looming barns full of Victoriana at Banowetz' Antiques are a complete antique district. Here are rolltops big enough to sleep in. Wicker high chairs on casters. Oak iceboxes. Iron bedsteads. Kitchen chairs for every hour in a week.

Banowetz' bills itself as the largest antique store in Iowa, and indeed, so jam-packed are its warehouses with the cast-off furnishings of a vanished age that you can get the feeling every farmhouse within a two-hundred-mile radius has been plucked and gutted like a chicken, cooked and eaten, nothing left but bones. Yes, there are great deals to be had — but at someone else's loss.

What corner pharmacy went under so that Jane could spruce up her new breakfast nook with ice cream chairs? Who lost his farm so Terry's patio could gain a giant birdcage and a couch? Nobody will deny it is swell that somebody is getting use out of that abandoned feed store on Main, but is an antique mall really the best way to revitalize small towns?

In recent years entire farm communities in Iowa—Walnut, Bellevue, Ladora, Bonaparte, West Branch, and McGregor, to name a few—have witnessed the conversion of prime main street retail space to antique stores and malls. Space that used to house the town's movie house, or bakery, or garden supply store, or café. Space for stores that sold new merchandise, things that catered to a known community, not carloads of tourists drifting through, following some so-called "antique trail."

No wonder, then, that local townspeople are not throwing a parade when these "new kids on the block" move in next door.

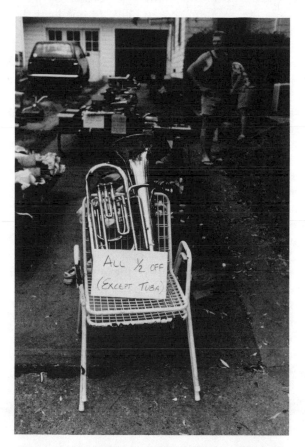

Fig. 14.3. Garage sales, like this one in Iowa City, are visited by dealers and neighbors both, and they form the base of the antique and collectibles markets. They are also an ever-promising source of bargains (except in tubas). (Photo by Drake Hokanson)

"Some locals almost have this 'you'll-never-make-it' attitude," one Bellevue dealer generalizes. "It's like they almost hope you *won't*." Her complaint is echoed by dealers from small towns all over: "They don't like us. And here we're bringing in new business. They can't see we're just as keen on getting this place back on its feet as they are."

Well, yes and no. For one thing, unlike most retail stores, antique stores in small towns sell lots of things local people can't afford. Then if that merchandise is locally procured, it can be all too remindful of better, sweeter times. Times, for instance, when every town had its own working dairy, as is suggested by the large collection of old milk bottles—Blue Grass from Fort Madison, Winters "All-Ways" Healthful, or Kennedy "Sweeter By Far" from Washington—in the antique store in Olds. In one light the Iowa antique store is a marvelous museum, but like all museums, it is also a tomb.

What ghosts are these? Driving through the little towns, you start to wonder—the drygoods store that used to be here—where do its customers go now? What happened to the owner? Did he sell out, go under, move on to greener, more suburban pastures? Is the boy who rode the toy John Deere tractor with the peeling paint a farmer now, or is he a meat-packer in Ottumwa, or selling headsets in L.A.?

Easy ironies, perhaps, but unavoidable—and in Iowa the more acute for being so newly felt. Yes, there have always been antique shops, or more precisely, local junk shops, places like "The Bargain Shop" in Wyoming, Iowa, with a carpet of The Last Supper in the window, and somebody's smashed-up guitar selling for a buck alongside a washing machine and a lot of mismatched plates. ("All prices subject to argument," the owner tells you cheerfully before you even get inside.) Thrift stores and consignment shops (racks of pantsuits, stacks of scratchy 45s)—these places are a fixture of small-town scenery as surely as the elevator and the water tower.

But the careful, conscious, unrelenting mining of the past— the antique shows and malls, the collectors' newsletters, the hoarding and the "finds"—this *is* new here, and unsettling. Not long ago, a woman from Olds whose family used to farm full time opened an antique store with her husband. And yes, the added income is welcome, "especially with farming being so bad, and it's nice meeting people, and learning about the trade"—but would she rather be home with the children and the chores? "You bet."

After all, Iowa is not Vermont, which suffered *its* great farm depressions in the early nineteenth century. Vermont is used to this. It started cashing in on its own natural and historic heritage—the flaming maples, the half-deserted towns—a hundred years ago. Turned a farmer's wasteland into the land of a thousand photo opportunities. And lo, tourism today—specifically, tourism that thrives on a sentimental passion with the past, the ruinous old barn, the country inn with letter-perfect reproductions of Windsor chairs in every room, the "old-time" auctioneer (with more New Yorkers on his mailing list than locals)—is an economic mainstay. Self-serving and unabashedly contrived, but it works.

But that is Vermont.

In Iowa, the game is new, and we are still sorting out the rules, working out who wins, who loses. And it is not easy.

On one hand, used stuff sells more cheaply in a depressed economy. Good news from the buyer's vantage. On the other hand, fewer local people can afford to buy. (An oft-cited example: before the farm crisis, antique farm toys—old tractors, baby combines—were big business. No more. The farmers and small-town bankers who bought them are backing off.)

On one hand, antique stores in small towns save old buildings that would otherwise be torn down. Thanks to these Johnny-come-latelys, the architectural integrity of that classic small-town *look* is preserved. On the other hand, who cares? If half the farmland in the fields at the back of town lies fallow, and farmers have to drive fifteen miles instead of two to buy supplies, big deal about the *look*. Who *needs* it?

On one hand, antique stores bring tourists. Iowa needs tourists. Everybody says so. But what if they only spend their money on antiques? And what about when those stores get antiqued out? What then?

One chilling example of the cut-and-run phenomenon is the village of Ladora, a farm town north of I-80 near Marengo. Here, all that remains of an antique "village" of five stores that beckoned buyers from as far away as California is a silent strip of boarded-over storefronts and grassy lots where buildings were punched out like teeth. Not one store is still in business—and longtime Ladora resident Carl Barb is not surprised.

"See, all these little towns depended on agriculture-supported businesses, and that's what kept them going. And now we're so depressed." Barb, a retired salesman of business machines, lost forty clients between 1982 and 1983 alone. In 1987 he says, "it would probably be up to 140. Ladora's so devalued you can't borrow to buy a house here. You can't pay people to invest. In '86 alone we lost the sundry store, Ike's Pool Hall, the Saddle & Leather Shop, the locker. As for the antique stores, well, their prices were too high and people stopped buying. And anyway, antique stores are nothing to be proud of. This town became a ghost town!"

A case in point: the day we spoke there was an auction in progress. Some nice things, too. Old bureaus. Glass-fronted oak bookcases. Bedsteads. It all sells out! All, that is, except the main event, the house itself. A steal at three thousand dollars—and nobody will touch it.

Yet you cannot blame it on antiques. The introduction of the antique trade into a small depressed town did not generate the problem, it has merely come to symbolize it—and the truth is, in Ladora, as in so many towns, the troubles started long ago. First there was the closing of the Ladora Savings Bank in 1931, then the opening of the nearby, traffic-thieving interstate, then a rash of fires, pull-outs, bankruptcies, and razings. And the buildings the antique stores took over were empty for years.

More importantly, for every failing antique town like La-dora there is a Walnut coming up great guns. Five years ago Walnut was as empty as a western stage-set between films. Today there is not an empty storefront on the block. Two well-advertised annual antique shows bring collectors from all over. High bidders throng the noisy auction hall. Fifty dealers from as far away as Omaha and Chicago rent nooks and corners in the malls.

Myself, I am not too keen on malls. I realize they are a godsend for the dealer who doesn't want the responsibility of running one's own store. Rent for space is nominal, you only work one day a week, it is pocket income, sometimes more. Plus you get to find out from other dealers what is hot and what is warming up.

But I am not a dealer. I do not have a dealer's card, and I do not buy things for the investment. I'm a citizen, a browser. And if I buy a wind-up polar bear or a deep-blue pitcher that looks like the prow of the *Normandie,* it's because I like them, I want to use them, show them off at home—and I miss the days when mere enthusiasts were accorded the same bargaining rights as dealers. I miss the days when every dealer's desk wasn't lined with a battery of standardized antique guides giving so-called "official" prices on everything from Royal Doulton to beer cans. Maybe I'm senti-mental, but I cannot help but think that if the old-style antique or junk shop was like the grocery store where they knew your mother's name and all her favorite cuts of meat, then the mall has got to be that efficient, sensible, and faceless supermarket that

drove the corner store out of business, only with this difference —
the supermarket was at least cheaper. The antique mall is not.

It is handy. And prettily arranged; indeed, the *hominess* of
some of these new malls is almost weird. Especially the ones that
have taken over old Victorian houses where every room is a kind
of shrine to the age of funky clutter and midbrow kitsch — you
can get lost in them, get to feeling like a housebreaker or a peep-
ing Tom. Isn't anybody *home?* But they are not homes, they are
malls, and there can be a sameness to the merchandise that blears
the eye (How many types of potato masher can there *be?*).

Even dealers sometimes wonder about the predictability, the
sheer redundancy, of some mall staples. Gesturing at a table full
of glass juicers, the manager of a Mt. Vernon mall voices a
private fear: "What if people start to think, 'there's so much of
this stuff, it must not be worth this much'?"

Hmmm.

What I do when the predictability of mall pickin's starts to
get to me is head out for the fleas. I'm a sucker for the fleas.
Especially the ones that only happen one, two, three times a year,
like Larry Nicholson's "Collectors' Paradise" in What Cheer. You
can *do* the looping lines of tables and booths at the What Cheer
flea market in the Keokuk County fairgrounds from noon to
dusk and still not reach the end of it. You can see dreck, you can
see state-of-the-art "klecked-bulls." And you can have fun, because the sellers here are not professionals. As promoter Nicholson explains, "Hardly any of them's making any kind of *living* at this. It's a part-time thing. They're looking for extra ways
to make money. I know a lot of guys here got laid off at John
Deere, for instance."

So if prices seem a little steep to start with, dicker on.
They'll drop. Make an offer, make a counter-offer. Walk around
and think about it. You might see it cheaper six tables up, and you
can always circle back. If the price is higher than what you would
see at a garage sale, it is still less than a mall, way less than a
store, and as for a show — well, that's moot. It will be a few years
yet before this stuff starts turning up in serious antique shows.
Wire baskets for deep frying. Two-sided harmonicas. A plaster
likeness of John Wayne on horseback. ("It's the first he's been out
of the house in years," his owner says worriedly. "He was made in
Mexico. I'm only selling him to make room for the dolls. The
horse is female — and so was *his!* Doesn't it look just like him?")
Toy tractors from John Deere, McCormack, Oliver. Bagatelles.
Old license plates. Old dentist's tools. Half-naked lady wrestler
printing blocks (antique pornography). A bubblegum machine.

Ad literature for Squibb's Dental Cream — the story of "The War Against the Germies" as fought by "The Tinies That Lived In A Tube."

Bricks. (Sound strange? A hundred years ago there were five hundred brick-making factories in Indiana alone.) Beaded purses. Shoe horns. Old valentines. Sheet music for the "Iowa Corn Song." A Roy Rogers wastebasket. Oil cans with pointy spouts like witches' caps ("use 'em for M&M's," the dealer suggests). Postcards of Coney Island at its peak. A rack for Life-savers, the kind you see in drugstores (great colors: I'll put spices in it). A lighter disguised as a miniature camera on a tripod: press the shutter-release cable and the flame darts out from under the viewfinder. Bombo the acrobatic monkey. A plate from the St. Louis zoo with elephants shuffling all around the rim. A peri-winkle Riviera plate for my sister. Yellow plastic corn holders I know I'll never use.

"What makes this a good state for fleas?" speculates a What Cheer regular from Ottumwa. "Everybody's poor and wants to sell everything, but then you got to do *something* with all the money you make selling, right? So back you go, and spend it all again."

And something else. The flea markets are a hold-out — a last imperiled stronghold for the easy unrepentant amateurs, the oc-casional unsystematic collectors who don't *care* about the market, who aren't looking for any *one* thing in particular, who just want to poke around and get a windburn, who buy a few things at prices they won't have to wake up later in a cold sweat about, and who see friends.

Fig. 14.4.   Aerial view of What Cheer flea market, at Keokuk County fairgrounds, May, 1986. (Photo by James Shepherd, courtesy of ClockWorks Events Magazine*)*

*Fig. 14.5.   The flea markets—a last imperiled strong-
hold for the easy unrepentant amateurs. A scene at a
flea market in Boone. (Photo © Joan Liffring-Zug,
from* Men 1950–1985*)*

A modern version of the quilting bee, that is how dealer
Judy Ball sees the role of the midwestern flea market. And it is
true, there is a sweet congeniality, a hang-loose laid-back holiday
vibration here that makes you half expect to look up and see
ferris wheels, or a guy selling burritos. You can almost forget you
are in the middle of the prairie on the outskirts of a town, itself
no more than a mining camp one hundred years ago.

Almost—but you don't. One way or another, the presence of the prairie manages to make itself felt. It could be a torrent, or a heatwave, or a gritty wind tugging at the tablecloths and rattling the plates. And maybe this is the thing I like best about the giant flea market at What Cheer. I have read about Iowa as it once was and what the pioneers put up with—babies disappearing in the panic grass and all that—and I have felt myself moved by all the relics in the antique stores, the rusty snippets of vintage barbed wire, the worn-out hoes. But until the first time I visited What Cheer on a hot May day in the middle of a burning windstorm, I never took it in. Never quite acknowledged the miracle of that pioneer persistence, hilariously revived in the spectacle of a hundred thousand bits of crockery and glass holding fast against a tidal wave of wind. I kept expecting people to clear *out* of there, pack up and leave—and no one did! You might have thought the wind was nothing but a trifle, so cheerily indifferent were the dealers and their clientele to its rough play. You might have thought that there was something about the stamina and vehemence of Iowa collectors that made this prairie gale look as mild as a rare spring breeze.

What cheer, indeed!

15

TRANSPORTATION
&
THE IOWA LANDSCAPE

Drake Hokanson

When I travel outside the state, people I meet often ask me where I'm from. "Iowa," I say. "Have you ever been there?" Most can differentiate it from Ohio or Idaho. A few rummage through their mental map file and come up empty-handed. Others tell me about their aunt in Rock Rapids or their brother-in-law in Albia and a visit long ago. One fellow who needed to write my home state on a gas credit card slip asked me how to spell it. Many of the people who have been across Iowa once or twice vaguely recall the state as a way point on a trip to somewhere else: "It was Des Moines, I think; that's where we got gas."

Of those who remember more about the state, most recall only idyllic farms, endless fields of corn, flat terrain, and little towns; they remember Iowa as a place they would rather pass through than stop to explore.

Traveling Iowans, too, overlook the state, even when they have a good opportunity to do otherwise. On a train trip across Iowa one recent fall, I watched pastel clouds race above me as yellow-brown corn flashed alongside, alternating with still-green trees and pastures. An Iowan in a seat nearby paused in a conversation and looked out the window for a few seconds. I was watching for prairie grasses along the tracks when he looked back at his companion and said with obvious boredom, "Some scenery."

He was right; according to usual tastes in scenery, these autumn fields were pretty ordinary. The view could never compare with that of the Colorado Rockies, New England in the fall,

Hawaii, or all the other places usually depicted in travel brochures.

Travelers in search of classic, calendar scenery overlook Iowa for good reason. Except for a handful of scenic spots, Iowa does not reveal her beauties to the casual tourist, the snapshooter, the vacationer looking for another Yosemite, another Oregon coast. Minnesota has five thousand lakes more beautiful than ours; the fall colors always seem better across the river in Wisconsin. So be it.

But for a traveler who is willing to look more carefully, an observant traveler who wants to learn about both the human-made and natural landscape of Iowa rather than simply "see scenery," the state offers many riches. To the student of landscape, wide-eyed deliberate travel by different modes can leave a surprising impression.

What can we see from the car, from the train, from a high- or low-flying plane? How will our impression of this state differ depending upon how we cross it or explore it? How did Iowa look to travelers years ago? What about Iowa's transportation landscape—its rail lines and highways?

The reason most travelers do not remember much about Iowa is that they have seen it only from the interstate. Today, almost everybody crosses the state on the four-lane highways at 65 mph in air-conditioned cars. As far as seeing and understanding anything about the state, that is not too different from not seeing it all by flying over it at thirty-five thousand feet with solid clouds beneath. Interstate 80 can take travelers from the Mississippi to the Missouri in about six hours; I-35 from Minnesota to Missouri in less than four. If a person has food in the car and spaces the bathroom stops just right, he or she might never stop or set foot in Iowa. Prone to long naps while someone else is driving, a traveler might miss it altogether.

These roads are fast, safe, and efficient, but the vernacular landscape—the storefronts, pastures, truss bridges, woodlands, streams, parks, farms, and other so-called obstacles are pushed back out of reach, back away from the surge of twenty-four-hour-a-day traffic. All one really sees from the interstates are the taillights of the traffic ahead, the gas gauge, and occasional chain food places and motels that look like every other one in the country.

Because of the interstates, we have learned to use our cars like 747s—we drive straight and fast from origin to destination and measure the pleasure of the trip with a stopwatch; the shorter the trip, the better.

But these wonderful machines work in other ways. We sometimes forget that they have the flexibility to stop, go, and turn wherever we wish them to. A car may serve its best purpose parked along the roadside at a shady place to keep your lunch while you spend the morning wandering a remnant of Iowa prairie on foot. The automobile, above all other modes of travel, allows us the greatest possibilities for adventure, exploration, observation.

The experiences of early automobile travelers provide an object lesson. Before the interstates, before bypasses, before paving came in the 1930s, motorists ventured into and across the state and carried away impressions and experiences that are far more detailed and tactile than most of today. These travelers had only the equivalent of our back roads to travel, and by necessity, they learned a great deal about the people and landscape of Iowa. And before hard paving was poured in quantity, auto travelers came to know the landscape intimately—in fact most cars and travelers became thickly covered with it whenever it rained.

Dallas Lore Sharp ventured into Iowa in 1927 on his way west from his home in Massachusetts and encountered the mud of Iowa's unpaved Lincoln Highway near Boone one wet day.

> Here was something new—a new form of motion, a new contact with the earth. I had skidded before this in Massachusetts, but never without some sense of the crusty globe beneath me, some expectation of bedrock. Here nothing—nothing even gritty geological, the very moral order of the universe without firmness or fiber! The car seemed about to dissolve, its reins no longer a frame of fabricated steel, but spilled and quaking jelly. And when it stopped going round, it lay sprawling in the elemental ooze of that Iowa road with about as much purpose as a mud puppy.

While bad roads were a particular problem in Iowa for many years, most adventures were of a more enjoyable nature. Automobile travelers of Sharp's day camped in shaded school yards, filled their tanks at tiny roadside gas stations, and filled their bellies at the same cafés and dining rooms the town residents did. Motorists encountered local color at every turn as they sought directions along unmarked roads, looked for a night's lodging, or dickered with a farmer over a fee for pulling a car from the mud.

From the high seat of an open touring car on a narrow road, the landscape of Iowa pressed close. A motorist traveling at a sedate 25 mph could study barn architecture, evaluate streams for fishing possibilities, or get a feeling for the character of a particular main street. Iowa's smells — not all of them pleasant — came directly to the motorist in the open car. The sounds of the countryside replaced the sound of the engine whenever travelers stopped to change a tire, which was quite often in the early days. Few people minded occasional delays; traffic was light, the rolling land beckoned, and there was adventure in the wind.

I drive to distant corners of Iowa fairly often and take delight in traveling the lesser state and county highways, the original routes that go through towns instead of around them, and even the gravel section-line roads. On any of them, the pace is slowed to trolling speed compared with the speedboat rate of the interstates and federal highways. Here I can find a pace and texture of travel similar to that of motorists of sixty years ago, without having to worry very much about getting stuck. On these back roads, my foot lightens on the accelerator, my head turns from the path ahead to see fields, old and new farm architecture, spindly truss bridges, scraps of prairie, rows of false-front buildings, rivers and lakes, railroads, parks, and grain elevators. I quickly become immersed in the trip and forget about the destination. I find myself turning in for a cup of coffee, not so much to stay awake but to see whom I might meet at the café.

Fig. 15.1.   The pace and texture of travel similar to that of motorists of sixty years ago. A gravel road in Poweshiek County in early spring. (Photo by Carol Kratz)

Iowa's automobile landscape intrigues me, especially the roadside landscape of earlier days. By far the best roads for finding clues to the early days of the auto are the old, bypassed routes of main highways. Along the former routes of U.S. 30 and U.S. 20 are many examples of early twentieth-century automobile service architecture: gas stations, cafés, garages, hotels, and motels. There seem to be more older farms along these roads as well, farms with old barns and two-cylinder John Deere tractors. These are the old highways that run through the downtowns of Jefferson, Webster City, and Belle Plaine, giving a traveler a view of main streets never seen from the new highway that runs out beyond the edge of town.

Belle Plaine is astride the old Lincoln Highway—now U.S. 30 across the country—and may hold some of the best examples of older highway landscape. Here, during a slow drive through town, I found places with many reminders of the great days on the Lincoln Highway, days before the new U.S. 30 was relocated several miles north. There are two cafés—the Lincoln and the Maid Rite—that stand beside or close to the old highway and evoke memories of the days when hamburgers were twenty cents and coffee was a nickel. There are the remnants of an old tourist court on the east edge of town, the Iowa and Herring hotels, and the E. L. Sankot garage, all standing to give a hint of what highway towns looked like to travelers years ago.

On the west edge of town is George Preston's gas station, a place where high-topped pumps once dispensed gasoline, and where today George shows off his collections of metal advertising signs, Lincoln Highway, and railroad memorabilia. This old station was once a main stop on the Lincoln, where George fixed tires and sold pop to motorists carrying license plates from distant states. Times are quieter now, and those days can be relived through George's recollections and artifacts.

It is because the main highway was moved from Belle Plaine instead of being widened and improved on the same route that the wonderful places there have survived. Because highway routes are often relocated in the process of improving them, we can often find several parallel and older routes of the same highway. The evolution of Iowa's highways parallels that of most of the rest of the country, and to a surprising degree, much of that process is still observable on the landscape. The braided paths of old major highways like U.S. 30 or U.S. 20 can be read as a chronology of highway development in the United States.

For my own observations of American highways, I have grouped them into four rough but simple classes based on their ages and characteristics. These categories represent the development of long distance roads for the auto from the turn of the century to the present. They can be useful aids to the observer of the highways of Iowa, or the highways of any state. My names for them are: early, mezzohighway, bypass, and interstate.

The early highways of Iowa were the same informal dirt and mud section-line roads that had carried buggies and wagons from farm to town. The highways among them were usually different only because they displayed the signs of some named highway or another. Sometimes they were actually in worse shape than the ordinary section-line roads because heavy auto traffic tore deeper ruts than horse drawn vehicles. Eventually some were improved and even paved with little change, but the corners were right angles and the paving quite narrow. This was the highway of the early Fords, the Maxwells, and the Overlands—the highway of the days when repairs were found at blacksmith shops instead of garages.

Fig. 15.2.   George Preston's gas station, once a main stop on the Lincoln Highway in Belle Plaine, is still "OPEN"—for memories. (Photo by Drake Hokanson)

Many have been improved to become ordinary-looking roads and streets; some have reverted to gravel section roads and a few have been abandoned outright, leaving little in the way of evidence of their important past. Pre-1925 auto guide books and old road maps are often necessary for finding fragments of these earliest routes. A 1913 *Huebinger's Pocket Automobile Guide for Iowa* allowed me to find a ten-mile section of the earliest Lincoln Highway between Dunlap and Woodbine in western Iowa. Look for the gravel and dirt road zigzagging along the foot of the bluff to the southeast of present day U.S. 30.

In general, look for scraps of narrow pavement—as narrow as sixteen feet—peeking out from under the outside of gentler curves, or taking the crooked way around or over some obstacle. Look for narrow bridges like the tiny Lincoln Highway bridge just east of Tama with the words "LINCOLN HIGHWAY" cast in its concrete side rails.

Fig. 15.3.   "Look for narrow bridges . . ." Sutliffe Bridge, over the Cedar River in northeastern Johnson County. An excellent example of the truss bridges built in the 1890s for wagon travel, it no longer carries traffic but has been preserved by local citizens. (Photo by Drake Hokanson)

Next in line was the mezzohighway, the highway of the great road-building boom of the late 1920s through the 1940s. Often these roads were built on entirely new alignments, avoiding some of the curves and grades of the original routes. Built of concrete, many of these roads in Iowa had those cursed curbs that ricochetted cars into opposing traffic. This is the highway of Burma Shave signs, of the Chrysler Airflow, mom-and-pop motels and cafés. Along the mezzohighway are found most of the relics of roadside nostalgia — old gas stations, neon, tourist courts, drive-in restaurants and theaters.

Sometimes our busy federal highways have been widened and rebuilt on top of these middle-era roads, pushing back the landscape, obliterating the "feel" of the path. But often a new route was built on another alignment nearby, leaving the mezzo-highway intact. A fine example is county road E-41 between Marshalltown and Ames, running some thirty-five idyllic miles through the middle of State Center, Colo, and Nevada. With close fences, narrow pavement and shoulders, the patched roadway undulates over the countryside, past farms, occasional tourist courts, and old gas stations to retain some of the feel of a highway in the days long before the interstates. This was the Lincoln Highway in its heyday; the present-day U.S. 30 is a mile or so to the south.

The modern U.S. 30 between Marshalltown and Ames represents the third type of highway, the bypass. For sound reasons of smoother traffic flow and improved safety, engineers have sought to move highways away from the centers of cities and towns. These newer two- and four-lane bypasses angle around the edges of even very small places, taking the highway off the main street. It is easy to find; in larger towns look for the suburban strip — shopping centers, giant auto dealers, fast food places.

The last of the four is the interstate. We all know it well because so many of our miles are spent on its oil-stained surface. It takes its lead from the bypass, finding a new route to angle past most cities without ever entering. It is the new "high iron," a path not bound by the old. On the interstate, we can cross the state and never see it.

For me, a fundamental rule of auto travel declares that the more primitive, narrow, and local the road, the closer will press the details of the landscape, and the more vivid will be the impression and recollection of the trip. A state highway can be memorable, a county blacktop is better, and a county gravel section-line road is best.

Iowa is blanketed with yellow gravel section-line roads, one to a mile, from one corner of the state to the other. They form a nearly perfect graph-paper grid and make a detailed road map of the state look like it was cut from a piece of window screen. These roads—and the land survey system that created them—give the Iowa landscape its familiar checkerboard appearance. In no other state is this grid of roads so ubiquitous; except for the northeastern corner of Iowa and places around streams and lakes, the grid covers the state.

And in no other state does the surveyed section-by-section grid have so profound an effect on our routes of land travel. The grid affects all roads, not just the gravel county roads. In Iowa it is hard to find a road of any sort that disobeys the grid for very long. Some highways follow railroads for a time, or wander along a stream bank, but eventually they return to the straight and narrow. Even the interstates are beholden to it, and a true diagonal road like Iowa 330 between Marshalltown and Des Moines is a rare item. It is Iowa's adherence to the grid that tells us that it will take an inordinately long time to drive from Sheldon to Mount Pleasant. It is the grid that tells us that the sun will be square in our eyes driving from Allison to Cherokee on a fall evening.

While such a rigid crosshatch of roads would hardly seem to whip enthusiasm for footloose adventure, it is along the thousands of miles of county gravel section roads that we can do some of our best wandering and can best see the agricultural landscape close up and in detail. It is from these dusty roads that the traveler gathers a real understanding of just how square Iowa is. Farm buildings, fields, main streets, rows of trees, cemetery plots—even streams—are made to follow the surveyed grid according to the cardinals of direction: north, south, east, and west.

From the gravel at 35 mph, farmsteads take on individual character; barns, silos, corncribs, machine sheds, and livestock buildings all make a specific impression. Some farms have great square houses with huge porches, some have new ranch-style homes; others have no houses at all. Names on mailboxes are legible at a gravel-road pace, and a farm dog will often spring from the ditch to bark at your tires as you pass. Fields, pastures, and woodlands stand out as elements of the landscape rather than mere blurs of color. A low spot in the ditch makes a minimarsh, complete with cattails and frogs. A windsock stands next to a low shed and a smooth hay field, giving clues about a farm family with an airplane.

Dallas Lore Sharp—when he wasn't fighting Iowa mud— took measure of the Iowa farm landscape from the Lincoln Highway, which in 1927 was nothing more than a gravel section-line road without the gravel:

Such mammoth barns! And such broods of lesser buildings round-about! Close by stands the house beneath a group of planted trees, often barricaded from the sweeping winds by outer walls of trees. Overtopping the trees and the roofs rise the windmill and the twin silos, adding a touch of Norman times, towers and keeps to guard the wide, flanking fields and the rich booty of the yards below: cribs of eared corn, stacks of hay and weathered chaff, swine and burly cattle, horses, mules, sheep, chickens, and machinery to outfit a feudal lord.

Armed with a rudimentary sense of direction, it is fairly difficult to get lost on the gravel county roads, and under certain travel conditions, they can get a person through when nothing else will. On a winter night some years ago, I was beset with an ice storm some ninety miles short of my destination in northwest Iowa. The paved roads quickly became 10-mph ice rinks, so I turned onto the gravel to find better traction. I figured that if I took the grid roads and drove about five miles west for every mile north, I would come out close to my destination. I could make about 30 mph on the gravel, and decided to drive until I came across something familiar. With poor visibility and freezing rain, I was turning off into parts unknown.

I kept loose count of my ratio of west-to-north miles, but for the sake of experiment, put away the map and ignored any clues to my whereabouts. I crossed an occasional paved road, a creek or two, and some railroad tracks. I had to jog from time to time at offsets and to avoid closed roads and any paved roads, and I passed through no towns and met no other traffic. After three hours, I had no idea of my whereabouts and was growing eager to see how my experiment was doing. Suddenly, I saw a familiar farm, then another and quickly oriented myself on roads I knew quite well, roads near my hometown.

Lindbergh's crossing of the Atlantic with only a compass and clock was certainly a greater feat, but I felt a sliver of the same satisfaction he felt when, after endless hours over the trackless North Atlantic, he made landfall at Ireland, only five miles off course.

Travel is the experience of rhythms, an exposure to repeated patterns of sight, sound, sensation, and activities. Some rhythms have a quick tempo, such as the one-per-minute section-line roads we cross when driving a two-lane highway, or the slap of the tires on the joints in a concrete road. Other rhythms play out slowly; a daily routine of stopping in some little café along the road for midmorning coffee, or for pioneers bound for Oregon in 1850, the cycle of the moon phases over the course of several months' travel.

But of all modes of travel, the railroad provides a rhythm, a set of cadences unlike any other. The sound and sensation of any train ride stays with me for days after the ride is over. The sway of the cars, the clickity-clack of wheels over the rail joints, the pole-dip-pole-dip of telegraph wires seen out the window, the air horn blowing for road crossings — all creep into my subconscious mind to be recalled for days. Is it any wonder that musicians have found so many of their rhythms along the railroad?

The cadence of the railroad creeps in unconsciously, drawing me to the window. The passing landscape is so different somehow, so much more interesting than that seen from a car. From an automobile on the interstate, the moving scene is just ordinary Iowa, but from the train it is much more dramatic, much more evocative.

I always take a book when I travel by train, but I never read during daylight, no matter how dreary the landscape. There is something mesmerizing about the dance of the wires and poles, the flash of backyards and creeks, industrial plants and bridges, rail yards full of boxcars marked with railroads with faraway names. I simply cannot take my eyes from it. Things are seen from the train in quick flashes as they pass; like snapshots, I see tiny details in the click of my mind's shutter, printed on my memory, microscopic dramas taken out of context to be remembered later with no regard to their importance.

Even though the train may be passing through some place I have been through by car, it really is a different landscape, seen from a different place, at a different angle. It is a separate place in part because the railroads do not follow the same lines as do roads. Railroads pay no heed to the grid. They concern themselves with gentle grades and smooth curves, not with some arbitrary survey system. Rail lines follow rivers, creeks, and ridges, or angle off in some straight line on flat ground, paying no attention to cardinal directions. From the train, then, we often see the grid at some oblique angle where farms or towns appear corner-first rather than straight on and square as they do from the highway.

The view from the railroad is essentially a backyard view. The tracks pass through the alleys of cities and towns, and around the backside of farms and businesses. Roads, on the other hand — even major highways — give us what amounts to a front-yard view of the landscape. We see the fronts of stores and houses; billboards and signs are directed toward us. I am reminded of the highways' frontyard view every time I pass a farmstead where morning glories climb the trellis on the front fence or the grass is mowed right to the pavement.

In the industrial Northeast on the run between New York and Chicago, Amtrak's Lakeshore Limited passes through the very heart of the cities of the rust belt; it looks as though every automobile, refrigerator, shopping cart, and steel mill ever discarded has found its way to decay along the tracks. But in Iowa the backyard view means that a rail passenger will see grain elevators, fertilizer plants, an occasional flash of a small-town main street, vegetable gardens, swing sets, and barking dogs.

In the Iowa countryside the land appears much wilder than it does from the highway. There are creeks and rivers and fishing spots where people seldom wet a line, great flourishes of prairie and woodland plants, long ago driven from the roadside by spraying and mowing. This is a view of fields and farmsteads from the backside, abandoned machinery, and untouched little pieces of ground, neither pasture nor woodlot—bits of land that intrigue the explorer in me but are gone before I have even really seen them. Once, in just such a parcel of land at the edge of a town, I spotted a treehouse, well camouflaged on the side facing the village and no doubt seldom seen from the ground. But from the train, the secret was plain; the treehouse stood open and near the tracks, seen and remembered by hundreds of people from far away who probably couldn't even recall the name of the town.

Fig. 15.4.   Following the river valleys and generally going around the hills, railroads were not laid out on the grid and thus organized the Iowa landscape very differently than highways. (Photo by Ray Kuefler, courtesy of State Historical Society of Iowa)

The angle of view from a train is different than from a car, as well. On a train we cannot ordinarily see where we are going, or where we have been. Instead, the world is seen perpendicular to the direction of travel. In a car we can look ahead and relate where we are with where we are going. A nearby farm is foreground to a distant town and a relationship can be drawn from their juxtaposition. But on a train the relationships among elements along the way are never seen; the landscape unrolls scroll-like—one element is gone before the next is revealed. The effect is very much like looking at a moving landscape painting—a sensation heightened by large, rectangular train car windows, and in Amtrak's double-decked cars, by a perspective from a good many feet above the height of an automobile window.

The path of the railroad often makes me want to come back for a slower, more detailed look on foot. Since passenger service in Iowa is limited to Amtrak running on the Burlington Northern line across southern Iowa and a Santa Fe stop at Fort Madison, a reconnoiter on foot is the only way to see most of Iowa's rail network. I can spend a day birdwatching, finding prairie plants, and learning a bit more about Iowa's transportation network by studying the physical structure of the railroad on the landscape.

From a first look, different characteristics of different lines are apparent. The main-line rails have long been called the "high iron" and for two apparent reasons. First, the embankment itself is often high in order to raise the tracks above possible floods and to better even out grades. The grades and curves will be gentle, giving the impression of the speedway that it is. During initial construction in the last century, most lines were built quickly and cheaply in order to get them operating and making profits. During the ensuing years and continuing through the present, the main lines, the busy arteries that carry the heavy trains, have had their grade and curve profiles improved as company coffers allowed. A branch line, on the other hand, will likely still exhibit the smaller, less developed physical features built into it by men with shovels and mules a hundred years ago: the curves will be comparatively sharp, the embankment narrow and the grade profile will more closely follow the terrain rather than seeking a level line.

The other reason for the term high iron is the height of the rails themselves. In general, the taller and heavier the rail, the heavier and faster the traffic using it. Rail size is measured in pounds per yard—65-pound rail is about the lightest rail still found in Iowa, and it is limited to old branch lines and a few yard areas. It stands about four and one-half inches high. The heaviest rail reported in the state on the other hand is 136-pound rail on the eastbound (north side) track of the double-track Chicago and North Western line between Clinton and Missouri Valley. This is the true high iron; the massive steel stands better than seven inches above the tie plates. In addition to being heavy, this rail is welded into quarter-mile or longer lengths, eliminating the joints at thirty-nine-foot intervals (and the familiar clickity-clack), making the smoothest possible surface for the pounding of heavy coal trains.

Most rail is stamped with data about the weight, manufacturer, and date of rolling; the stamp usually faces the center of the track and often carries additional information decipherable only by workers at the steel mill. Look for it on the inside of the rail (the web) between the base and the top. An example: "CARNEGIE 1909 ET 70A" notes Carnegie as the manufacturer, 1909 as the year the rail was rolled, and seventy pounds per yard as the weight. In the case of "11525 RECC ILLINOIS USA 1948," the first three digits of the number are the pounds per yard.

Fig. 15.5.   The main-line "high iron" of the Chicago and North Western running parallel for awhile with a mezzohighway (the old Lincoln Highway) near Boone. (Photo by Drake Hokanson)

As much as I like the back roads, and as much as I like a trip across the state by train, I like Iowa best as seen from a small plane flying low above the corn, cows, and rooftops. I sometimes fly the breadth of the state, carefully avoiding the tall radio towers, and never climbing beyond a thousand feet above the ground.

On the best days when I don't need to be someplace at a particular time, and when the air is clear enough so that details stand out undiminished on the horizon, I follow a crooked line from point to point at a pace slow enough to take care of flying business and still leave plenty of time to watch the land beneath. A stream draws my attention and I follow it a few miles, or a town with a big elevator off to the left looks interesting so I point the nose there. No road grid controls my course, no iron railroad. With a chart in my lap it is hard to get lost, and little airports are still common, airports close enough to town for a walk downtown to the café.

Even from the low altitude of a thousand feet I can scan the horizon and take in miles of territory at a single glance—a whole county or two spread beneath my wings, landforms, towns, and grids to read like a map. But for me the appeal is directly below, far beyond those silly wheels that hang in space beneath me and so out of place above the trees. Looking downward brings the view that only flying can—blending the shapes, colors, and details of the land into an endless mosaic.

The strongest impression is that of pattern and texture. The landscape below becomes an abstraction on a painter's canvas, designs in stippled paint, smooth strokes, dilute washes, and bare fabric. Patterns of row crops become corduroy; even and smooth here, a bit tattered and missing a row or two in places where the planter box ran out of seed and the farmer took awhile to notice. A rough pasture becomes matted wool; a suburban neighborhood becomes rows of blocks, all with the same gray roofs and white ventilators. Each yard is a small patch of a different shade of green depending on who laid sod, who used fertilizer, and who watered.

I circled a farmer deep plowing a triangular field of hay one day. As he plowed around the ever-shrinking island of grass, he left a growing swath of fresh soil to dry in the sun. The soil near the center of the field that was most recently turned was wettest and darkest; each swath outward from there grew lighter by steps, making a delicate gradation from dark to light, from center to edge.

A town appears as a pattern of squares and rectangles inside other squares and rectangles. Section roads and highways feed into the grid pattern that city blocks, parks, and industrial plants follow closely. Lines of trees along the boulevard, the blue-green swimming pool with black lane markers, each house, and every building — all are lined up according to the ever-present grid. Anything set at angles, like the new high school at the edge of town, stands out clearly as an aberration in the nearly comprehensive pattern.

The grid, as it is from the railroad, is usually seen obliquely because the course of an airplane over the land need not follow a ground-based pattern. But to follow a grid line from the air, to line the compass up on a square direction, is to know the grid in a way that cannot be done from the ground. Wolfgang Langewiesche, banking his little plane to follow a section line in the Midwest one day back in the 1920s, noted:

> First it was a dirt road, narrow between two hedges, with a car crawling along it dragging a tail of dust. Then the road turned off, but the line went straight ahead, now as a barbed wire fence through a large pasture. . . . Then the fence stopped, but now there was corn on one side of the line and something green on the other. Next it was a narrow dirt road again with farms on either side, and then suddenly, a broad highway came curving in, followed the line for a mile, and curved away again. For a short stretch it didn't consist of anything, but the grass, for some reason, was a little greener on one side and a little more yellow on the other. Again it was a hedge until it broadened and became a road, dignified itself, and became for a few blocks the main street of a small town, filled with parked cars; people stepped out of stores to look at me. Then it thinned out again. When I climbed away and resumed my course, I left it as a fence which had cows on one side and no cows on the other. That's a section line.

Langewiesche came to see and understand details in the landscape of the Midwest because he saw its beauty from close above the ground, something jetliner travelers can do only during approach and departure. But from six or seven miles up, the cruising altitude for long-distance jets, some other aspects of the Iowa landscape are apparent that are not so from the lower altitudes. On a day when there are no clouds below and the visibility is good, the sweep and uniformity of Iowa's agricultural landscape can be seen in total. Undulations in the terrain melt into absolute flatness from this height; even the bluffs of Allamakee County look like faint shadows. The grid is there with all its expanse, and the landscape becomes a vast quilt of farmland with darker spots that denote towns. The roads have nearly disappeared; all that is left are the largest land features — major rivers, cities and towns, a lake or two, an interstate highway inter-change.

From there Iowa becomes a map of itself, an infinitely de-tailed drawing by a cartographer who misses nothing. From here we can see the grand spread of Iowa; below is Des Moines; off the wing tip is Minnesota. Or Missouri. Or Illinois. Or Nebraska. We see the rivers in western Iowa flow in different directions than the rivers in the east. We see the billiard-table flat Missouri River floodplain abutted against the bumpy Loess Hills, not so much as a difference of elevation but as a difference in texture. The view becomes an abstraction of landscape, a place that is no more real than a map of someplace we have never been.

The impression of Iowa from thirty-five thousand feet is in some ways similar to the impression of Iowa gained through cas-ual glances at the passing scenery from the interstate. Similar also is the impression of Iowa seen from a train window between pages of a good novel, or the impression of anyplace when a traveler doesn't slow down and take time to observe and remem-ber. It will be a remote, abstract landscape—a place prone to stereotypic recall by travelers who passed through but never looked. A blank space on the map or at best a place of fuzzy details, Iowa becomes a landscape to be passed over, a place to ignore.

A train is a wonderful place to read, and the interstate is an excellent place to roll along in overdrive and listen to music, but consider what you are missing.

Fig. 15.6. From the air, the landscape quilt of Har-per and surrounding fields, Keokuk County: row crops like corduroy, rough pastures like matted wool, and the roads and fences the seams. (Photo by Drake Hokanson).

16

IOWA:
BICYCLING HEAVEN

John Karras

Every summer since 1973 thousands of people have come together in Iowa to spend the last full week of July riding bicycles
from the Missouri River or a tributary on the western border to
the Mississippi River on the eastern border. The excuse for this
annual passage is a festive event sponsored by the *Des Moines
Register* called RAGBRAI (the *Register's* Annual Great Bicycle
Ride Across Iowa), followed by a Roman numeral, as in
RAGBRAI–XV (a truly silly acronym, which I can say without
fear of contradiction because I made it up).

Many of these thousands (at least ten thousand on
RAGBRAI–XIII) have come to Iowa from all over the United
States and from many foreign countries as well. And strange as it
may seem, many have done RAGBRAI again and again. Why?
What madness induces them to torture their bodies on hard little
bicycle seats across as many as 540 miles of Iowa countryside in
one week?

The simple answer is that there is hardly a better place anywhere for riding a bicycle—the secondary road system is terrific,
the small towns are frequent, the people are almost over-
whelmingly friendly, and the Iowa countryside is both varied and
lovely. Add to all that the total cooperation from the Iowa
Highway Patrol and you have an unbeatable package. Indeed, I
am not sure RAGBRAI could happen in any other state; that is,
that any other state has the happy, though accidental, combination of factors that permit RAGBRAI to work. Certainly, many

ride organizers in other states have tried to duplicate it, with only partial success.

I will be referring to RAGBRAI a lot in this discussion of the joy of bicycling in Iowa, not because I want to promote the ride any further (Lord knows, it needs no more), but because the ride wraps up in such a neat package all the pieces that make cycling in Iowa a joy.

Donald Kaul, a *Des Moines Register* columnist, and I started what came to be called RAGBRAI in 1973. At the time we had no intention of founding the most successful newspaper promotional event of the second half of the twentieth century, nay, perhaps in all of history. No, our aim was much more modest. We simply wanted to ride our bicycles across the state and were looking for some gimmick to get the *Register* to pick up our expenses. RAGBRAI was the result. (The first ride, incidentally, was called simply The Great Six Day Bicycle Ride Across Iowa. The second one was called the Second Annual Great Bicycle Ride Across Iowa. It didn't take long to figure out that if we kept going in that vein, the acronym for the fourth ride would be FAGBRAI, and nobody wanted that to happen. Thus, RAGBRAI with a Roman numeral.)

Even that first bike ride in 1973 produced an instant, authentic folk hero. His name was Clarence Pickard; he was eighty-three that year and weighed about the same number. He showed up in Sioux City with a Schwinn woman's bike that must have weighed forty pounds and a determination to ride across his state. How much had he ridden? "Around the block in Indianola," where he lived, he said.

He wore a pith helmet covered with duct tape, a long-sleeved shirt, and trousers, despite temperatures all week in the high nineties and low hundreds. Of course, we all figured he didn't have a chance—that he would either quit or die. We were so wrong. He was featured in stories in the *Register,* and by the time the ride reached Des Moines, elementary schools were letting children out to stand along the road and watch for Clarence. By the time the ride got to Davenport, he was a hero. He told me years later that he wanted to demonstrate that older folks who still have their health can do anything they put their minds to. They might have to do it a little slower, but they could do it. Clarence died 10 years later, struck by a car while crossing a main street at night in Indianola. He was a fine gentleman who made a major contribution to RAGBRAI's early success.

I would like to think the event has been a success because of the cleverness and canniness of those of us who plan it and carry it out each year, but the real credit belongs elsewhere—with the state and its friendly people, with the Clarence Pickards of Iowa.

Let's take, one at a time, the factors that make RAGBRAI or any cycling excursion a wonderful experience.

The Roads

Iowa has 14,326 miles of paved secondary roads—the blue roads on the official state highway map—according to the Department of Transportation. If you put them together with the state's additional 10,105 miles of primary highway, Iowa has enough two-lane pavement to circle the earth.

Most of the secondary roads carry light traffic and are surfaced acceptably enough for cycling. Many of them once were part of the state's primary system, and some still are paved, though rough and cracked, with the original 1920s or 1930s concrete. Others are smooth, new asphalt. Whatever, they give the state a marvelous network of possible bicycle routes. This extensive road network is the reason RAGBRAI has not had to repeat one route in fifteen outings.

Fig. 16.1.   RAGBRAI Riders in early morning, east of Harlan. (Photo courtesy of Des Moines Register)

There is a widespread misapprehension, even among Iowans, that the state is flat. That is a motorist's perception, not a cyclist's. Iowa's roads rise and fall a lot, and indeed, one of the great discoveries that first-time RAGBRAIers make is just how hilly the state is. Even the flattest areas—in northwest and north central Iowa—are gently rolling.

We have heard cyclists from Colorado complain about Iowa's hills, and they weren't kidding. True, Iowa has no mountains, but it has more than one hill up to three miles long in the northeastern, so-called unglaciated area, and many steep but short climbs in the southwestern Loess Hills that cry out for mountain gears. I recall once coasting westward out of the Loess Hills toward Pisgah and touching the brakes as my speedometer hit 40 mph. The Des Moines River valley is especially precipitous, bringing curses to the lips of, near tears to the eyes of, and burning pain to the legs of more than one struggling cyclist.

The Towns

Actually, the townspeople.

The first time we did RAGBRAI in 1973, the best we hoped for from people along the way was disinterest, the worst, hostility. You can imagine our amazement at finding people waiting to welcome us in the towns and along the roads. And as the bike ride has grown in number and tradition, the welcomes have continued and grown more elaborate. Towns vie to see which can put on the greatest show.

Cooper, then with a population of fifty, astonished the bikers several years ago with a small cannon welcoming them into town, food stands everywhere, and a marvelous taped message about the town and its residents playing over several loudspeakers mounted on poles and in trees. The next year, Tingley, with a population about two hundred, closed off its main street and lined it with food stands, plus the senior citizen kitchen band decked out in their red and white uniforms.

The riders are charged for almost everything now, but I do not know of one instance when prices were increased for RAGBRAI, or of one instance of attempted price gouging. Furthermore, the townspeople in the overnight communities try to outdo each other in hospitality. Many take cyclists in for the night, many others permit cyclists to camp in their yards, and still others are just plain friendly and accommodating. Occasionally, astonishingly so.

On a RAGBRAI several years ago, two young men from

out-of-state (I think Chicago) found themselves about five miles out of the most recent town when one of them developed bike trouble. They stopped at a farmhouse and asked the woman who came to the door if it would be possible to get a ride back into the town to get the bike fixed.

"Just take my car," she said.

"Lady," one of the astounded young men said, "you can't give us your car. You don't even know who we are."

"Oh, you can't be too bad if you're riding bicycles. Here, take my car." Which they did. And they brought it back, too.

For their part, almost all of the riders are courteous and pick up after themselves.

Finally, Iowa has a rich variety of ethnic backgrounds that is reflected in the communities and in the pride townspeople take in those communities. The people of tiny Elk Horn (population 748), for example, bought, disassembled, transported, and reassembled a windmill from their native Denmark. Kimballton, Elk Horn's sister Danish city a few miles to the north, has a replica of Copenhagen's famed little mermaid in the city park. In Stanton, a southwestern Iowa town settled by Swedes, all the houses are painted white. Pella and Orange City are proud of their Dutch heritage. And so it goes around the state. You will get green beer on St. Patrick's Day in Emmetsburg and kolaches (delicious filled pastries) in the Czech towns of northeast Iowa.

I mentioned the highway patrol's cooperation earlier. The fact is that the patrol became intimately involved in RAGBRAI the second year, and primarily because of the vision of one man — then Lt. Robert Glenn, head of the Community Service Officers group, and since retired from the patrol. Each of the thirteen patrol districts has a community service officer, and these were the men Glenn enlisted to work on RAGBRAI.

Glenn, a bicyclist, rode one day in 1973 from Ames to Des Moines and immediately recognized the public relations potential of the bike ride for the patrol. Thus, he had troopers working the second year, directing traffic at major intersections, driving the route and helping riders in distress, and generally being useful and friendly. The upshot was that for many members of a generation of Iowa teenagers and college students, the first friendly cops they had ever run into were the patrol officers on RAGBRAI.

Those were the years, you may recall, of Vietnam protests, of Chicago police beating up and gassing demonstrators at the 1968 Democratic National Convention, the Cambodian bombing protests, and the slaughter at Kent State University — years of conflict and confrontation. And here came these kids on the bike ride, and what did they see? A uniformed police officer stopping semis so they, the kids on bicycles, could cross U.S. 30 in safety.

The public relations effect for the patrol was terrific. The lesson for the youngsters was even more terrific.

Fig. 16.2. Tavern in Ionia, Chickasaw County, suddenly surrounded by resting riders, August, 1977. (Photo courtesy of Des Moines Register*)*

The Scenery

All right, let's be right up front with this. Iowa is known for corn, hogs, beans, and cattle, not scenery. We have no ocean shore, no mountains. Indeed, we have hardly any forest left, and most of the wetlands in the north central part of the state have been drained and cultivated.

Having said that, let me add that Iowa is a beautiful state. It is, however, a very gentle kind of beauty, not readily appreciated from a car as, for instance, a distant range of mountains or the Grand Canyon. Iowa has few breathtaking vistas, few golly and gee-whiz views to offer the motorist. But from a bicycle seat, this is a beautiful state, indeed.

The Loess Hills of western Iowa were mentioned earlier.

There are no rocks in them, or in much of western Iowa, because the soil was laid down by wind as the last glaciers melted. The Loess Hills, which extend all the way along the state's western border from Missouri to Sioux City, are extremely challenging, but unspeakably lovely to pedal through.

My favorite area for cycling, however, is northeast Iowa. It is an area of limestone outcroppings and deep valleys. Some of the loveliest bike rides follow roads along the edge of the bluffs high above the Mississippi River, others wind through wooded valleys along clear streams or follow a high ridge from which folds of valleys stretch on either side as far as the eye can see. This is not to say that other areas of the state are without beauty or charm. Almost everywhere, even among seas of corn and bean fields, small surprises — a lovely little lake, a verdant river crossing, a lovely country church — crop up several times in any day's ride.

I can still remember vividly the first long-distance excursions my wife and I took in the late sixties, and our surprise and wonderment, our sense of discovery, if you will, at realizing for the first time in the ten years we had lived here how pretty the Iowa countryside actually is. Another vivid impression, and something I had experienced previously only on wilderness camping trips, was a sense of being in close contact, almost a part of, the countryside. On the bike, you feel the wind, you feel every rise and fall in the road, you smell the crops and the fresh-cut hay and the livestock, you feel alive and a part of things. Biking is being there. Driving is like watching TV.

One of our routes in those days was a twenty-five-mile loop north out of Bondurant, into and out of the Skunk River valley, then east past Chichaqua Wildlife Refuge to Farrar, south into and out of the Skunk River valley again, then west paralleling Interstate 80 back into Bondurant. We found the hills challenging enough, although someone driving a car probably wouldn't even notice them, and the scenery lovely.

We now ride regularly west of Des Moines to Waukee, a round trip of about twenty-five miles, for breakfast. It is a ride we have taken a thousand times, yet it never is exactly the same. Alas, though, for cyclists. The developers are building houses further and further west of Des Moines, pushing the country further and further away.

Several years ago, in the early days of RAGBRAI, my wife and I did a series of weekend or three-day trips, just the two of us, to various parts of the state. We would leave our car somewhere, carry extra clothing on the bikes, and stay in motels or old-time hotels. Unfortunately, or perhaps fortunately, most of the old railroad hotels now house permanent residents. I recall the fire escape in our room in the Hotel Lansing was a length of two-inch manila rope with knots at appropriate intervals and one end tied to a leg of the radiator.

One such trip, from Marengo to Vinton, turned out to be a two-day battle against particularly vicious headwinds. But we stayed the night in Garrison with a potter and her husband who, in typical Iowa fashion, offered us beds.

Another trip introduced us to the glories of northeast Iowa. We rode from Marquette to Waukon, taking state highways to Harper's Ferry, then county roads X-42 and A-52 into Waukon. There is a stretch of A-52 that sits on a high ridge between Paint Creek on the south and Village Creek on the north with a view guaranteed to take your breath away. Fields fall away on both sides, red barns dot the valleys, and folds of other ridges and valleys undulate north and south to the end of the world. From Waukon, we rode to Lansing, then along the Mississippi River back to Marquette.

Another three-day ride took us from Fairfield to Keosauqua to Mount Pleasant and back to Fairfield. The area around Keosauqua along and above the Des Moines River is gorgeous.

One of the oddities of our cycling experiences occurred on that ride, in Lacey-Keosauqua State Park. We were riding through the park early in the morning, my wife several hundred yards ahead of me, when a fully grown doe leaped out onto the road between us and went loping along for at least a half mile. When my wife first glanced back, she thought she was being chased by a dog, but finally realized it was a deer.

A relatively new factor in Iowa is the development of what is becoming an extensive network of biking and hiking trails, most of which use abandoned railroad rights-of-way. Wisconsin was the first state to develop such linear parks, but Iowa has assumed leadership in the area. The longest of the trails, the Cedar Valley Nature Trail, runs about fifty miles between Cedar Rapids and Waterloo. The second longest, the Heritage Trail, runs twenty-five miles between Dubuque and Dyersville. These, like most railbed trails, are surfaced with sifted lime over a rolled base. The surface is not perfect, but is certainly acceptable.

What could become one of the great trails in the nation, however, is being developed by the Army Corps of Engineers along the Des Moines River north of the city. By the summer of 1988 the trail totaled a little over twenty miles of asphalt surface. If things go as now planned—that is, if Congress ever appropriates the money for plans already approved—the trail will be paved all the way from Lake Red Rock near Knoxville in the south to Fort Dodge in the north.

But why ride a bike at all? Why subject oneself to the pain
of that hard and narrow bicycle seat, to the discomfort of bend-
ing over in that unnatural 10-speed position, to the grinding
agony of working endlessly against a headwind, or shivering
when caught by a cold rain about thirty miles from home?

Fig. 16.3.   The hiking and bicycling trails of Iowa.
(Maps courtesy of Des Moines Register*)*

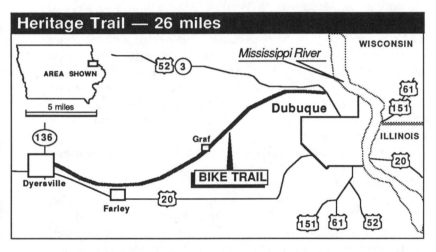

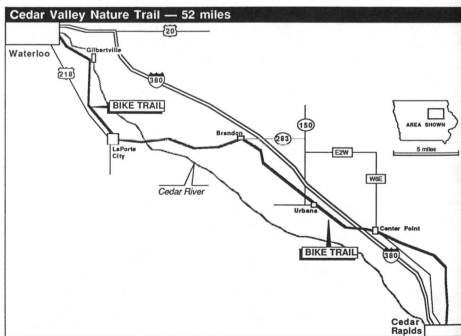

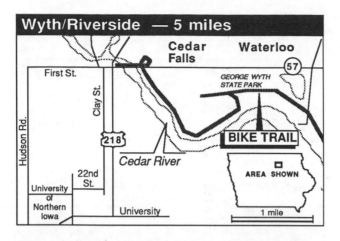

Wyth/Riverside — 5 miles

First St.
Cedar Falls
Waterloo
57
GEORGE WYTH STATE PARK
Clay St.
Hudson Rd.
218
Cedar River
BIKE TRAIL
22nd St.
University of Northern Iowa
University
AREA SHOWN
1 mile

Duck Creek Parkway — 6 miles

AREA SHOWN
1 mile
80
61
80
Harrison St.
Davenport
Brady St.
74
Hickory Grove Rd.
Kimberly Rd.
6
NORTHWEST PARK
Duck Creek
Locust St.
DUCK CREEK PARK
BIKE TRAIL
Mississippi River

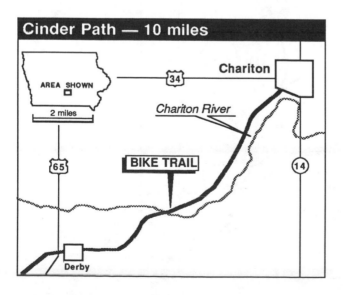

Cinder Path — 10 miles

AREA SHOWN
2 miles
Chariton
34
Chariton River
65
BIKE TRAIL
14
Derby

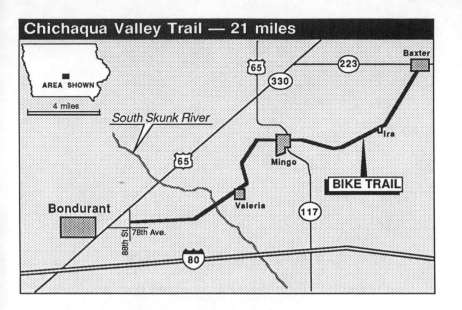

Chichaqua Valley Trail — 21 miles

AREA SHOWN

4 miles

South Skunk River

Baxter

Ira

Mingo

BIKE TRAIL

Bondurant

Valeria

88th St

78th Ave.

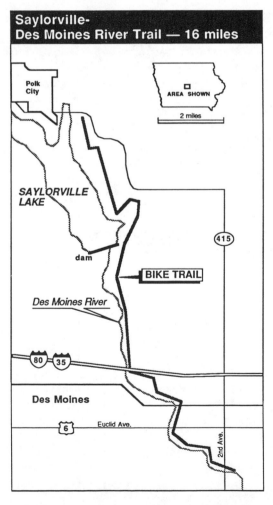

Saylorville-
Des Moines River Trail — 16 miles

Polk City

AREA SHOWN

2 miles

SAYLORVILLE LAKE

dam

BIKE TRAIL

Des Moines River

Des Moines

Euclid Ave.

2nd Ave.

The Whys
How many reasons do you need?

Let's start with considerations of health. Of course, we all know that hardly anyone does anything only because it's healthy. Thousands of people all over the world continue to smoke cigarettes even though there is by now incontrovertible proof that smoking cigarettes is a health disaster. The same holds true for eating hot dogs, potato chips, most fried fast foods (because they drip with cholesterol), and so on and so on to the point of terminal boredom.

Let me put it another way. If someone advised me (and I believed the advice) that bicycling would shorten my life by five years, would I stop riding? Well, I am pretty sure I would give it some thought. But I am also pretty sure I would decide that five more years of life don't mean all that much if the quality of those years is to be diminished by unacceptable restrictions on my activity. In short I think I would prefer to live five years less biking than five years more watching TV (a kind of living death, after all). Likewise, I would not elect to add five years to my life if I had to stop reading. Nor would I choose five more years if a condition of the addition were Alzheimer's disease. So the question of doing something because it's healthy, or at least life-extending, is, at best, ambiguous.

But how about thinking about activity in terms of it making you feel better. Now, then, we are onto something. And here I can speak with the authority of experience.

I can tell you without equivocation that once you get past the initial discomfort that accompanies any new physical activity (in biking, this means a sore rear end, stiffness between the shoulder blades, a weakness in the muscles above the knees, perhaps nagging pain in the elbow joints, and numbness in the hands for about the first 150 to 200 miles), you will enter a new world of physical euphoria that nonathletes don't even know exists. And if you put in enough miles in any single season (without trying to do them too fast and thus really injuring yourself) you will enter the athletic equivalent of Nirvana. I have been there several times, both jogging and riding the bike.

I am not at all sure what happens physiologically—I think it has something to do with the production of endorphins (hormones)—but the sensation is that of shifting into overdrive. The strange thing is that it happens suddenly, without symptoms, without warning, without premonition. You will be riding or running along, struggling through the miles or your workout, and all of a sudden everything changes. If you are running at the time, you will suddenly have the sensation of floating, your feet merely kissing the surface. If you are bicycling, you will suddenly find yourself going faster than you have ever gone before with a fourth of the effort. Again, I really don't know what the physiological process is, but I do know it works, it happens.

Such sensations have to be earned anew each season, but fortunately there is a fitness carryover from one season to another. That is, if you are starting from step zero this summer, you will be starting from step two or three next spring. And if you are interested in mechanistic considerations, bicycling is rated as one of the top five aerobic conditioning exercises. (I put that in just in case such statements turn you on.)

But enough of health talk. There are many other reasons, most of them less important than good health, for taking up bicycling in Iowa. I have already touched on several of them, such as our marvelous system of roads, the railroad rights-of-way that have been converted to public trails, the feeling cycling gives you of being in touch with the environment, and the feeling of well-being that comes with physical fitness in any form.

Fig 16.4.   A leisurely ride over the Cedar River on the Cedar Valley Nature Trail. (Photo courtesy of the Black Hawk County Conservation Board staff)

It's also a great way to meet mostly nice people (male or female, depending on your preferences). You will find these people, typically, in the state's bicycle clubs, of which there are a bunch. Iowa is full of bike clubs with huge membership lists because of the interest in cycling generated and nurtured by RAGBRAI. Likewise, we have a lot of very sophisticated bike shops in the state for the same reason.

Now, I must warn you, there are a lot of cycling nuts out there. Like anything else, cycling generates its fair share of cultists. That's fine if you like cults and cultists, or if you have a predilection for the same. To the cycling cultist, of course, everything else in life is secondary to mileage. I must admit, I can talk gear ratios and pedaling cadence and stem length and tire pressures and high-tech equipment with the best of them, but at the same time, I have other interests in my life besides bikes and biking. Cultists do not. So you have to have a care. Beyond that, the place to meet these people (besides on RAGBRAI, where everyone seems to be tan and beautiful) is in the bike clubs.

Fig. 16.5.   Riders enjoying the tree-lined section of the Cedar Valley Nature Trail. (Photo courtesy of the Black Hawk County Conservation Board staff)

The biggest, as you would expect, are in the large cities. Some in fact, are mere shadow clubs, organized expressly for signing up with and participating in RAGBRAI. The year-round clubs, however, have full programs of rides throughout the season. Some dedicated cyclists (I think of them as nut cases) ride throughout the year, going to great lengths and expense to protect toes, fingers, and noses from frostbite. The clubs schedule rides most weekends and often during the week, also. Many clubs grade the rides according to experience, stamina, and ability.

Whatever your tastes or abilities in cycling, if you want companionship seek it at the club nearest you. Even if you are a rank beginner, the chances are excellent that the club, especially if it is a large and well-established one, will have rides and other riders for you. And no matter where you live in Iowa, there are bicycle paths or roads less traveled, accompanied by gently enrapturing countryside to make the legs pump and the heart sing. Once you get over that sore butt, that is!

The names and addresses of both major and minor Iowa clubs:

Alta — Royd Riders/Storm Lake, James F. Black, 610 Johnson, Alta 51002

Ames — ISU Cycling Club, John Fish, 107 State Gym, ISU, Ames 50011; Friends of Central Iowa Biking, Dennis Jones, 1500 Truman, Ames 50010; Team Skunk, Tom Brumm, 3920 Quebec, Ames 50010

Audubon — Free Wheelers, Dick Goodrich, 202 Walnut St., Audubon 50025

Boone — Bicycle Club, Sherwood Selim, P.O. Box 524, Boone 50036

Burlington — BikeBurlington, P.O. Box 1135, Burlington 52601

Cedar Falls — Rainbow Cyclists, 3018 Rownd St., Cedar Falls 50613

Cedar Rapids — Hawkcyc Bicycle Association, P.O. Box 223, Cedar Rapids 52406

Charles City — North Iowa Touring Club, Bill Neal, P.O. Box 233, Charles City 50615

Clarion — Clarion Chain Gang, Jack Jenkins, 104 N. Main, Clarion 50525

Clinton — Riverbend Bicycle Club, M & W Schwinn Cyclery, 129 Fifth Ave. S., Clinton 52732

Council Bluffs — Pottawattamie Pedalers, Steve Elliott, 1405 Longview Drive, Council Bluffs 51501

Davenport — Quad Cities Bicycle Club, P.O. Box 3575, Davenport 52808

Des Moines—Team Skunk, Tom Brumm, P.O. Box 2325, Des Moines 50310

Dubuque—Dubuque Bicycle Club, Tom Bechen, 2510 Mineral St., Dubuque 52001

Emmetsburg—Emmetsburgers, Gregory C. Hoyman, 2216 Main, Emmetsburg 50536

Estherville—Bike Buddies, Bill Ridout, 703 First Ave. S., Estherville 51334

Fort Dodge—Fort Dodge Wheelmen, Deb Larsen, YMCA 1422 1st Ave. S., Fort Dodge 50501

Iowa City—Bicyclists of Iowa City, P.O. Box 846, Iowa City 52244

Iowa Falls—Green Belt Bikers, Cindy McDonald, 523 Railroad, Iowa Falls 50126

Keokuk—Keokuk Bike Club, P.O. Box 161, Keokuk 52632

Keota—RC Bike Club, Nadine Greiner, Box 112, Route 3, Keota 52248

Marion—Marion Bike Club, Thomas L. Begley, 1807 5th Ave., Marion 52302

Marshalltown—Iowa Valley Bicycle Club, Trisha L. Hlas, 208 Olson Way, Marshalltown 50158.

Milford—Okoboji Bicycle Club, Terry Bauer, 902 8th St., Milford 51351

Monticello—Monticello Bikers, Bernie Barker, Box 271, Monticello 52310

Muscatine—Muscatine Pedalwheelers, Wiladene Yankee, 1744 Devitt, Muscatine 52761

Ottumwa—Spoke Folks, Chuck Manson, 627 Crestview, Ottumwa 52501

Perry—Perry Bike Club, Patty McKee, 1717 Evelyn, Perry 50220

Rockford—Rockford Bike Group, Jim Schumburg, P.O. Box C, Rockford 50468

Sioux Center—Sioux County Bike Club, Dave Eekhoff, Route 1, Box 64, Sioux Center 51250

Sioux City—Siouxland Cyclists, Dave Kass, 1418 38th St., Sioux City 51104

PART
VI

Maps

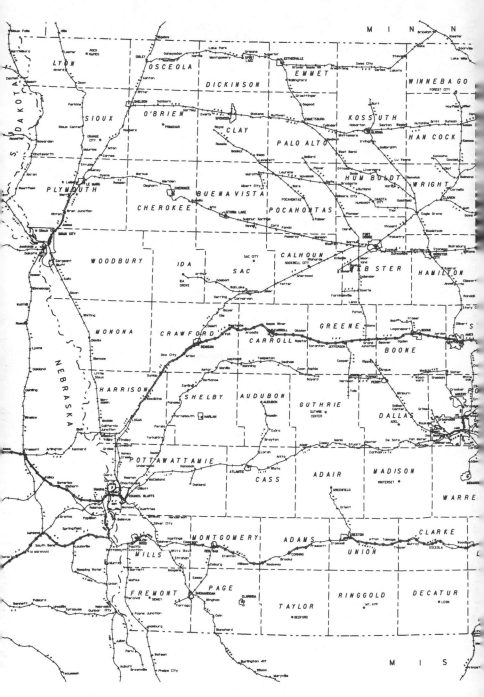

Iowa Railroad Map, 1987. Total mileage is 4,160, down from 8,173 in 1970 and well over 10,000 in 1930.

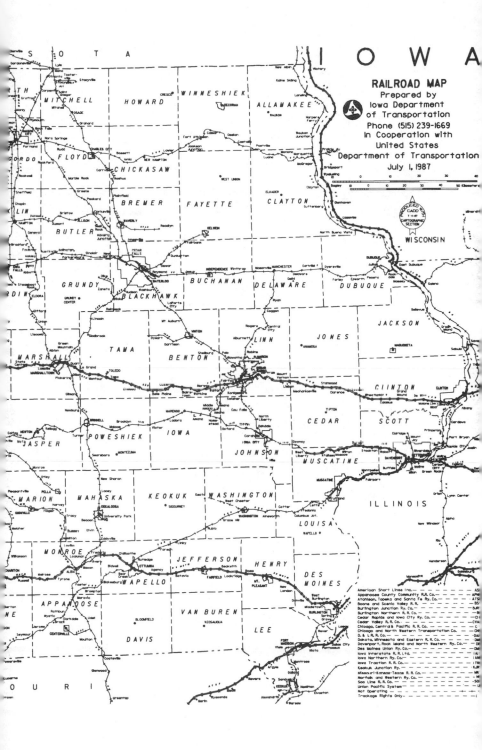

RAILROAD MAP
Prepared by
Iowa Department
of Transportation
Phone (515) 239-1669
In Cooperation with
United States
Department of Transportation
July 1, 1987

American Short Lines Inc. —
Appanoose County Community R.R. Co. —
Atchison, Topeka and Santa Fe Ry. Co. —
Boone and Scenic Valley R. R. —
Burlington Junction Ry. R. —
Burlington Northern R.R. Co. —
Cedar Rapids and Iowa City Ry. Co. —
Cedar Valley R. R. Co. —
Chicago, Central & Pacific R. R. Co. —
Chicago and North Western Transportation Co. —
D. & L R. R. Co. —
Dakota, Minnesota and Eastern R. R. Co. —
Davenport, Rock Island and North Western Ry. Co. —
Des Moines Union Ry. Co. —
Iowa Interstate R. R. Ltd. —
Iowa Northern Ry. Co. —
Iowa Traction R. R. Co. —
Keokuk Junction Ry. —
Missouri-Kansas-Texas R. R. Co. —
Norfolk and Western Ry. Co. —
Soo Line R. R. Co. —
Union Pacific System —
Not Operating —
Trackage Rights Only —

317

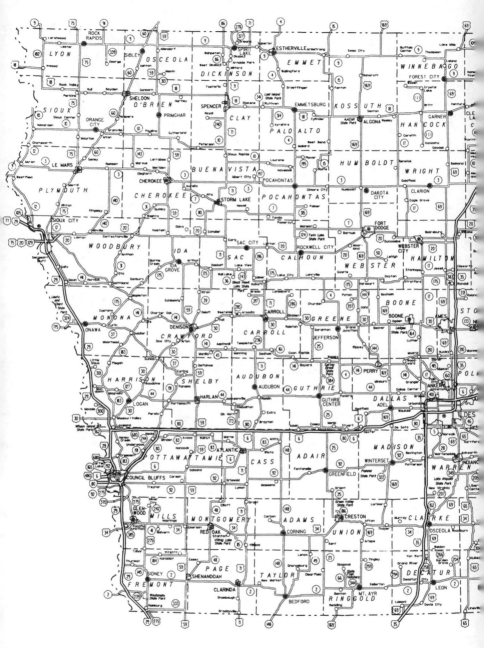

Iowa State Highway Map, 1987.

318

I O W A

STATE HIGHWAY MAP

Prepared By
Iowa Department
of Transportation
Phone (515) 239-1289
In Cooperation With
United States
Department of Transportation
January 1, 1987

INTERSTATE HIGHWAYS
U.S. HIGHWAYS
STATE HIGHWAYS
COUNTY SEAT

Contributors

▽

Robert Bunge is professor of the Lakota (Sioux) language and culture at the University of South Dakota at Vermillion and professor of the Dakota language, culture, and psychology at Morningside College, Sioux City, Iowa. He is the author of *An American Urphilosophie* (University Press of America, 1983) and numerous articles on Native American language, thought, and culture.

Paul Christiansen is professor of biology at Cornell College, Mt. Vernon, Iowa, where he teaches botany. His research and field interests are in prairie ecology, establishment of prairies, and prairie management. He is a native Iowan from Mitchell County.

Amy Godine was born in Boston and is a graduate of Hampshire College. After working as a journalist in Portland, Oregon, she came to the University of Iowa Writers' Workshop and remained in Iowa City another year as a Michener Fellow. Her fiction has appeared in *The North American Review, Another Chicago Magazine,* and other journals.

John B. Harper is a life-long resident of Iowa and a faculty member in English at the University of Iowa, where he specializes in teaching American drama. A frequent actor and director of theater productions, he also organizes workshops and play festivals for the Iowa Community Theater Association.

Harriet Heusinkveld retired in 1985 from teaching at Central College, Pella, Iowa, where for many years she was professor of geography. She is presently writing a history of the Des Moines River Greenbelt under the auspices of the Rock Island Army Corps of Engineers. She has also spent a number of terms teaching in the Yucatan and has written on Mayan folk literature.

James Hippen, professor of history at Luther College, Decorah,

Iowa, is an expert on the history of American industry and technology. A major current interest is the history of Iowa bridges.

Drake Hokanson teaches in the School of Journalism and Mass Communications at the University of Iowa. A writer and photographer, his special interests are physical and cultural geography and the history of transportation, and his work has appeared in many publications in Iowa and elsewhere. His book *The Lincoln Highway: Main Street Across America* was published in 1988.

Loren N. Horton has taught at all levels from public school through junior college, college, and university. His doctoral dissertation was a pioneering study of early Mississippi rivertown architecture. Research and writing have included works on urban planning and development on the American frontier, historical architecture, historical archaeology, material culture, and ethnic influences on demography. He is now state historian for the State Historical Society of Iowa.

John Karras has been a serious cyclist, off and on, since the age of nineteen, when he spent the summer on a fifty-pound one-speed bicycle. In the last twenty years, as cofounder of the *Des Moines Register*'s Annual Great Bike Ride Across Iowa (RAGBRAI), he has cycled literally all over the state. In a previous life, he was a newspaper writer and editor, and he still contributes regularly to the *Register.*

Cornelia F. Mutel is a graduate of Oberlin College and has a master's degree in environmental biology. A writer of educational materials for the University of Iowa's Institute of Agricultural Medicine and Occupational Health, she also engages in natural history writing and is active in efforts to preserve Iowa's remaining natural areas. She is completing a book on the natural history of the Loess Hills.

Robert F. Sayre is professor of English at the University of Iowa. His interest in the Iowa landscape began between 1973 and 1980 when he lived in rural Johnson County. He is the author of *The Examined Self* and *Thoreau and the American Indians* and edited Thoreau for the Library of America series of American authors.

Don Scheese is a graduate student in American studies at the University of Iowa. His projected dissertation, for which he has won a Ballard Fellowship, is on *Inhabitants of the Land: Thoreau, Muir, Leopold, and Abbey and American Nature Writing.*

Dorothy Schwieder received her Ph.D. from the University of Iowa in 1981 and has taught history at Iowa State University since

1969. She regularly teaches a course in Iowa history, which also represents her main research area. Her most recent books are *Black Diamonds: Life and Work in Iowa's Coal Mining Communities, 1895–1925; Buxton: Work and Racial Equality in a Coal Mining Community* (as first author); and *Iowa, Past to Present: The People and the Prairie* (as first author).

Lowell J. Soike completed his Ph.D. in history at the University of Iowa. Since 1974 he has been staff historian with Iowa's historic preservation program. His book *Without Right Angles: The Round Barns of Iowa* (1983) is the first book in the series, The Changing Iowa Farm: Agricultural History Through Buildings.

Jon Spayde grew up in Fairfield, Iowa, and in Iowa City. A graduate of Harvard and Stanford, where he studied Japanese, he currently works as a travel editor and writer in New York.

Philip E. Webber is professor and chairman of German at Central College, Pella, Iowa; he also serves as co-chairman of linguistics and regularly teaches Dutch. His many publications on language and ethnic studies include a chapter on German and Dutch craft traditions in *Passing Time and Traditions,* and he is the author of *Pella Dutch: The Portrait of a Language and Its Use in One of Iowa's Ethnic Communities.*

Index